T0129318

EAGLE SCOUT TO KILLER

A NOVEL BASED ON TRUE EVENTS

K S ALAN

authorHOUSE®

AuthorHouse™
1663 Liberty Drive
Bloomington, IN 47403
www.authorhouse.com
Phone: 1 (800) 839-8640

Published by AuthorHouse 06/11/2018

ISBN: 978-1-5462-4619-0 (sc)
ISBN: 978-1-5462-4618-3 (e)

Print information available on the last page.

CONTENTS

PREFACE

This book is graphic and violent, because that's what "war" is. It's not a romantic adventure. Soldiers do not acquire PTSD and Moral Injury from participating in peaceful endeavors.

Although this book is centered on the Vietnam War, it is not meant to be a war story. Do you know the difference between a "war story" and a "fairy tale?" A "fairy tale" starts out, "Once upon a time." A "war story" starts out, "No shit, there I was," and that's the only difference. From there on, it is all the same.

This book is about the emotional toll and lasting effects of the horrors of war that afflict combat Soldiers. It is the story of the transformation of a young Eagle Scout into a warrior, and the lifelong memories and scars that burden him. These types of traumatic events will haunt combat Veterans, for the rest of their lives.

This is not an anti-military book. The military itself is made up of brave, loyal, unselfish men and women, who leave their homes, and risk their lives to make sure we are safe and that democracy is preserved. I am proud of my service to this country and of what I did. If there is a fault with the military, it is not with the individual Soldier; it's with the politicians and senior leadership that sometimes take their eye off the ball and the goal of the mission.

It is my hope that when you read this book, you are not looking at whether the war was right or wrong, but rather, that you try to understand the moral struggles Soldiers face in combat. It will become clear how "doing the right thing" in war, conflicts with the idea of "right and wrong" we were raised with. Hopefully it will shed more light on the difficult and often impossible choices we are forced to make, especially for those of you who have been lucky enough never to have experienced combat and been faced with such grueling decisions.

When you're young and in war, you don't realize you have two lives to take care of; you have your physical life and your emotional life. At that age, your only concern is with your physical life. You give no thought to your emotional life and how it will be effected years down the road, as you grow older. You worry about going through life without an arm or leg, but you never considered what it will be like going through life having your soul wounded, and living with PTSD and Moral Injury.

As you read about my transformation from and Eagle Scout to Soldier, know that in war, we don't have the luxury of choosing between right and wrong; we must choose between bad and worse, and those are our only options. There are no heroes in this book, only people who have been thrust into the depths of hell, and made it out alive.

A PROFESSIONALS
THOUGHT ON THE BOOK

Kurt's VA - PTSD Therapist
Dan Bishton

This not a war story, this is Kurt's story. It is the story of his transformation from an idealistic Eagle Scout, into a warrior and a killer. It is a story about what happened to him, what he did, felt, and saw, and the memories and invisible scars that he bears, as a result. These are scars he will carry for the rest of his life. I know this because I am Kurt's therapist, and have been for 10 years. This book is part of his therapy.

When I met Kurt, he was 65 years old, and having intense panic attacks that came out of nowhere. He didn't associate them with his military experiences or Vietnam, at first. In fact, he could not associate them with anything, which is why they were so terrifying.

War survivors often push their memories deep into their minds. They separate the true narrative of what happened from the feelings and images that were present. This is why they can sometimes tell a horrific war story, as calmly as you would describe a trip to the grocery. It also means those feelings can burst out without the story, or the images can play out in their minds eye, or in a dream.

The feeling one gets in a panic attack is the same as if you looked down and saw a cobra slithering across your carpet, coming right toward you, except there is no cobra. You might not know whether to fight, flee, or freeze, and you would have only a split second to make the right decision or die. It can also feel like a full regiment of armed enemy Soldiers about to run right over your position, and you have no place to run. Sometimes in combat your own death is so close, it's like that cobra you saw going right up your pant leg! If you survived it, it would only be because you were lucky. You get all of this training, but in an actual battle, you may have only a few seconds to make the right decision or it will be your last one. Sometimes there is no right decision, there is just luck, fate, or God's will.

This book is also about the emotional cost and lifelong effects of combat PTSD and Moral Injury, which burden most Soldiers who were unfortunate enough to have faced the horrors of war. The brutality, terror, and utter loneliness that is "war," are both experienced and imposed on combat Veterans. The carriers of combat PTSD include the young, naïve and optimistic, and some not so young, who re-enlist and go back for the second, third, and sixth tours. The conditions that produce PTSD in an individual are not restricted to upbringing, age, race, gender, or education. Situations of intense danger, where life, death, and intense pain or disfigurement hang in the balance, are the perfect cauldron for PTSD. War is a factory that mass produces it.

The focus of this book is Kurt's journey from Eagle Scout, to Soldier, to killer, to civilian, to trauma survivor. It is about his effort to reclaim his soul, unite with the person he was before, and learn to live with the person he became in battle. A lot of Soldiers who go off to war zones develop PTSD. You don't have to be in combat to get it. Just the proximity to the conditions of war can do it. Bearing witness to the wholesale violence of war is sometimes enough. Just ask students in one of those school shootings who never saw the attacker, but heard the shots and screams of those students and teachers in the line of fire.

Kurt, bless his Eagle Scout heart, stayed in the military for 24 years before he retired, and his PTSD went from simmer to full boil.

I hope reading this book will help you see how doing the "right thing" in war, directly conflicts with the moral instruction of a person's entire life.

The struggle and pain this can cause, will continue until they draw their last breath. People who have never experienced combat or been forced to make decisions causing such moral conflict under those circumstances, should not pass judgment on those who did.

DEDICATION

This book is dedicated to my wonderful wife, without whom I would never have survived after coming home from Vietnam, confused, scared, and angry. I hate to think where I would be had I not met and married her. She put up with all of my problems and was always there for me. It was her love and example that kept me from falling into the trap of drugs and alcoholism. She is truly the most loving and caring person I've ever met.

When I could only see the bad in people, she always saw the good. I needed that example, because I had become very cold, emotionally. She put up with my behavior, even though she didn't know or understand anything about PTSD. She is the perfect example of what love and goodness are in this world. She endured with me for 30 years, before I was able to find any real help through the VA.

I have a good church and friends that are part of my support system, but it is my wife who is responsible for anything good in me and for anything good I have done. She reminds me daily through her example, of what I can and should be. She deserves all the rewards, medals, and anything I have earned, for her showing me love and support through all of these years. We just celebrated our 50th wedding anniversary. That is the greatest accomplishment I have had in my life.

Without her love and support, I am sure I would've been dead by now. She didn't understand but she was always there for me and never passed judgement on me. She sacrificed so much *in* her life and *of* her life, because of my actions. I believe she is the angel that God sent to save my life.

PROLOGUE

What Really Happened at the Gulf of Tonkin

I am Kurt S. Alan, codename, "Coconut." As a result of being a member of a detachment assigned to an operational group assisting the Central Intelligence Agency (AKA: "CIA," "The Company," or "Christians in Action"), I have knowledge of, and did participate in, many operations that were deceptions throughout the course of the Vietnam conflict.

It was mid-February 1964, and I was at a meeting in Saigon at the U.S. Embassy. Coleman, the CIA Station Chief, was there and called the meeting. The U.S. Ambassador, a U.S. General and four others with him, the President of South Vietnam, the head of Vietnam's police, six other Vietnamese who I didn't know, (four were in military uniforms), three Company men, and four of us, were present. We were Soldiers that worked for The Company. Everyone wore polite smiles and nodded in greeting to each other. Everyone, that is, except Coleman. Nondescript in many ways, Coleman had the look of a 40 year old professor, with round eyeglasses and slicked back hair. He was stone-faced, no smile, and his piercing black eyes were all business.

All the talk was about how the war was going and where to go from here. In the end, the conclusion was that it was going to take a lot more U.S. combat troops if we were going to defeat the North. The General, the Vietnam President, and the U.S. Ambassador were going to recommend to

President Johnson that he increase the U.S. forces in Vietnam. Coleman was in agreement.

The next day, we met again. This time it was only Coleman, two of his men, and the four of us at the meeting. Coleman was worried that President Johnson would not commit more troops. We discussed what we could do to persuade him to increase troop levels, but no one had a good idea. Frustrated, Coleman ended the meeting saying that we should all think about it and if we came up with an idea, to contact him.

Coleman was right. Johnson did not want to increase the troop level, and things were not going well with the war. It was obvious that the Vietnamese along with U.S. advisors could not defeat the North and maintain control of the free South.

We had another meeting on 5 May 1964. This meeting was not at the Embassy but at a house about half a mile from the Embassy; Coleman and his men were the only ones there again with the four of us. Coleman demanded our attention with his direct stare, and said that he had a plan to persuade Johnson to send more troops and hit North Vietnam from the air. He went on to give us a history lesson.

In Cuba in 1899, when the Battleship U.S.S. Maine blew up, the U.S. used this as an excuse to attack Cuba. Later, we found out that the boiler had blown up. In 1915, the Germans sank the Lusitanian, and likewise, we used this as a reason to go to war in WWI. On 7 December 1944, when Japan attacked Pearl Harbor, we went to war in WWII.

Coleman reasoned that it appeared any time someone attacked our ships, we went to war. So we needed a way to have one of our ships attacked by the North Vietnamese to escalate this conflict. He told one of his men to find out where all of our ships were at present, and where they would be assigned in the future, then he told us to stand by and he would get back with us.

We met again on 10 May 1964, at the same location. In his calm, self-confident, determined way, Coleman said it looked like we could arrange an attack on one of our ships sometime in July. I asked if we were going to let the South Vietnamese in on this, and he said, "No we don't need them, and we don't want them to know anything about it."

I said, "Well if we don't use the South Vietnamese, who is going to be manning the attracting PT boats (armed patrol boats), U.S. personnel? What if something goes wrong, and one of the boats sinks and they find Americans on the PT boat?"

He said, "Don't worry about it because all the boats will have Vietnamese aboard them." He then told us to come back the next day with two of our guys and three of our Vietnamese counterparts, and he would fill us in on what was going to happen. As we left the room he said, "You are going on a mission."

The next day we boarded a C-130 (military transport plane) and proceeded north to Hue. At Hue, we picked up a "slick" (transport helicopter) and a Company pilot, and headed west. Even with the doors open on the chopper, it was hot. The wind blew in like the heat from a furnace. We made a stop at the village of Ko Va La Dut. It was a small village in Vietnam just east of Laos, where we picked up another Vietnamese who also worked for The Company. He had about 10 other armed men with him. He looked to be about 35 or so, and had a big smile. I didn't know his real name, but his code name was "Bull".

Bull didn't look like most Vietnamese. He was only about five foot five, but was built more like a Korean. He had dark hair and eyes, but his face was wider. He was stockier than most Vietnamese. He had wider shoulders and larger biceps, like an American. Looking past his easy smile, I could see that he was a very determined person. I found out later that in spite of his friendly demeanor, he was all business all the time.

Bull got on the chopper with us and we flew west to the village of Co Ka Va, just inside Laos. We landed and Bull said, "Stay at the chopper. I'll be right back." Since we were in Laos, I set up a perimeter. In about 10 minutes, Bull came back and told us to follow him. We went into the village and entered a small hooch (straw/mud hut).

In the bigger cities like Củ Chi, there were hard-packed roads and more substantial buildings. The buildings had doors, windows, and power poles running along the streets. Out there in the small villages, the buildings were made of mud and straw. Most didn't have doors or windows, and they were spread out, not close to each other like in the cities where two buildings would share one wall. This hooch had one door opening and two window openings, but no real doors or windows. There was no ceiling, and you could see light coming through the thatched roof in some places. I told the guys to take up defensive positions around the hooch, and Song (one of my Vietnamese bodyguards) and I went inside with Bull.

Bull walked over to a man and shook his hand. I couldn't see this person very well because it was dark in the hooch and Bull was standing between us. There were two other men there, one on each side of the man to whom Bull was talking. They were in North Vietnamese khaki uniforms with AK-47s (Russian assault rifles). Bull said something to the guys and they turned to face me, and he introduced me to them.

Bull didn't speak much English, and as he started to introduce me, the main man walked over to me from about 10 feet, and in almost perfect English said, "Hello. It's good to meet you. I am General Fong," as he put out his hand to shake mine. I looked into his eyes, searching for a sign to see if I could tell what he was thinking. If I shook his hand, I would have to take my hand off my weapon and my finger off the trigger, and I didn't feel safe enough to do that. I looked at the other two men with him. I was worried one of them was going to raise his AK and fire at us.

I had been told I was going to meet someone from the North Vietnamese Army, but I never thought it would be a general, and for sure not General Fong. He was the number three or four man in North Vietnam under Hồ Chí Minh. He was in a dark green, short-sleeve shirt, with red tabs on the collars and gold emblems on his shoulders – a three-star general. He had no rifle but a side arm in a holster on his right side. He looked to be in his mid-40s, and there were gray streaks around his temples and through his mustache and goatee. He was extremely thin but a little taller than most Vietnamese, five foot seven or eight. He was very soft spoken, but exuded tremendous confidence.

In the moments that followed, my mind was jumping back and forth. I knew I was there to meet with someone who was to help the CIA with the attack on our ships, but I never thought I would be face-to-face with one of the high ranking leaders of the North – the enemy. I certainly never dreamed it would be a meeting with a general, who had helped kill some of my men!

I didn't understand just what was going on. Was this for real, or was it a trap? I looked at Bull and wondered if he was really one of us, or part of a deception? There were just a few of us, and we were in Laos. With the exception of Coleman, no one even knew we were there. If we were killed or taken as POWs (Prisoners of War), no one would come to help or even know we were missing.

Bull seemed relaxed and had a smile on his face, as did the General. Did that mean things were okay, or that they were happy that they had us where they wanted us? Conflicting thoughts flew back and forth in my mind, but the relaxed body language of Bull, the General, and the two NVA Soldiers (North Vietnamese, People's Army of Vietnam) told me things were probably all right. They didn't have their weapons at the ready or their fingers on the triggers. They didn't seem nervous. None of the little signs were present that people exhibit when they are about to take action. I instantly looked at Song. This was one of those times when having someone like Song with me, gave me confidence that we might survive all this.

Song had been with me for about a year at that time. He was only 18, but he had already lived two people's lifetimes. The VC (Viet Cong, Vietnamese Communists) had killed his mother and father when he was 12, and cut the unborn baby out of his sister while she was still alive, killing them both. He was not just my bodyguard, but also my friend whom I trusted with my life. He was like most Vietnamese, but taller at five foot seven or eight, with black hair and dark eyes. Most of the time he had a smile on his face. His face was rounded and he had wider shoulders than most, more like an American. I had to keep reminding myself he was just a boy, because he was the fiercest warrior I had ever known. He had earned my trust many times and had saved my life a time or two. He was good at reading people, and this was a time when his skills would be of great value.

I found him staring at me now. Our eyes met, and I could see he was as worried as I was. He backed up a step, looked at the two guys with the AKs, and I heard him flip the safety off his weapon. I quickly moved my M-16 to my left hand and pointed it up in the air and kept my left trigger finger on the trigger with the safety off. With a smile, I slowly reached out my right hand and shook the General's hand. I said, "It's good to meet you, General."

I was worried he would grab my hand and reach for his handgun, or try to hold me as the two other guys started shooting. When he shook my hand it was with a firm grip, but not a grip strong enough to hold me. I looked him in the eye as we shook hands. He smiled, let go and stepped back a step pointing to a table and said, "Let's sit and talk."

We both sat down and I laid my 16 on the table pointed to the left, so the barrel was aimed at the two guys with the AKs, and the trigger near my right hand. Song and Bull were to my left about 10 feet away and a little behind me, and the two North Vietnamese Soldiers with the General were to my left toward the front.

We started with some small talk, and he asked in his quiet tone where I was from in the States. I told him I was from a small town in Indiana, so I was sure he wouldn't know where it was. "How far is that from West Lafayette," he asked. Surprised, I said, "About 100 miles north of there," and asked how in the world he knew anything about Indiana. He told me he had gone to Purdue University where he learned to speak English, and was an

Agricultural Engineer in Hanoi before he was in the army. I was amazed and thought, "How small this world is!"

The General began to talk about the war, and from the way he spoke about his people and his home, it was obvious that he loved his country. I couldn't understand why he was helping us. He asked what exactly we needed from him. I told him about Coleman's plan to have North Vietnamese PT boats attack a U.S. ship in the Gulf of Tonkin, so that President Johnson would have the support of the American people and Congress to increase U.S. troop levels in Vietnam.

This whole situation seemed surreal. I felt very uncomfortable telling this man our plans, but Coleman told me to tell the man I was to meet everything, and that he could be trusted. I sure hoped he was right. After listening to the plan, the General said he could make it happen, he just needed to know when and where. I told him I didn't know that yet, so we agreed to meet again later when I had the time and place for the attack. It was strange. We shook hands, and we left. It was an eerie feeling, me shaking hands with a North Vietnamese general.

When we returned to Saigon, I met with Coleman and told him what had happened at the meeting with General Fong. I said, "Sir, I don't understand all of this, but if this attack works and we increase troops and air strikes, then we should win this war."

"That's right," Coleman said, in his straightforward, positive way.

"Okay," I said. "That's good for the United States and good for the South Vietnamese, but it would be bad for the North and General Fong. So why is he willing to help us win the war?" I could tell by the way the General had talked that he loved his country and he had power and money, so I didn't understand his eagerness to help us. It looked to me like he might have been a spy, and I didn't see any reason we should trust him.

Coleman answered, "It's because the General loves his country that he is helping us. He loves his country but isn't a fan of communism or Hồ Chí Minh. He thinks that if this war keeps going it could destroy his country and even now, Hồ Chí Minh is mistreating his people to win the war. His people are suffering great hardships to keep this war going."

General Fong had been telling the other generals that they should not attack the U.S. personnel or the United States would get more involved, and they would win the war causing the NVA to lose everything. So Coleman said if we could pull this off and get a lot of our troops over there to win the war and drive the VC out of South Vietnam, then Hồ Chí Minh should lose his credibility and control. General Fong would take the lead in making peace with the South and stop the war, thereby saving the people of the North and South from all the hardships they were suffering.

Coleman went on to explain that we would provide aid, food, and money for the new government in the North. If this worked, it should shorten the war and save lives on both sides, hopefully getting rid of communism in the North, and helping to stabilize that area of the world to stop the spread of communism everywhere. "This is important for the South, General Fong, his people, and us," he continued. As Coleman told me this, I saw the look of sincerity and determination on his face to do whatever he thought necessary to win the war for our country. At the same time, I knew that in his drive to accomplish his goal, he would be absolutely ruthless.

Coleman said General Fong was taking a big chance, and that if anyone in the North found out what he was doing, he would be a dead man. Of course, if anyone found out what we were doing, we would be making little rocks out of big rocks in Leavenworth for the rest of our lives. I knew that whether this worked or not, we must take it to our graves, all of us. That's why as few people as possible, could know what we were doing.

On 19 July 1964, Coleman contacted me with the information General Fong was waiting for. He said I needed to meet the General at the same place I did the last time, on 22 July 1964, at 1500 hours. I didn't know how Coleman contacted General Fong, but I thought it had something to do with Bull. This was not unusual. We all worked together and each of us had our own contacts on the side that the others didn't know about.

I met General Fong for the second time on the 22nd, at the same place, with the same people. I told him at the end of July, and the 1st of August, a carrier task force with the carrier Ticonderoga would be in the Gulf of Tonkin. On the 30th and 31st of July, the Marines were going to use Nasty Boats (small, fast boats) to attack a base on the island of Hon Me, just off the shore of North Vietnam. Those operations should go on for a week or so. The destroyers, Maddox and Turner Joy would enter the Gulf of Tonkin, but remain in international water, to provide security and electronic surveillance for the Nasty Boats.

We thought that when the Nasty Boats attacked, everyone would expect the North to respond. If they used PT boats and went after the Nasty Boats they would be in the area of the Maddox or the Turner Joy. This would be a great opportunity to attack one of the destroyers in international waters. It would be up to General Fong to decide when and where, but we thought this would be a good opportunity.

I asked him what he thought and if he felt he could do it. Silently, he got up and walked out of the hooch. He continued to walk around outside for about 20 minutes. When he returned, he sat down and said in a quiet voice, "I think I can make that happen." We agreed to meet back there on the 10th of August at the same time for an after action report.

On the 2nd of August there was a report of the destroyer, Maddox, being attacked in the Gulf of Tonkin in international waters by North Vietnamese PT boats. On the 4th of August, the Maddox reported being attacked, a second time by three or four PT boats that fired torpedoes and 50 Cal rounds at them. The report stated that they were not hit by the torpedoes but were hit by a 50 Cal round. The Maddox returned fire and said it hit two of the PT boats and aircraft assisted in the attack on the PT boats. They reported that one PT boat was dead in the water and burning and three PT boats were damaged and headed back to shore.

Well, this worked. The Los Angeles Times urged Americans to "Face the fact that the Communists, by their attack on an American vessels in international waters, have themselves, escalated the hostilities," and Congress passed the Gulf of Tonkin Resolution and gave President Johnson a blank check to escalate the Vietnam War. By 1965, there were about 100,000 U.S. troops in Vietnam, and by 1966, the troop level was up to almost 400,000. It looked like we would win this war, and General Fong would soon be in power in North Vietnam.

I met with General Fong again on the 10th of August. I asked him what had happen on the 2nd and the 4th. He just smiled and said, "Well, what happened was not what the American news and military reported." He went on to say, he had used the attacks from the Nasty Boats to go out into the Gulf with the PT boats. When the Nasty Boats headed for international waters they had pursued them, and made a run on the destroyer that was out there. I guess it was the Maddox, but we didn't know which one it was and didn't really care. Unlike the United States who reported that there were three or four PT boats, he said, "We only used two, and never fired a torpedo. We did fire our 50 Cal machine guns, but neither one of our two PT boats were ever hit."

I told the General what the Maddox had reported. We both had a laugh about what they claimed, what the news reported, and what had really occurred. We both agreed that whatever really happened didn't matter, all *that was important was that the whole world thought the North had attacked our ships in international waters. It looked like our plan had worked and that we should soon have many more troops in the country and air strikes going on. However, since Vietnam was one-day and 12-hours behind U.S. time, Coleman was concerned that someone would discover that the CIA had identified targets for retaliatory air strikes before the Gulf of Tonkin incident occurred.*

General Fong said that he hoped the time would soon come when his people would see that, peace with the South was better than a long, hard, war, and that we would meet again soon, as friends. I said I hoped so, too. We shook hands and I never saw General Fong again, until 1985.

I grew up being taught to never lie, but here I was perpetrating a lie on the U.S. Congress, the President, the Pentagon and the American people. It truly seemed then, like the right thing to do. After all, Congress and the American people were safe at home, and I was there witnessing the atrocities of war: the butchering, the killing, and man's inhumanity to man. It seemed unfair then and still does today, that people with no personal involvement in the war should be making life and death decisions about the war. So there I was, having a conflict between my oath as an Eagle Scout and my oath and loyalty as a Soldier.

CHAPTER ONE

To DC

It was July of 1985, and I was on my way to Washington, D.C., following a phone call from The Company. I had passed mile marker 110 eastbound on the Pennsylvania Turnpike, the last exit before the tunnels. There was a tunnel about 15 minutes off to the east; the first of three or four tunnels on the way to Philadelphia. The mountains were beautiful, but it was hard to get and keep a good radio station because of them.

I came to the first tunnel, and knew I always lost my radio signal when I came out on the east side. It was time to put in a CD and listen to some vintage music. This was the highest area of elevation, then it was all downhill toward the Atlantic Ocean into DC.

It was time to get off at the exit for Breezewood, PA. That was the busiest exit on the turnpike. It was always busy, no matter what time of day or time of year. Most of the time I got off there and headed east on US Hwy 30, to Gettysburg.

I enjoyed the trip from Breezewood over the mountains to Gettysburg. It was beautiful all the way. I also loved Gettysburg. Whenever I was in the area, I would always go over there to walk around. I don't know exactly what it was, but I could always sense something special when I walked through the battlefield. It was as if I could feel the presence of all the men who had fought and died there.

I had planned to stop at the Gateway Travel Plaza at the Breezewood exit to grab a bite to eat and get fuel. I had been stopping there for 20 years, so it felt like home. From there, I would get on I-70 and head for DC. It was 1600 hours, and I had to meet Colonel Raines the next day at 1100 hours, so I needed to find a place close to DC to stay for the night. It was only about 125 miles into the city and it should've been an easy drive. It was rush hour; everyone would be coming out of town, so there shouldn't be much traffic going in. It would be a madhouse tomorrow morning when I was trying to get into the city, though.

I thought I would try to stay at Fort Detrick near Fredrick, Maryland. Fredrick was where I needed to get off of I-70 and head south on I-270 to get to DC. Fort Detrick was on US Hwy 15, just a few miles north from where I-70 and I-270 cross. It was easy to get to and it cost less to stay on a military base. It was safer, too, since there was a lot of security. This was where our main biological weapons were developed. There was also a PX (Post Exchange: store for military personnel) if I needed something.

The next morning at 0700 hours, I was only about 50 miles from where I was supposed to meet Raines, but it was rush hour. I would need all three hours to get there. I had just passed Gaithersburg. They had a good airport for small private planes. In the past, there were time when I had flown my plane into that airport so I could get to a meeting and back home in the same day.

I was at the northwest corner of DC where I-270 and I-495 meet, when I took I-495 east and got off on Connecticut Avenue heading south. I passed the National Zoo and turned on 17th Street NW and continued south. I could see the White House to my left.

You could never find a place to park around the Mall, so I was going to park in a lot just south of the Treasury Department. From there it would be a nice little walk to the Mall. I was supposed to meet Colonel Raines at the Natural History Museum on the north side of the Mall.

Walking north on 14th Street I saw the Holocaust Museum across the street on my left. What a special place. The last time I was in DC, I spent the whole day there. You could feel a real spirit within. That holocaust may be over, but there are still many more going on all over the world. How could one group hate enough to kill everyone in another group? I just didn't understand.

The first building I came to was the American History Museum. I needed to continue east to the next building. This was the Natural

History Museum, my favorite museum on the Mall. I walked up the front steps and into the rotunda. To my right front was the African Elephant. I first saw the elephant back in 1960 when I was here on my senior trip. I walked over to it to wait for the Colonel. There were a lot of people admiring the elephant. The little kids liked to just stand and stare at it. A Boy Scout troop from Ohio was there that day.

It was about 1045 hours and there were a lot of people there, with dozens of school kids wandering about. It was 1985, and I hadn't seen nor talked to Raines since 1972, until he called me last week asking me to come out to talk to him about General Fong. I couldn't imagine what The Company could need me for now and what, I wondered, could General Fong have to do with anything? I hadn't had any contact with General Fong since 1964 when he helped us with the Gulf of Tonkin attack.

CHAPTER TWO

The Rotunda

There he was. He looked about the same, a little older, but then it had been over 20 years. Raines had gained some weight and his hair was streaked with gray. Our eyes met, and a smile came to his face. I smiled, too. Then it seemed like no time had passed. It was 20 years ago, and I was back in Nam. There was a lump in my throat. I could feel the heat and see the palm trees, just like the last time I was with the Colonel.

"Hi, Colonel Raines," I said. "It's been a long time!"

"Yes," Raines agreed, nodding his head. "Let's walk and talk."

He looked at me, then his eyes glanced to his left and he started walking in that direction. I waited until he passed me on my right and he was 20 or 30 feet ahead of me. I then checked the surrounding area to be sure he wasn't being followed before I turned to walk behind him.

He moved into the Dinosaur Exhibit. There were a few people there. Raines stopped and looked at some of the exhibits, then walked over to the Ice Age area and stood near the Wooly Mammoth. There were people there, too, but they were moving around and looking at other things. They appeared to me to be nothing more than ordinary tourists.

I was next to him then. I looked directly at him with questions racing through my mind. He turned his head, looked at me with a smile, and again said, "It has been a long time, Kurt. Good to see you!"

"Yes," I agreed, "a very long time - It's good to see you, too, Colonel."

He laughed, "I'm not a colonel anymore. I'm just a working guy, with no title."

"Well," I said, confused, "if you're no longer a Colonel, and I'm no longer a Sergeant Major, what was so important that I had to come to DC to meet you here," as I leaned back against the wall, crossing my arms over my chest.

"Well, I'm not a Colonel, but I still work for The Company. Look Kurt, what I need you for *is* important. I don't think there's any danger here in DC. I could have met you in my office at Langley, but I would just as soon not have others there see you."

"You look great by the way," he added, smiling again. "You're still strong and fit, I see, and you've kept that golden hair the ladies always liked," as he laughed.

"Yeah, thanks Colonel," I said, laughing with him, but I knew there was truth to this. I still noticed women giving me a second glance from time to time.

"Well, you know it's true," Raines went on to say, "It isn't just your hair or your build, but that way you walk with such ease and confidence. I think the women like that, and your icy blue eyes . . . or so I've heard them say." He laughed again, having fun with my embarrassment.

"Whatever," I thought, as I laughed along with Raines. What other women thought of me didn't impact my life. I'd been married for a long time to the love of my life. She was the only woman I was interested in.

"I'm hungry," Raines said, breaking into my thoughts, "How about you?" Glad to be changing the subject, I said, "Yeah, I could use something."

"Then let's go downstairs and sit, eat, and talk," he said.

"Okay," I thought, "I love this museum, but it sure costs a lot to eat here. I could feed two of us a whole meal back in Indiana for what it cost just to buy a sandwich in this place."

"Let's sit over there in the back," Raines pointed.

"Okay," I said, "that's fine with me." Personally, I always preferred to sit with my back in the corner. I always wanted to see what was going on around me, no matter where I was.

Once we were seated, I jumped right in with the questions. "What could you possibly need of me Colonel? I'm older now and I've changed a lot in the years since I last saw you . . . and what has General Fong got to do with anything?" Raines shook his head as he laughed and said, "Kurt, you always did get straight to the point no matter what!"

"It's like this," he said. "Do you remember that General Fong helped us at the Gulf of Tonkin, because he didn't think that Hồ Chí Minh and communism would be good for his people? Well, it turns out he was right. From 1975 when they took over the South until now, things have not improved for the people. He has stayed in good standing, and he and his family have been all right, but back in April the Vietnamese approved a new constitution to replace the one from 1975. The new constitution reasserted the Communist Party role in both government politics and society.

The Vietnam People's Army is organized on the same line as the Chinese Peoples Liberation Army. The General's problem is that the new people in power are looking into the lives of all the older government people and coming up with reasons to get rid of them. The new government is more interested in power than the welfare of the people. The General is worried that they might find out something about his involvement with us, but even if they don't, he is sure they will come up with some reason to get rid of him anyway. If that happens he's worried about what will happen to his family when he has no power."

"Okay," I said, "I can see his problem, but what does any of that have to do with me?"

"He wants us to get his family out of Vietnam," Raines explained.

"And the General, himself," I asked.

"No, he's not worried about himself; he just wants to get his family to the United States."

"Okay, Colonel, I can sure understand that, and we owe him a lot for his help. But again, what has any of this got to do with me?"

"Well Kurt, General Fong is worried about the authorities finding out that he helped the Americans, but he's also worried about who we send to rescue his family. I don't know where he got the idea, but he feels he can't trust The Company. Imagine that. He's worried because of what he knows about the Gulf of Tonkin and the fact that we never released the true story to the public. The truth would cause a lot of problems for The Company and the Administration. He's worried that it would be easier and better for us to have the guy we sent to rescue his family just kill him and his family instead."

"You know," he continued, "that *would* be good for us and a lot easier than getting them out. There are people in The Company who would agree that terminating him would be the right thing to do. That's why we're not meeting at Langley. I want as few of The Company people as possible to know about this."

"Well, okay, I can see that, but where do I come in to all of this?"

"Because," Raines answered, "I need someone from outside The Company who I trust to go get them out. More importantly, General Fong wants you to be the one to come and get his family, Kurt. He said that you are the only one he would trust with their safety."

"Really," I asked in surprise. "Why does he trust me, Colonel? I only worked with him one time at the Gulf of Tonkin."

"I don't actually know the answer to that," Raines said. "He just said that when he shook your hand and looked into your eyes he saw an honorable man, a man who would die if necessary to complete the mission. I totally agree with him on that, Kurt."

"Okay, he trusts me, Colonel, and I trust you, but the General is right about The Company. He and I are the only ones still alive who were at the Gulf, and that makes us a liability to them. I trust you, but you had to get the plan approved and the money for this mission from someone above you. All they would have to do is get us in there and then contact the Vietnamese to tell them we were in country. We would just disappear off the face of the earth. No one would ever know, and their liability would be gone."

"I've thought of that Kurt, but it was so long ago and there are no records of what happened. No one who had first hand knowledge about it is left in The Company. There's nothing but old rumors floating around the agency. Just to be sure, I didn't use the General's real name. I told the Deputy Director for Operations about the General's son being an Intelligence Officer in the Army of the Peoples Republic and that he would trade information that he obtained from his son in exchange for asylum for his family in the U.S., that way the General is an asset to us rather than a liability."

I sat back in my chair to take in what Colonel Raines had just told me. Looking up at him moments later I said, "You know, Colonel, I'll need some time to think about this."

I thought to myself, "Look at all the people here just walking around and enjoying the day and the museum. I love it here and I have a good life in this great country. I'm safe and relatively happy, and no one is shooting at me. Even better, I'm not shooting at anyone else. Why should I go back there and risk my life?" My thoughts raced on, when I suddenly realized - this was the answer.

I went to Vietnam the first time to try to give the Vietnamese people the same freedoms and life we had, but we failed. We not only didn't do that, but we left all the Vietnamese who helped us behind to be killed or tortured by the thousands, after we had already burned and destroyed a lot of their country. I couldn't even get Song, my own bodyguard and friend out. I didn't know what happened to Song at that time, but the others all died because they had helped us – no, because they had helped *me*. They were my friends. So for them, if I could do this and get a few people out of there to give them the life I have here, maybe in some small way I would have won the war and helped to make up for leaving Song and the others behind to die. I had never forgiven myself for that. Maybe this was a way to help make up for it.

I turned to Raines and sighed. I realized then that I had to do this.

"Okay I'll do it," I told him. "When do I go? How do I get in and get them out? There are a lot of things I'll need to know!"

"No problem, I have everything ready and in place," Raines told me, as relief spread across his face.

He paused and then added, "I hope you're still proficient with weapons, Kurt."

"Yeah, absolutely! I run a security company now and I also train SWAT teams."

As I was telling him this, I was thinking, "What is it with me?" Most of the guys who were in Nam couldn't wait to get home, and when they did, they melted right back into their old lives. Not me. I just couldn't fit back in. There was something in me; I don't know what it was. I tried to join in and enjoy life. I got married and found a good job, but I hated it. I just couldn't get into mundane things like paying the light bill. I hate to say it, but I missed the war – maybe not the war itself, but something. I know it was not fair to my wife. She couldn't understand, and I couldn't explain.

Anyway, as far as going back was concerned, I suddenly realized that I not only wanted to go rescue General Fong and his family, I needed to do it!

"Good," Raines smiled. "I can't say I'm surprised. I don't think you've changed that much at all, after all this time . . . do you remember Ron Albright?"

"Yeah, sure," I said. "He went to Bangkok after he left Nam and was running a bar there, as far as I know."

"You're right, and he's still running that bar," Raines smiled, "but he's been working for us all this time. That's where you're going to start. When you get there, he will fill you in on everything you need to know, then he will get you in and out of Nam."

"Do you still remember Bull, Kurt?"

"Bull? Do you mean the Vietnamese guy who set up the meeting with General Fong in Laos?"

"Yeah, that's him," Raines responded. "He'll be the guy who will be with you all the way in and out of Nam. He can also come out with you and back here if he wants. You see after the war, he stayed in Laos and Cambodia providing us with Intel (intelligence)."

"Okay," I said, "but there's one more thing. I want to bring the General out, too."

"Well, I would like that as well, but the General isn't sure he can arrange to get both himself and his family out. If it comes to that, he wants you to take the family, and leave him."

"Look Colonel," I said, looking directly into his eyes, "I will get everyone out including the General. I am not going to leave anyone there again, even if it costs me my life – so when do I go?"

"Right away," Raines smiled. "You need to be in Bangkok in 72 hours."

"What? It takes 12 hours just to get back to Indiana, and 24 hours on a plane to Bangkok!"

"You're right, Kurt, so you had better get going," he laughed. "I have your ticket out of Chicago."

"Come on," he added, "We have a few other things to do here first before you can leave. We'll take the Beltway around to I-295 and go up to Fort Meade to the NSA to get your new ID and documents."

CHAPTER THREE

JFK Remembered

"Okay," Raines laughed, "Smile for the camera. Now you're Paul Carper, a tourist going to Bangkok for fun in the sun. Here's a credit card in his name, and it has $10,000 on it for a start. We'll keep all you need on it. Let's get you back to your car now and on your way."

As we were leaving I saw Raines talking to two men. One of them turned to look back at me and smiled. I smiled back, and I knew I had seen him before, but couldn't remember when or where. It came to me later. I had seen this guy with Coleman, when we talked about how to assassinate people. It was back then that I learned what I know about the JFK (President Kennedy) assassination.

I was at Fort Gordon, Georgia, when JFK was killed. What I know, I learned when I was in Vietnam in 1967 while working for The Company. As part of what we were doing for Operation Phoenix, we talked about the best ways to assassinate someone. Of course what we did in Vietnam was not the same as you might do in the United States or some other country. In Vietnam we were at war, so a person getting killed was not noticed the way it would be somewhere else.

At one point we talked about assassinations in the States or in a country that was not at war, and how to do them. There were 10 or so of us military men, and two of Coleman's men. The Company men were 35 to 40 years old, and said they had been with The Company for a long time. We talked about the School of the Americas at Fort Benning. This was the U.S. Army training school that trains Soldiers and military personnel from Latin American countries in subjects such as counter-insurgency, military intelligence, counter-narcotics operations, and political assassinations.

There are many ways to execute an assassination. First, you need to decide if you want everyone to know if a person was assassinated, or if you need to make it look like an accident. It's very hard to make it look like an accident, especially if it's someone with power and money that is worried about being assassinated. Most of the time, you may want people to know in order to scare other people, or it just may not matter if anyone knows. In that case, it's a lot easier to do if you don't have to make it look like an accident.

There are many ways to assassinate someone: poison, explosives, and shooting. I'm going to talk only about shooting, as this relates to the JFK assassination. If you are targeting someone who is not in fear of being killed and has no security, then you may be able to get close to him or just walk up to him and shoot him. It's different when looking to assassinate high profile people with power and money and lots of security, who are worried about being killed.

Of course every assassination is different due to location and security, but there are a few standard rules to follow for all assassinations:

1. Everyone involved in the mission should keep the mindset that if they fail to terminate the target, then they themselves will be killed.
2. Use three shooters: one shooter is the driver, and the other two are to take the kill shots.
3. Take no long shot, never over 300 yards. You don't have to depend on the shooter being a great shot or the wind and the environment being just right for the shot.
4. Go, only if everything is a "go." Be willing to walk away.
5. No one is left behind.
6. Everyone on the team must agree that the goal is worth the risk.

We were talking about how a good assassination would work using these rules. Most people assume that you try to rely on the first shot to be the kill shot, but that's not the case. It's great if that happens, but you don't count on it at all. Most of the time the target is well protected as he moves, but security starts to break down after the first shot. They will try to move the target to a safe location. If the first shot hits the target, security will head for a hospital.

You would place the first shooter so that after he shoots, the target will move away from him. The first shooter is called the "driver," because his job is to make the target move or run, driving him to the spot where the other two shooters are waiting. Most of the time, security will try to get between the target and the first shooter and move the target away from the shooter. This will leave the target vulnerable from the front. You place shooters #2 and #3 somewhere that you think the target will be heading after your first shooter has fired at him.

During our meeting, we talked about different ways to do that, and used the chalkboard to draw how it might work. One of The Company men drew a plan on the board to illustrate. The first shot came from a building from the rear of the target car and did hit the target, then all the security went to the back of the car to get between the target and the shooter. The car sped up and drove away so fast that it left most of the security behind and had no security in the front. They drove right past shooter #2, who had the kill shot from the front at only twenty yards. The car then went past shooter #3, who didn't have to shoot. Since everyone was looking at the building, everyone else just walked away. "It was perfect," he said.

As I sat there looking at the board, I said, "This looks like Dallas when they shot JFK." The two Company men looked at each other, smiled, and walked away. We all went to eat, and when we came back, I was standing outside the room waiting for the other guys when I heard the same two Company men talking in the classroom. I couldn't hear everything, but I did hear one of them say, "Dallas was a perfect mission, wasn't it?"

A few days later I was alone with Coleman, and I said, "If Dallas was an example of a perfect hit, where do you think the kill shot would have come from, the grassy knoll?"

He said, "No, from the storm drain. It leads to a safe area about half a mile away."

"And where would shooter #3 have been," I asked.

"Just beyond the overpass, but he didn't have to shoot," Coleman explained.

I said, "What do you think about Oswald?"

"I think he was a good guy who worked for us. How do you think he got a job in that building weeks before anyone knew the route JFK was going to take?"

I asked him why he thought JFK was killed, and he said it was because of Vietnam. He went on to explain that the war wasn't really about Vietnam, but about the Communists taking over the whole world. They had been *taking a country and then using it as a base to take the countries next to them – The Domino theory. They had been taking one country at a time for a long time, and the Intelligence Community decided that the next country they tried this with, was where we were going to go in and stop them. The next country just happened to be Vietnam.*

Coleman said that we didn't care about this country as a country, it was just the place we needed to make a stand against communism. But JFK had changed his mind and was going to pull us out of there, and he had let us down at the Bay of Pigs. Coleman went on to say that LBJ (President Johnson) didn't like this war, but he knew he had to stick with it, or else.

Coleman never said anything about it after that, but Dallas was used a few more times when we talked about assassinations.

CHAPTER FOUR

Hồ Chí Minh's Birthday –
The Day Skinner Died

Driving away, I realized that I had just enough time to stop by the Vietnam Memorial Wall. The first two times I had been out there to go to the Wall, I couldn't bring myself to go up to it. It was as though it was surrounded by a force field. It wasn't a bad force field, but an emotional one. I just sat on the grass about 50 yards from it, and then left. Since then I had been up to the Wall, and when I touched it I could feel the presence of all those men.

"Today is a beautiful day," I thought, as I stared at panel 20-E, "It's been a long time, friend. I think of you every day." It was Hồ Chí Minh's birthday, and we had a cease-fire. How dumb was that, to have a cease-fire on the birthday of the enemy's leader. "I tried to get to you that night, but the firefight was so intense I just couldn't. They killed most of us. I don't know who lost that night, you or me."

"They took your body away that day and I don't even know where you are, but I can feel you here. I still carry my Special Operations group coin, and when I rub it I can feel all the guys. I don't know if they buried you with your coin, so I'm going to leave my coin here at the Wall for you, my friend."

It's been a long time, but I can still remember it all . . .

It was about 0900 hours, and Song came over with a villager from An Lộc. The villager said there were VC in the village. I asked him how many there were, what kind of weapons they had, did they have uniforms, and did he know what they were doing? He said that sometimes there were 50 or so of them, and that he didn't know much about weapons, but he knew that all the VC had rifles. He also said that some of them did have uniforms and he thought he heard them say they were with the 48th Battalion. He didn't know what they were up to, only that they would go out in both the daytime and at night, and then come back. Many of the villagers of An Lộc were sympathetic to the VC and were giving them information about the area and feeding them, and the VC knew about us being there. He had heard them talking about our village, and about us.

Well I knew we had to check this out. I couldn't let the VC be that close to us and not take them out. An Lộc was only about five klicks (kilometers) away from us. I relied on Song to know the villagers. I asked him what he thought about this guy and he said that he believed he was telling the truth, but that he could be VC or a sympathizer. He said it could be a trap. Either way, we had to go check it out. If there were 50 or more VC and they had uniforms, then I would need more than the four or five of us. I called headquarters (HQ), and went up there to talk it over with them. If it was a trap then we needed to be ready, but even if it wasn't, we needed to take the VC out and clean the village of any VC and their sympathizers.

I told the Colonel I thought we needed to go there and stay for a week and see what was going on. He agreed. I told him I would need some regular army troops to go with us, and he said I could have 20 or so from the unit up the hill from our village.

I went up the hill and talked to Chuck. He was the 1st Sergeant for the unit. Chuck was a true Soldier. He was in his late-30s during the Vietnam War, but had served in Korea before that. He came from Newark, New Jersey, and talked with a heavy Jersey accent. He always spoke loudly and used a lot of profanity. Standing about five foot nine, weighing 220 pounds; he had a beer belly. He loved the Army and believed his main mission there was to take care of his men and lead them into combat. His nickname was DBB, Delta Bravo Bravo. He was hit in the belly during the Korean War and it looked like he had two belly buttons, so we called him Double Belly Button.

It was always great to see Chuck, and hang out there for a while listening to him. I told him my plan about the village, and he gave me 23 men, two 60s, a 50, lots of ammo, and two medics. I decided to take Song, Tuk, and

Skinner with me. That would make 27 of us, and that should've been all we needed to take out 50 VC.

The next day we got everyone together and I gave them a briefing. The plan was to get as close to An Lộc as we could, without being seen. We were going to sit there for a day to observe what was going on in the village, who was coming and going, and when. Once a pattern was established, we would engage them, and kill as many as we could. When we had control of the area, we would move into the village to set up there and stay for five to seven days. While we were there, we would talk to the villagers and try to create some kind of rapport with them. We needed them to know we were there to help them, and assure them that we would be there if they needed us.

It was 0600 hours, and I held a final briefing before we started out. I told the guys if they had any questions or any input, this was the time to come out with it. I had to tell them I didn't know why, but I didn't feel good about this. We needed to take it really slow. I reminded them that we wouldn't get more money or get to go home sooner if we got it done faster. We needed to be on our toes all the time. I said, "Slow and easy! Don't take any chances. Fire if you need to, kill them before they can kill one of us." It was only five klicks (about three miles) away, and we had all day to get there and set up, so again, slow and easy was the way to go.

We could see that there was jungle most of the way so we were going to stay in there and off the trails. Everyone checked and secured their gear to make sure they weren't making any noise. We stayed close to each other. I didn't want anyone in a position where someone else on the team couldn't see him. In order to maintain visuals on everyone, Song and I were going to take point. Skinner and Tuk were going to bring up the rear and make sure no one came up behind us.

Skinner and Tuk made a good pair. Skinner was a good man. He and I had gone through training together, and he loved being a Soldier. He was five foot eleven, but he was only about 160 pounds. He was thin, but strong. He looked like a Soldier with his short brown hair and square chin. There was a Special Forces tattoo on his left arm. If he was around, you had to be sure you checked your boots before you put them on. You never knew what Skinner might have put in them. In spite of his sense of humor, he was a fearless warrior.

Tuk was one of Song's friends. Like Song, the VC had killed most of Tuk's family. He was a few years older than Song, probably 23, or so. He was very thin, but quite strong. Unlike Song, who was full of shit and always ready *with a joke, Tuk kept to himself, and was quiet. I paid both of them to provide protection for me.*

I told Sergeant Williams, the senior NCO (non-commissioned officer) for Chuck's men, to keep someone on both flanks (sides), and we would keep one of the 60s up near the front, and the other 60 near the back. We kept the 50 in the middle, and positioned the RTO (regional transmitter operator) with the PRC-25 (back-pack radio transmission device) with the men, and Skinner and I both took a PRC-6 (walkie-talkie) so we could keep in contact with each other, and with them. We needed to make sure we were ready to call in air or ground support if we needed it. We couldn't get out far enough with a PRC-6, but we could with the PRC-25.

If we got hit on the way, Williams and his men would take action. We all knew what to do because we had been in firefights before. I reminded the guys not to worry about Skinner and me. If they couldn't see us or didn't have contact with us, then they would just do what they needed to do to get things done.

I told Skinner that we were going to be in the jungle, so we had to get four of the 12-gauges (shotguns) for us and four CARs (carbine rifle, short version of M-16). We needed code names, so I set them up as follows: William was "Black One," I was "Coconut," and Skinner was "Slim." Our gunships for air cover were "Firebird One," and "Firebird Two," and our artillery battery was "Big Bang Two." I wanted two men pacing, because we needed to know our status at all times. Radio checks would be every 15 minutes, starting at 0700 hours. It was then, 0650 hours.

Off we went. We were headed out Gate 4 and then it was only about half a mile until we could get into the jungle. Once everyone came through the gate, I told them to wait there. Song and I were going out to make sure that no one was out there watching or waiting for us, because we knew the whole thing could be a plan to get us out in the open. Song went out and to the right, and I went left. I told the men to work their way to the jungle and I would meet them there.

I took off with my 12-gauge slung on my back, and the 16, magazine-in, with a round in the chamber and the safety switch on. There were two men walking into our village, and I didn't see anyone else except Song, to my right. We agreed all was clear, and decided to check into the jungle about 50 yards deep, then return here.

"Black One, Coconut," I said. "All clear. Move out and join up with us." Black One gave the all clear, and Song moved into the jungle about 25 yards

to wait for me. We prepared to move out, and I told them to remember to stay close.

Damn, it was so hot in the jungle with no breeze and so dark. I was glad we had the other guys with us for the firepower, but you couldn't move 27 men through the jungle and be quiet. If it were just Song, Tuk, Skinner, and me, no one would have ever known we were there.

We had gone about half a mile when it was time to stop and have a look around. I told Black One to take a break, and that we were going to have a look up ahead. I sent Slim to go look around, and we would go again in 15 mikes (minutes).

Slim reported that they were back and it was all clear. I told Black One it was clear, and it was time to move out. I told Song I would stay there and keep the rest of the men in sight, while he went ahead a little. I thought it would work well if one of us stayed out front while we were moving, at least for a while, so that's what we did. I stayed, and Song went on in front of us for about half a mile.

I put my hand up, and everyone stopped. I lowered my hand for everyone to get down. I told Song to stay put, and I moved back to talk to Sergeant Williams. We were about half a mile from An Lộc. From now on, we were going to move very slowly and try to get to a point in the jungle that was about 300 yards from the village. I told Black One to stay there with his men and wait until Song and I checked that area out. Song and I took off to see what we could see. After a few minutes, I told Black One to bring his men up. We had found a good spot to stop and monitor the village.

The jungle was thick and the villagers didn't like to come into the jungle. It was full of snakes and bugs and there was nothing they needed in there. This was as close as we could get. The last 300 yards were clear of jungle and out in the open. I had everyone move into the jungle about 25 yards and set up a perimeter. It was now 1500 hours. We were going to be there the rest of today, tonight, and all the next day and night. That was a long time for regular army troops to sit, eat, and be quiet. I told Williams that all he and his men had to do for now was stay in place until we were ready to enter the village. As long as no one saw us, we should have been safe there. I wanted the men to get some rest, but continue to keep the 60s set up and ready to go. I had them set some Claymores (mines) out around our perimeter and keep the men tucked back in the jungle until we needed them.

From 1500 hours until dark, all we saw were villagers going in and out of An Lộc. With binoculars, I could see men with rifles walking around. At one point, there were three men with rifles, two of them in uniforms. They came out to the edge of the village and talked, but didn't leave. Not much went on during the night. At daybreak we could hear and see villagers moving around. I could see smoke from the fires and villagers leaving, but no sign of VC.

At 0918 hours, two men with rifles in NVA uniforms came to the edge of the village. Soon, there were about 20 of them, all with weapons, some with M-1s (WWII vintage American rifle), but most with AKs. They started to move out of the village and down the main route. As they moved north, the trail came within 50 yards of where we were hiding in the jungle. There were 18 of them, and all but two were in NVA uniforms. They must have felt safe because they were talking and moving as if they were just out for a walk. Most of them didn't have their weapons in a ready position and didn't seem to be worried about anyone being around.

At 50 yards, we could hear them talking but couldn't make out what they were saying. They slowly moved up the trail until Song and I could no longer see or hear them. I hoped that maybe they would be back later in the day, and that would be our chance to ambush them. We continued watching the village, and could see a few men with weapons, but we couldn't tell how many.

I told Williams to bring his men up to the edge of the jungle and get ready to hit the VC when they returned. He set up the 60s, one at each end of our line, with the 50 in the middle. We put four men and some Claymores behind us, just in case someone came up from behind. I had Tuk move north into the jungle so he could see the VC coming back, that is, if they came back by the same route. It was all open area between us and the village and the trail that they would be using, so we couldn't set up Claymores without giving away our position. We would have to hit them from right where we were. At that point, they would be about 50 yards from us and about 300 yards from the village. There was no place for them to hide, except a field. The village was at a 90 degree angle from the direction we would be shooting, so there would be less chance of us hitting the villagers when we fired at them.

We waited and watched. The people in the village went about their daily routines. At 1524 hours, Tuk came up and said the VC were returning. Everyone knew to wait until I fired, but they also knew it was okay to fire before me, if they needed to. Each of us would to take someone in our own field of fire, so we were not all shooting at the same guy.

I could see them coming from my right. Just like when they left in the morning, they were still walking along and talking, as if out for a walk. Three or four of them had their weapons at the ready, but they didn't look like they were worried about anything. After all, they were almost back to their village and "safety," or so they thought.

I was at the left end of our line. I wanted to take the first shot, and I was going after the first man in line, hoping he was the leader of the group. I waited until the whole unit was in the middle of our kill zone and I took aim at the man I thought was in command. He was young, maybe in his mid-20s. He had an AK and a pistol on his left hip, meaning he was left-handed and was carrying his AK in his right hand. He was wearing an NVA khaki uniform with red markings on the collar, and as he walked, was talking to the man on his right, with his head turned that direction. He was only 50 yards away, and I was sure I could hit him in the head. With the first round you just need to make sure you hit them, you can kill them later, but you need to get a round into them right away.

He was still talking to the guy to his right, and his upper body was turned about 30 degrees to the right, so I could see his back. I put the sights on his back just below the shoulders. I was about to squeeze the trigger when I thought, "Here I am about to kill a man I don't even know. Does he have a wife, a family?" In fact, all of them were about to die and didn't even know it. I asked myself, "Where the hell is God? Where is the God they told me about in Sunday School who loved everyone and would bring peace to the whole world? Why are we killing each other on this earth?" Then Song nudged my arm, and when I looked at him, his eyes were asking, "What are you waiting for?" He was right! I was here to liberate the oppressed, and these were the oppressors. I was certain God was not going to come down right now and stop the killing, so at least I could stop those men from killing anyone else.

That was how I kept pulling the trigger. I thought, "I'm not killing anyone – I'm saving lives!" I put the sights back on him and squeezed the trigger. I saw his body lunge forward, as if someone had kicked him between his shoulders; blood splattered on the khaki uniform of the guy he was talking to when he was knocked against him.

When everyone opened fire, the noise was so loud you couldn't think. It was as if everything was in slow motion. I could see the VC being hit and blood splattering everywhere. I would acquire a target and fire, and when everyone was down, I kept putting rounds into them. I used two magazines, firing 36 rounds. After we had stopped, the 60s kept firing. They kept raking the bodies. You could see the dirt flying as they went over and over the pile of VC.

It seemed like a long time before the firing stopped but it was actually only a few minutes, and then it was over. I could hear the men on the 60s changing the belts of ammo and the other men putting in new magazines and letting the bolts go home on their 16s. I looked at the VC, and no one was returning fire. One was on his knees and some were making noises. When I looked to my left I saw the people looking at us from the edge of the village.

I stood up and asked my men if anyone was hit, but no one was. The VC really never had a chance to return fire. I motioned for the men to move out to the VC. Song and Tuk were the first there. All of the VC were dead, but five. Within 10 minutes, two more of them died, and the medics worked on the other three. I took Song, Tuk, Skinner, and four of William's men, and headed for the village. Williams and the rest of his men picked up the VC weapons and checked the bodies for papers.

When we entered the village, the people didn't know what to do. We started to talk to them, and the first thing I asked was if any of them were hurt. "No," said one of the men. Song and Tuk talked to the villagers and found out that three of the VC who were left in the village had run out the other side and were gone.

I called HQ, and the Colonel came out in a chopper. We had the villagers bury the VC. Choppers brought us more ammo, food, and medical supplies. The VC had been living here, so this was a village we needed to give some attention to. Our goal was to get the villagers to stop supporting the VC, but we needed to know why they were supporting them. Was it out of loyalty or fear? We soon learned that they had helped the VC out of fear. Once they knew we would protect them, they started helping us, so we needed to spend some time here.

The Colonel and I decided we should stay there for a week and work with the villagers to see how things would go. The village had about 500 people in it, and had a main meetinghouse with a courtyard. The rest of the village was built around the other three sides of this meetinghouse. The Colonel took the three wounded VC back with him.

We set up an HQ in the meetinghouse, a Van Fong. This was the only building that wasn't mud and straw. It was a stucco building with a real door, windows, and a tile roof. I put the RTO and Song there with me. We built seven bunkers in a semicircle in front of the Van Fong facing the open field where we had killed the VC. The bunkers were three feet in depth. We didn't put tops on sand bag bunkers unless we were staying for a while. In fact, we just dug foxholes if we were only staying 24 hours, and only filled sand bags and put them around the foxholes if we were going to stay for a day or two. In this case, we were going to stay for a week, and that would give the VC time to bring in heavier weapons, so we were going to put a top on those bunkers with at least two layers of sand bags. It would be a big job, so we paid the villagers to fill sandbags and help build the bunkers. We had three feet of sandbags around the hole.

For the next four days we worked with the villagers. We treated 30 to 40 of them each day for various medical conditions. We even delivered a baby and talked a lot with all of the people to see how we could help them. The people were friendly, but things just didn't seem right. No one would say much about the VC who had been living in the village. No one seemed to know anything about them, what unit they were with, or what they did. That seemed strange. In a village this small, everyone should know everyone, and what is going on.

Song and Tuk brought two people in and said they were VC, and that they were telling the VC in the area what we were doing in the village and how we had our defenses set up. He said he was sure that they were not villagers but VC. This was about 1900 hours on the 18th of May. Like a lot of other dumb things going on, we were going to have a cease-fire on the 19th, because it was Hồ Chí Minh's birthday. This was the man who was trying to take over this land, killing everyone, and we were going to honor his birthday. What a bunch of shit!

It was about 0400 hours and I couldn't sleep. I walked outside and knew something was wrong. I didn't know what it was, but I knew something was wrong. Then it hit me. The village was dead quiet. There was not a sound. There were no fires and no voices. Everything was dark and quiet. I went back into the Van Fong with Song and the RTO and told them to stay awake, then I went to each bunker and told everyone to stay awake – everyone. With three men in each bunker they slept two hours and were up one hour, but I wanted everyone up all the time now. I walked back to the Van Fong and stood there looking out over the bunkers and into the dark field.

About 0430 hours I heard a bugle blow, and then there were massive explosions and the bunkers blew up. All but two of the bunkers were gone. Nothing was left but sand, blood, and body parts flying everywhere. Then 200 or 300 VC came charging at us out of the darkness. I turned and ran inside the Van Fong. Fire was coming from everywhere, not only from the field, but from everywhere in the village! My first thought was that they were coming for the prisoners we had. When the bunkers blew, it killed 20 of us right then, and I was not going to let them have the prisoners. I told the RTO to call for some help and medivacs.

Song and the RTO were on the ground returning fire. I took my 16 and looked at both of the prisoners. I could see the fear in their eyes, and I thought, "You can't just kill them!" Then, I thought about my men who had just died. I told myself there was no way that they were going to die so these guys could live. I pointed the 16 at the one on the right, and he just closed his eyes. I pulled the trigger, and his head exploded. The other had his hands tied behind him but jumped up and ran for the door. I pulled the 16 up to my chest and pulled the trigger. He went flying out the door and into the dirt. I went over, and he was lying on the ground on his face. Blood was running out of his mouth, and he was not moving. I shot him two more times in the back. It made his body jump, but he was dead anyway.

I went back in and asked the RTO if he had gotten a hold of anyone. He said that the company on the hill above our village about five klicks away was coming, and that there was a gunship in the area coming to help. Since there was a cease-fire for Hồ Chí Minh's birthday, HQ would not authorize artillery support and would not send air support.

I looked out into the courtyard, and realized the villagers had planted 155 mm rounds under our bunker while they were helping build them! The only two bunkers that didn't blow up were on each end. The only reason they didn't blow was because the lines had been too long to carry the electrical charge. One of the bunkers that was left had a 60, and it was being fired continuously. The bunker with the 50 on it was gone, and that was the bunker that Skinner and Tuk were in.

Fire was coming from everywhere, not just from the field in front of us, but from everywhere inside the village, too. Song and the RTO stayed in the Van Fong and fought from there. I ran to the bunker on the left side of the courtyard. Williams and one other man were in there. Both of them had been hit but were still able to keep firing the 60.

I looked to the rear towards the village, and there was a large group of men running at us. I wanted to just let go with my 16 on full auto, but that was not very effective. You waste a lot of ammo that way. So I took aim at one of them and fired, then got another one in my sights and fired again. I was getting one with every round, but it was hard because there were so many coming at me. As I got one in my sights, I saw a bandage on his right upper arm. It was a boy who I had helped yesterday, and I put that bandage on his arm. I thought, "You bastard! I helped you, and now you are trying to kill us!"

We couldn't kill them all. As they ran by us, they would throw grenades in our bunker and we would jump out. While we were out on the ground, they would run by and throw the grenades on the ground near us, so we would jump back in the bunker. We were killing a lot of them, but there were too many. I ran to the other bunker and found two men still alive. I grabbed them, and we ran back to the other bunker. With five of us in one bunker, it was easier to keep the VC off of us. I ran back to the Van Fong and got on the radio. It was DBB, the 1st Sergeant up on the hill. He was about half a mile away to the east, and was getting ready to enter the village. The gunship was overhead now, too.

Firebird called and asked for a "SIT-REP," (situation report). I said, "We are under heavy attack and vastly outnumbered. We have lost 20 men, only seven left, and all seven have been hit. We are low on ammo, in hand-to-hand combat, and in danger of being overrun." At that moment, Firebird said, "Coconut, are you able? I say again, are you able?"

I told him to stand by. I had to think. I was firing and couldn't hear anything but gunfire, and this was the most important question that I had ever had to answer. How could I, a young man from Midwest America be here, and have to answer a question like that? How did my world get so messed up? This was one of those things everyone talked about in training, but you didn't really think the time would come when you would actually have to make this type of decision.

Everything in the Army was stated in short-form, and so was this. Just like the words "SIT-REP" and "Intel," but all of them had a longer meaning. I'll bet no one, including most of the normal Soldiers in the Army, would understand the importance of the question Firebird asked me, or how crucial a "yes" or "no" answer would be. It meant life or death.

I thought about what "Are you able," really meant. He was asking if we were still able to resist. If I said, "No," then that would mean I didn't think we could survive and Firebird would start to fire on our position and kill everyone, including us. This would be better than being taken as a POW or killed by the VC. If I said, "No," then not only would I die, but I was giving the command to kill my men, also. How in the world could it come down to one little word "No," that could end my life?

I always told myself that I would never think of such a thing, but here I was thinking about it now. If they got their hands on us, it would not be good, but I just couldn't say, "No." If my men and I were going to die, we were going to die fighting. I said that then, but I knew if we ran out of ammo, our only hope would be to fight in hand-to-hand combat. That is not something to look forward to. We would be better off killed, than to be taken prisoner.

But we weren't dead yet, and with Firebird up there and DBB and his men on their way, I thought we had a chance to survive. This was one of those times when time seemed to stand still. It must have been only a few seconds as this was all flashing through my mind. I replied, "Yes, I say again, yes, we are able!"

Song and I were in the Van Fong, and I had a magazine full of tracers to fire into the air.

"Firebird, this is Coconut! See if you can see me. I hear you. You are to my right front at about a quarter of a mile." He told me to go ahead and mark my position, so I fired one tracer round every second. "I see you, Coconut," he replied.

I told him if we were going to survive he needed to shoot up everything around us. We were taking fire from everywhere, even the village.

"The whole village is VC. I say again, the village is VC. No friendlies in the village. Kill everyone! I am designating the village as a black zone!"

A black zone was a "free fire zone." You could kill anyone in the zone. In order to save ourselves, we were going to have to kill men, woman, children, and anything that breathed air. While that may sound harsh, that responsibility falls on the conscience of the VC. They were the ones who put their people in harm's way.

While my friends back home were making decisions about what movie they wanted to go see, I was halfway around the world, making life and death decisions for myself and others; I was so scared, I would kill or do anything to survive at that moment. I knew when I got back to Indiana no one would ever understand this. Hell, I didn't understand this, and I was there. At that point I didn't care about the politics of the war or what people back home thought, I just needed to survive the next few minutes!

I called the bunker and they fired up in the air with tracers. Firebird identified them and made a pass over us firing two mini-guns. This stopped the mass assaults on us, but the VC had a mortar (weapon that launches projectiles) to our right front about 400 yards out, and that was a problem. I called Firebird and told him about the mortar, and he asked if I could mark it for him. I loaded a 16 magazine with 15 tracers and fired at the mortar, but it was too far, and I couldn't hit it. At least it gave him an idea of where it was. Just then, the VC fired the mortar and Firebird saw it go off. He made a hot run and hit the mortar with two, three-inch rockets. We were still taking a lot of fire, but at least they were not rushing us now.

DBB called, "Coconut, are you ready for us to come in?"

"Roger, DBB, come on in. Everyone is in the one bunker or the Van Fong."

He had 150 men and was coming in from the east through the village. I told DBB that everyone in the village was VC and to kill them all, don't worry about innocent villagers. In about 10 minutes I could hear a lot, and I mean a lot, of 16 fire coming from the village. The fire coming at us from the village stopped, but we were still taking fire from the field in front of us. Firebird said he had a volunteer in a slick with him, and he was ready to come in for our wounded. I told him we needed light, so he said he would drop flares. The flares lit up the whole area like midday.

There were dead VC everywhere. Thank God for Major Black, who was patrolling in the area, and in spite of the cease-fire, still responded to our distress call! We told him the LZ (landing zone) was too hot for him to land, but he shouted, "To hell with the hot LZ!" As heavy as the ground fire was, he dropped off his men to protect them and single-handedly flew his chopper right into the courtyard shouting, "Tally ho and away we go!"

We started to throw everyone who was wounded into the chopper. It was taking a lot of fire, but Black just sat there and waited for us to fill it up. He flew in three times, taking out the dead and wounded. By the time he came back for the last time, DBB and his men had come through the village and had it under control.

It was starting to get light; the VC had broken contact and were on the run. I was looking in all the bunkers, or what was left of them. Everyone in the bunkers that were wired was dead. Out of the 27 men we entered the village with, only seven of us were alive, and everyone had been hit.

When it got light, there were a lot of choppers coming in. We threw all of our dead in the choppers. I went to the bunker where Skinner had been. Skinner and I had gone through training together. We had promised that if one of us died, we would be sure to bury them with our SF Coin. I found Skinner, but his legs were gone. I pulled him up into my arms and just held him for a while, then I carried him to the chopper and said, "Goodbye."

A lot of people from HQ had come in by now, and I couldn't find Tuk. I was looking for him when DBB came over and said that Tuk had been killed. He said Tuk had been lying in a hole when he and his men came through the village. Tuk knew DBB, and when he saw Chuck, he made a noise, but when DBB turned, he just saw a Vietnamese with a weapon. He didn't realize that it was Tuk, and he fired and killed him! When he told me what he had done, this big hardcore 1st Sergeant who had fought in Korea and now in Vietnam, turned away with tears in his eyes.

There were dead VC everywhere, and some that were not dead yet. I saw Song over by the Van Fong with two VC. He was asking them what unit they were with and how many of them there were. They were not saying anything. As I walked across the courtyard I had blood running into my eyes, and I was so angry I couldn't think. The chopper was leaving with Skinner, all my men were dead, and all the villagers we had helped, had turned on us. My head felt like it was going to explode!

I looked up into the sky and yelled at God. I called him everything I could think of, and then I shot into the sky and told Him He was nothing in my life anymore, and that I didn't believe in Him. I walked over to Song and the VC. I took the 45 pistol out of Song's hand and aimed it at one of the VC and asked him where their camp was. He just looked at me and said, "Go to hell! You are an American, you can't shoot me."

I put the 45 down to my side and looked at Song and then looked at the chopper that was taking Skinner away. It was as though a calm came over me, and the rage left, but I knew I had to do something to avenge the killing of my friends. I looked back at the VC, pulled the 45 up, pointed it at his eye and pulled the trigger. I then pointed it at the other VC and asked him where their camp was. He started to tell us everything he knew. I handed the 45 back to Song and turned around to walk back across the courtyard toward the field. When I turned around there were six or seven guys looking at me including the Colonel, but they just turned away and went back to what they were doing.

When I got near the Colonel he said that the VC body count was about 200. I just looked at him and didn't say a word. I went over to where there was a can of 16 ammo. I loaded up all my magazines and called for Song to come over. I told him to get ammo and come with me. Song and I spent the next three or four hours or more, following blood trails. As soon as we found a wounded VC, we killed him. We killed another 17 VC that day, just following blood trails. Song and I then returned to our village.

Remains of Bunker in An Lộc

CHAPTER FIVE

❧

Back to Southeast Asia

"Damn! It is 1500 hours, and I'm just leaving DC. There's going to be a lot of traffic, and I have to get clear back to I-70 and Breezewood, then onto the Pennsylvania turnpike to get back to Indiana."

Normally, this was a long, boring 12 hour trip home, but not this time. I had so much to think about; I was sure the time would fly by quickly. It had been so long since I had been there. I hoped I could remember some of my Vietnamese. It was always hard to tell my wife and kids I had to leave, and not be able to tell them where I was going or what I was doing.

I decided to stop at the rest stop in Ohio and get something to eat and drink. "I guess I had better enjoy this hamburger, it may be my last one for a long time." That's another thing I would miss, our good old American food. They didn't have good milk in Nam, either.

My flight had just departed O'Hare in Chicago, and I was glad to be going back on another mission. I realized I had always been a better Soldier than I had been a husband or father. This trip was just another reminder. I kept telling myself, "I have to remember my name is Paul Carper."

The trip over there was much easier now, than back the '60s. It took about 24 hours to get to Vietnam. I remember that we left Chicago about

0800 hours, and we kept up with the sun all the way. We finally landed at about 1000 hours in Vietnam.

The earth rotates at about 500 mph at Chicago, and that is about how fast the plane flies, so you stay at about the same time all the way there. I remember it was hard to sleep, and I was so tired when I got there. I still had to go all day before I could get any rest. It was different now than back then. I made six trips to Vietnam in those days, and each time the plane was full of Soldiers. I took all different routes back, from the East Coast and West Coast, and sometimes over the Pacific. There were a few times I even flew over the Atlantic to get there. No matter which way we traveled, we landed in Saigon, but this time I was going to land in Thailand and then 'back door' into Vietnam from there.

I hated plane seats. There was never enough room, and it was 19 hours to the Philippines for our layover. I liked that I had a window seat and could lay my head on the window to try to get some sleep, but it was a problem when you had to head for the bathroom and step over the other two people. The food wasn't bad now, either. It was better than on my trips to Nam 20 years ago.

There were all kinds of people on this plane. It looked like a lot of Thai's and quite a few Americans. I would guess most of the Americans were on vacation, and a few were probably businessmen. Everyone on the plane had a story, but I bet not one of them was going to have a story like I was going to have. Unless something unusual happened to them, they would all go home safe and sound and have nice stories to tell everyone back home. Even if I made it back alive, I would never be able to tell anyone about this trip. It made me think about all the operations that were going on each day. Most of the world went on day-to-day and never knew anything had even happened. With all the people in the world (about five billion at the time), each day a very small percentage of people did things and made decisions that affected everyone else in the world. Meanwhile, all of us went about our lives completely unaware of it.

I didn't think most of the people in the world *wanted* to know anything. They just wanted to go about their business, plodding along day after day, thinking everything in the world was okay. What I was going to do would not change the world, but it would cause a bump in the road if people found out about what we were doing and the involvement General Fong had at the Gulf of Tonkin.

CHAPTER SIX

Landing in Bangkok

"Please fasten your seat belts. We will be landing in Bangkok in 30 minutes."

This was the first time I had looked out and seen the jungle in 20 years. The last time I saw it was when I was leaving Vietnam, and I was in shock because we were abandoning our mission and our friends and allies.

It was Tuesday, April 29, 1975. Armed Forces Radio had broadcasted the code to let everyone know the city was about to fall. It was a dumb code, "The temperature is 105 degrees and rising," followed by eight bars of "White Christmas." I remembered all the array of emotions I felt then, and everything I was thinking as we left. It was as if my whole world had collapsed that day.

I ran all over Saigon trying to find Song. The whole city was in chaos with people running everywhere trying to find a way out of Vietnam. American civilians, Vietnamese citizens, and third-country nationals, being loaded on transport planes at Tan Son Nhut Airbase. They were to be flown to United States bases on Guam, Okinawa, and elsewhere. I could see the fear in everyone's eyes. The military had left, and those who could not get on a plane or helicopter heading for ships off shore, were on bicycles or anything they could use to try to get out of the country. Some were getting into boats to try to escape, and hoped that they could get out to sea and have the U.S. Navy pick them up. Unfortunately, many of those boats were not made to be seaworthy, and there were too many people on them. Most of them sank before they got very far.

As far as I was concerned, the U.S. was committing war crimes by leaving all those people behind to be killed or put into camps, because they had worked for us or helped us in any way. All three Presidents: Kennedy, Johnson, and Nixon, had made public statements saying they would never let the people of Vietnam down, would never allow the Communists to take over their country, and we would never abandon them. Yet, here we were, leaving them to be tortured and killed.

Song was supposed to get there so I could take him out with me. I got to one of our safe houses on the northwest side of Saigon, but Song wasn't there. One of his friends was there and said that Song had gotten stopped between Củ Chi and Saigon by a VC force. They had killed the other three who were with him, and he was wounded. He had squatted down with a grenade behind each of his knees, and when the VC came up to him, he stood up and died along with five VC.

God, I couldn't believe it! My friend was gone! It was as if a part of me had died right then. Song, who had been with me through thick and thin, always had my back, would've given his life for me in an instant, was dead, and I wasn't able to save him!

If I didn't get back and get on the chopper, I would be left there. I would have stayed and died if I could have saved him, but it was too late. By the next day the VC would own the city and if I was still there, I would been killed.

I had to get back to The Company house. The military had stopped taking anyone out and the Army personnel themselves, were all out of Saigon. The assembly point for us was 22 Gia Long Street, opposite the Grall Hospital. It was about half a mile from the U.S. Embassy and where the senior Company personnel lived and worked. The military and State Department had all gone and had left many of the Vietnamese behind.

We were still using a Huey (helicopter) to take locals out to ships. I remember after I got home there was a famous picture of a helicopter on a roof with Vietnamese climbing into it to get out of Saigon. The headlines said it was an Army helicopter on top of the U.S. Embassy taking the last of the Vietnamese out of Saigon. In fact, it was a CIA Air American Huey on top of CIA Headquarters taking some of the Vietnamese allies out, not the Army on the Embassy.

Here I was, back in Bangkok again. The heat was just as intense as I remembered, but the airport was different. There were a few security guards but not many military.

Hey, there's Ron now. He is older and a little heavier, but I would know him anywhere! He must be about 45 by now, just like me. We were both six feet tall, but he was still smaller in body size, like in the past. He was born and raised in New York, and had always been quiet. He was usually talking about his girl and the car he had back in the States. Ron really never wanted to be in the war, but he was a good Soldier. He was always there when you needed him.

I shook his hand and looked into his eyes, but that just wasn't enough. At the exact same time, we both put our arms around each other and stood there for a moment. "Well, here we are again." It was a different time, but the same place and the same enemy.

He said, "Kurt, it's great to see you again!" Turning to the side, he introduced me to the Vietnamese gentleman standing behind him. "This is Ton, Kurt. He's been with me for 10 years. He knows everything I know and will keep you out of trouble here, so listen, and do everything he tells you to."

I looked at Ron with a question in my eye and he knew just what I was asking without saying it. "Don't worry he knows about you and what you are here for. He came out of Vietnam back in '75. I trust him with my life, and so can you."

We climbed into a car and headed for the Jade Elephant, Ron's nightclub. It was a few blocks northwest of the center of Bangkok, about a block east of the river. The airport was about 12 miles northeast of the center of Bangkok, so we had about a 30 minute ride to the club. It all looked about the same as in the past. The streets were full of people on bicycles, and there were a hundred people in every vehicle. I could see that there were a lot more locals dressed like Americans, and many more Americans on the street. Ron said that the tourist business was the biggest income the country had now.

I needed to concentrate on the mission, and I had to be fearless. I couldn't be too cautious, or I might foul things up. I would have to stop worrying about the past and the people I couldn't get out the last time, and start concentrating on this mission from now on. This was a good thing. I began thinking; it was the mission that got me here, and the mission would allow me to get the General out of Vietnam, so maybe I would have saved someone after all.

After maneuvering down several more congested streets, we arrived at the Jade Elephant. Wow, what a place! This was impressive! Two large jade elephant heads circled in gold braid about five feet high, stood at each end of the building. There was marble for the street tiles in front of the building itself, with a small elephant head in the center of each tile. The lights were just like in Las Vegas, and there were lots of them. The front door must have been five feet wide and was made of teak with an ivory inlay. A beautiful girl with long dark hair and a very short skirt was passing out flyers advertising the drink specials inside.

"It's such a beautiful place Ron! I feel sorry for you though," I said, sarcastically. "It looks like you're living a hard life!" Then I laughed, shaking my head in amazement.

"Thanks, Kurt," Ron said, proudly. "Ninety percent of our customers are American. They know they can come here, have fun, and be safe. They can have almost anything they want: drinks, music, girls, gambling - almost anything-except drugs."

"Hey this is great inside, Ron!" I was in awe. Everything was beautiful. There was marble everywhere and mirrors from the floor to the ceiling. The bar must have been 50 feet long and looked like it was made out of solid teakwood. There was a ballroom with a glass ball hanging from the ceiling just like in the seventies. Wow, what a restaurant, too, with glass tables and gold chairs!

"This is the main bar area, Kurt, and the room over there is what we call Little Las Vegas. Guess what we do in there?"

"Man, Ron, it actually looks like Vegas in there, and I bet you take their money just like Vegas, too!"

"You bet," he said as he laughed.

"We also have a great restaurant, both Thai and American food," he continued. "Here let me introduce you to some people. This beautiful little lady is Lilly! She's in charge of all the girls. This is Tom Smith, and he's my manager. He was in the Air Force and ended up here after the war." Then he said, "Everyone, this is Paul Carper, my cousin from Ohio."

"Kurt, let's go back to my office and catch up on old times."

"Man, this is quite an office, too. I like the two-way mirrors, Ron. You can see what's going on in every room. Let's see, nine TVs? You only have two eyes!"

"That's so we can see outside the building as well," he said smiling smugly. Then he turned to Ton and said, "Make sure no one interrupts us, okay?" Ton agreed, and left the room.

"I like all your security cameras, too, Ron." This was totally impressive. I was amazed at what he had accomplished for himself since the war.

"Yeah, we can see everything that's going on in the Club and everything outside for two blocks in all directions."

"Doesn't the Thai government mess with you?"

"No, we make sure we stay out of any local politics, and they like the money we bring into the city. And . . . of course, we pay the right people to take care of us. It goes without saying that they don't know about our connection with The Company. The U.S. Ambassador and a lot of his people come here, and I go to the embassy as well, so they don't think anything about embassy people hanging around here. As a matter of fact, the Cultural Attaché is really The Company man."

"I see," I said, nodding my head. "What a sweet setup."

"Here's a key for that closet in the corner, Kurt. Only Ton and I have a key to it – and now you."

"Okay thanks, Ron. What's in it," I asked, as I reached my hand out for the key.

"Go ahead Kurt. Open it up and see."

"Whoa," I said, impressed again. "This is a better armory than we had back in Nam, Ron."

"Go ahead and take a 45, Kurt. You shouldn't need it here, but we can't take a chance that a local punk would try to rob you and mess up this whole mission. Don't go anywhere alone. You'll be staying with me at my home tonight. We can work on the mission tomorrow, but for now let's have something to eat, and then you can get some rest. I'll have Ton take you to my house."

It was nearly four hours later, and I had been gearing myself up emotionally for the last three hours since Ton had dropped me off at Ron's house. Before every mission I always had to start staging up psychologically. Now it was time to focus on the mission and put aside thoughts about non-essential things. I had been going over the various scenarios in my mind of expedient actions that might be necessary during this operation. It was nearly time to put the rounds in the chamber, and when that happens, my personality changes. My focus is entirely centered on accomplishing the objective.

Kurt and His Team's Weapons

CHAPTER SEVEN

To Cambodia

At 0800 hours, Ron, Ton, and I got down to business. I asked Ton how we were going to get into Vietnam. It was about 400 miles from Bangkok to the border of Vietnam near Tây Ninh where we would need to enter. I also wanted to know how many men we had, and if anyone knew when and where we were going to meet General Fong.

Ton said he had it all worked out, but there was someone there who wanted to go into Nam with us. He told him it would have to be my decision. Before I could ask who it was, Ton said he was right outside, and then called him in.

"Oh, my God, Robe! Robe Martz, is that you? I haven't seen you for what, 15 or 16 years? Wow, it's great to see you! Are you still with The Company?"

I envied him. It was a hundred degrees, and there was nothing out of place on him. He was still so damn handsome, about five foot nine, brown hair, and of course, looking totally together. He was my age, but he looked like he was thirty. He reminded me of the Fonz from Happy Days. He could find a woman in the middle of the jungle! Robe always hated the jungle, so I figured he wouldn't want to go on this mission. He might get dirty. Ha! On the other hand, he may have been a pretty boy, but he wasn't a sissy. He would be there and kill if he needed to.

"Sure am," Robe answered, breaking into my thoughts, "but I'm here on my own this time. I just want to go in and help, if I can."

"Are you sure you're up to it, and you really want to go in with us? There's a good chance we won't make it out. Besides, when you were in Nam you worked with Coleman at HQ and didn't go out in the field much, not to mention, you were a lot younger then," I said with a grin.

"Yeah, I know, Kurt. You're right," Robe said, smiling back at me. "But I just want to do this. It's like a need." Robe suddenly looked so serious. I could see how sincere he was and how much this meant to him, and I could relate. I crossed my arms and walked around the room wondering if I really needed to be responsible for another person's welfare, with all that was to come.

"Okay, Robe. I would love to have you, if you're sure you're up to it. By the way, how's your head," I asked, trying not to laugh.

"What about my head? Oh! You remember the mortar round?" Shaking his head, he said, "It's okay now."

"Ron, I don't think you were there that time, so let me tell you about it. You don't mind if I tell this, do you Robe?" Robe shrugged his shoulders, knowing he had no choice.

It was back in '67. We were at the club, and at about 2100 hours they came and told everyone to go to the bunkers, because we were going to get hit. We sat in the bunker until about 0200 hours, and then they said it looked like we were not going to get hit after all, and to get some rest. So we all went to our tents. Robe's tent was about 100 yards from mine. At 0400 hours, the first round came in! It came in with about 10 others. They weren't too close to me, but one threw Robe right out of his bunk!

I was running over to see if he was okay, and was about 30 yards from his tent when I saw him coming out. He was staggering, had his helmet in his hand, and was about to put it on when a mortar or 122 mm rocket hit about 50 yards to his right, front. I was coming from the other way, so I was about 80 yards away from it when it hit. I was blown back, and as I fell back I saw Robe being picked up, and he flew backwards into his tent. I remember seeing his helmet come flying over the tent.

I got up and ran to Robe. He was in the back of the tent under a pile of cots and shit. I can still remember the look on his face. He looked at me, and I could see in his eyes what he was thinking, "Are we dead?"

I said, "No we're alive, but you have a lot of blood running from your head!" He just looked at me. The blast was so loud he couldn't hear anything.

I just patted him on his head and smiled. He looked me in the eyes and smiled. We made it to one of the bunkers and stayed put until the attack was over. It was then that we found out that he actually had six or so holes in his head! It was a good thing it hit him in the head, because if it had hit him anywhere else, he might have been hurt. Ha!"

Everybody laughed and laughed, except Robe, who looked a little embarrassed. "Hey, Robe," I said, "don't forget, we have to get up early, so try not to have too much fun tonight. Don't forget where you're sleeping! Ha!" Then I said, "Hey, everyone, let me tell you how Robe use to find his tent back in the war!"

Robe covered his face with his hands and said, "Thanks a lot Kurt, but I don't think they really want to know!" With that he started to exit the room.

"Oh come on Robe, I'm sure they'd like to hear this story. Don't leave!" Robe just shook his head and turned back for the inevitable laughter to come.

"It was back in Nam," I continued, "and Robe's tent was on the right side of an active combat runway on the south end. One night he got so drunk he had to crawl down the white line in the middle of the runway until he got to the end, and then roll to the right to find his tent! They found him the next day halfway between the runway and his tent. I told him then, it was a good thing no plane landed in the night or he would've been road kill!"

Everyone laughed, and I added, "There's no runway here, so if you crawl down this white line, you'll be in the street and be road kill for sure! Ha!"

Robe couldn't help but laugh along with everyone else, but Ton, in his straightforward way, said, "Okay we've had our fun. Now, let's get down to business. This is how it's going to go down. Ron will stay here and run interference for us in case someone gets on to us here. Kurt - you, Robe, four of my men, and I are going to the border of Vietnam and Cambodia about 20 miles from Tây Ninh. Bull and his men will meet us there and take us into Vietnam to get General Fong. We will leave at 0500 hours, tomorrow. Our primary weapons will be AKs. There is a lot of ammo around and more weapons and parts if we need them. If or when we fire, it will sound like AKs and not 16s. We'll eat local food, taking medical supplies, and a lot of morphine."

Now it was my turn to brief them on communications. "For radios we have Motorolas for our walkie-talkies and an Iridium satellite phone that works almost anywhere in the world to get back to Ron, The Company, or the military, if we need to. Robe, you make copies of all the phone numbers for The Company and the military and see that Ton, Ron, and I all have the numbers. Make sure Bull gets a copy, too, when we meet up with him. Everyone, try to commit them to memory, so if we get nabbed, no one can find the numbers. I have taken them off the phone memory, so if the Vietnamese get the phone, they can't get The Company's or our military numbers. We need to make sure if something goes wrong, they can't connect us to the U.S. Government. Along with all of that, make sure you don't have anything on you that would identify you. No papers of any kind. If the time would come that you need to call this satellite phone, the number is 88163155186."

"It's 0550 hours," I said, "Everyone on the boat!"

Then, I asked Ton about the boat and crew, and he said, "The boat's 45-foot, and it's sea worthy. I wouldn't want to be out in the middle of the Pacific with it, but it's good as long as we stay along the shore all the way. As for the crew, they're all Vietnamese who got out in '75. They don't know who you or Robe are or what we are doing, only that they are to get us into Cambodia and wait for us. This thing will run from 12 to 15 knots, and it's about 300 miles to where we're going to switch to another boat and head further up the river. It should take about 24 hours. I hope to be near the river by no later than 1200 hours tomorrow, that way we will have light going up the river. This is going to be a long ride in a small boat, especially since it goes up and down with every little wave."

"Robe," I asked, "do you know who General Fong is and why we need to get him out?" Robe shrugged his shoulders and said, "Well, all I know is that he had something to do with the Gulf of Tonkin."

"Yeah," I agreed, "he was the North Vietnamese General who helped set up the attack and provided us with the North Vietnamese PT boats. We need to get him and his family out of there."

Handing him my AK and looking him straight in the eye, I said, "Robe, listen very carefully. You didn't go on operational missions back in the war. Are you sure you understand the risks of this mission? This is not academic. This will be a real life and death operational mission."

Robe looked down at the weapon in his hands and then up at me. He looked down again at the AK for several seconds, but when he looked up at me a moment later, I could see the determination in his eyes. In a quiet voice, he said, "I do understand Kurt. I understand the risks, but I want to go."

"Well, let me spell out the rules for you then, just in case. When we get to the river you can stay with this boat if you want, or go on with us. That will be your decision."

I looked up to stare directly into Robe's eyes. "You see, the General risked his life in hopes of stopping the war. As for me, the U.S. failed all the South Vietnamese when we left them to die at the hands of the North. This mission is a way that I might be able to get someone out and give them a better life. At the same time, though, we can't be the cause of an international incident. That means we can't be caught alive or leave anyone behind alive."

Silence hung in the air and I could see Robe was considering my words.

"You're my friend Robe, but make no mistake, this mission comes first. I will kill you and everyone on this mission, if it becomes necessary. What worries me the most about you, is that you need to be able to do the same. If I get hurt and can't get out you need to kill me. Do you think you can do that Robe? Think about it for the next 24 hours. I know Ton, Bull, and the others can do that. They have killed before. Don't get on the next boat going up the river into Nam if you have any doubt about this, okay?"

"Why did you come back again, Kurt," he asked. "It can't be for the money. The money can't be worth the risk."

"Yeah, you're right," I agreed. "It's never been about the money for me. It's always been about freeing the oppressed. As corny as that sounds, it really is the reason. I'll tell you about the time when I first understood that."

I was part of the Special Operations Forces in Vietnam. It was the fall of 1966. I was part of a six-man team assigned to the 25th Infantry Division at Cù Chi. We had started an ambush school and trained the 25th LRRP (long-range reconnaissance patrol teams).

I had only been in Vietnam about three months this time, and I was out trying to gather intelligence from a small village about three klicks north of Cù Chi. I was with a platoon from the 25th ID (infantry division) out of Cù Chi. The village appeared to be a normal village, and there didn't seem to be anything going on or anything out of place. The men from the 25th searched all the hooches for weapons or signs of VC. I was there with three other men from my unit. The village had about 200 people and they were all just going about their jobs. I was talking to the village chief, and he didn't seem to be uneasy and didn't know much. He said that sometimes VC came through the village but didn't stay, and he didn't know where they came from or where they were going after they left the village. He said this was a small village, and most of the villagers had never been more than a few miles away from their home. Most had never even been to Củ Chi, and it was only about three or so miles away.

The men from the 25th didn't find any weapons or anything out of the ordinary, and we were about to leave the south end of the village when firing broke out! We all took cover, returning fire. It didn't sound like more than four or five shooters. It was unusual for a small force like that to attack a larger force. We had about 30 men with us.

I had moved back and was standing behind a small hooch. I was not in a position to be able to return fire, because I couldn't see where the fire was coming from. Then I felt someone pulling on my shirt, and turning around I saw a little woman standing there. Her skin was wrinkled and dried from the sun. Her teeth were black, probably from chewing sugar cane, and most of them gone. She was only about five feet tall, and very skinny. There was a look of panic in her dark eyes and tears were running down her cheeks. She was pointing and saying something, but she was talking too fast. I couldn't understand her. I could speak some Vietnamese, but I couldn't understand them when they talked so fast. I did understand enough to know that it was something about her son.

I turned and looked to where she was pointing. I could see a small boy curled up in a ball on the ground next to a hooch about 50 feet away. He wasn't really in any danger because the fire had all but stopped, and he wasn't in a position to be hit anyway, but the hooch was just mud and straw, and an AK round could go through it. I turned back and saw that the mother was still crying, and she started around me toward the boy. I put my hand out and said, "No," but she tried to push by me. With a smile, I pushed her back again, and said, "I go."

I turned and ran over to the boy. There was not much firing at all now, but I still had to keep down in case of a stray bullet. I knelt down on one knee and held my right arm out to him. He was crying and had dirt on his face from hiding his face in the ground. His tears were mixing with the dirt and making mud. He jumped into my arms and threw one arm around my neck and the other around my waist, burying his face in my chest. I would *guess he was about 6 or 7 years old. He was very thin and felt like a spider monkey hanging onto me.*

The firing had stopped, and the men from the 25th were walking around. I knew it was safe to move. I grabbed my 16 by the carrying handle in my right hand and took the boy back to his mother. When we got to where she was standing, she was still crying and had her hands up to her face. The boy jumped out of my arms, and the mother knelt down, throwing her arms around him. They were both crying.

As I watched this scene, a strange feeling came over me. It was like I was not in a war or a strange place. It was as if I was seeing the people for the first time. It was just like being back in Indiana. This was a mother and son, and they were real people. Up to this point it was just like training, only with real bullets. I always told myself that I was here to free these people, but those were just words until now.

I turned to see where everybody was, and I was about to move out when I felt that same pull on the back of my shirt. I turned around and there was the mother and the boy. She looked into my eyes and said, "Thank you," for her son's life. At least that's what it meant in Vietnamese. Then she reached out and grabbed my left hand and kissed it. When she did that, a tear ran down her face and onto my hand.

I hadn't really saved the boy, because he was never actually in danger of dying, but when the mother looked into my eyes, it went straight to my heart. I can't explain exactly what it was, but my life changed in that moment. I turned away, and we headed back to camp. I couldn't stop thinking about what had happened.

I'm not sure about all of my feelings. I can only compare them to other feelings I've had in my lifetime. It was a combination of the love of my mother, winning a big ball game, and doing something good for someone, yet it was bigger than all of those put together. I knew I had just done something far better than winning a ball game, making money, or anything a man could do in life. I had been training for war, but for the wrong reasons. Sure I wanted to do good for the people, but I think what I wanted most was the thrill of combat, and to be something special in the Army, earning medals, and all that.

Now I knew even at this young age, what I wanted to do with my life. I understood what it really meant to free the oppressed. I was young, but I thought of what I was going to tell my kids and grandkids someday about my life. Do I set them on my knee and tell them about some big business deal

I made? No, this was what life was all about – taking care of people. I don't know how good of a job I have done since then, but I really have worked at it.

Up to this time, I was just killing the enemy, but from that day forward, I never killed anyone. Every time I shot, it was to save someone. The enemy was killing my friends, and I had a responsibility to use whatever means necessary to keep them safe.

I earned many medals and received a lot of recognition for my military service. I have never made much money in my lifetime, but to that mother and little boy, I was someone special and they loved me. Sometimes that was all that kept me going in life after I came home. Of course, as I said before, after the war, I didn't feel like I fit back into society. War seemed to be the only place I did fit in. No one would ever know or understand how I felt, except for my fellow warriors. All of the money a man could have and all the medals the military could bestow upon someone, could not give me the satisfaction I felt by helping that poor, innocent little child.

Now, here I am in the same place in 1985 about to kill bad people to save good people, again. It was 0830 hours the next day when we passed Kampot, Cambodia. Kampot was on the southern coast, and the river we were going up was about 15 miles toward the southeast at the village of Khum Angkor, so we should be there in an hour or so. It was 0945 hours. Looking around, I couldn't believe how strange this was. It looked just like it did before and yet there were no Soldiers. The war had been over for years, and no one was looking for an American to shoot. The only Americans here were on vacation, although I doubted there would be many around this part of Cambodia.

It was good to finally stand on land and get off that boat. The weather was good, but it had been a rough ride, and I was sick to my stomach. I don't know if it was just me, but it seemed like the Vietnamese people aged in a funny way. They seemed to stay the same age until they got to be 45 or 50, and then they all looked about 90. This was how it was with Bull. The last and only time I saw Bull was in Laos in 1964. He looked a little older, but I still recognized him.

"Bull," I shouted. We shook hands and hugged.

"It's good to see you again, Kurt," he laughed. He still had that great smile.

"You, too, Bull!"

Funny, the first time I saw Bull I was worried he was going to kill me, and now he was the one who was going to keep me safe, or at least I hoped so.

"I see you have four men. Are they going with us?"

"Yes, they will be with us throughout the mission."

"Do they know where we're going and what we're doing?"

"They know everything," he said. "They have been working on this for over a year now, going in and out of Vietnam and making contacts. We have over 30 others in Vietnam and Cambodia to help us. They are all looking forward to getting a little revenge on the Communists. Let's get everyone on the boat now. We have been using this boat for six months to move rice and food up and down the river, Kurt, so no one will think anything about seeing it on the river. You and Robe should stay down with the supplies under cover when we get near a village, though. The villages have too many people standing around. We are going to stop at the village of Kampong Trach, about 10 miles up the river. It's a small village, and that's where we're going to pick up most of our supplies and weapons."

"Damn," I thought, "I had almost forgotten how hot and humid it was over here." It was hot on the first boat, but we were at sea and had a breeze the whole time. No breeze here, and it must've been 100 degrees with 90 percent humidity. My shirt was wet, and I had sweat running into my eyes from my sweatband, just like old times.

"Well, we have all the supplies on board now, Kurt, so let's get going," Bull said. "It's about 90 miles to where we're going to enter into Vietnam, so it's going to be a long hot trip up the river. It will take us around 20 to 24 hours."

CHAPTER EIGHT

Operation Cherry

It was 1130 hours the next day.

"Coconut," Bull shouted.

Wow, it had been a long time since anyone had called me Coconut. I couldn't believe Bull still remembered it. It sounded good to hear it, and somehow made me feel like a Soldier again.

"Coconut, we will be in the village where we'll be unloading in about an hour. At that point we'll be about three miles from Vietnam and about 25 miles from Tây Ninh."

It had been a long and boring trip to this point, but now it was time to change my mindset and get into my "get the mission done" mode. Time to clear my mind of anything but the mission. I had been thinking about home on the boat trip, but I couldn't afford to be thinking about anything but the mission now. I needed to think about Song and all my men who the Communists had killed. This was the time to be ready to kill quickly and without mercy or hesitation. Only completing the mission and getting the General and his family out could be on my mind now. We would get him out, or I would die here in the mud of Vietnam.

"Hey Bull, what's the name of the village where we're going to unload?"

"Phumi Bat Tras," he answered.

Oh, my God. I couldn't believe it! I was here before. I could see the village coming into view up the river. There were people on the river and on the banks. Little kids were playing in the river and washing the water buffalo. The village stretched out along the river, and there were mud and straw huts in the jungle along the river. It looked a lot like it did the last time I was here, but that was not a good time then, for the villagers or for me. I can still remember how it all began.

It was back in '67 as part of Operation Cherry.

It was June of 1967, and Operation Junction City had ended. General Westmoreland had tried to seal the border from Vietnam into Cambodia and force the 9th (about 10,000 or more VC), to engage with us, using our air, artillery, and firepower to inflict large casualties on the enemy. Unfortunately, most of the VC had slipped back across the river into Cambodia. They would break up into small groups and disappear. We were not allowed to follow them into Cambodia, or for that matter, even fire across the river into Cambodia.

Once in Cambodia, the VC were free to regroup, re-supply themselves, train, and get ready to come back into Vietnam and hit us again. Officially, the government of Cambodia was saying that they were not supporting the VC, but out in the countryside the VC had a lot of support. Some of the villagers helped VC because they were sympathetic, some out of fear, and others because they needed the trade to survive. Whatever the reason, it was a safe haven for the VC, and there was nothing "official" we could do about it.

We were in War Zone C, about 80 to 100 miles northwest of Saigon. This was near the end of the Hồ Chí Minh Trail. The trail started in North Vietnam and ran though Laos and Cambodia, ending here.

Officially, we could not be in Cambodia, but The Company had us doing recon there. We had located a large camp about two or three miles inside Cambodia near the village of Phumi Bat Tras, 20 or 25 miles west of Tây Ninh, Vietnam. We had taken pictures and given a report to Coleman, and he gave it to the U.S. Ambassador to Vietnam, who passed it on to the U.S. Ambassador to the United Nations. The U.S. Ambassador presented it to the Security Council. There, the representative for Cambodia said that the camp did not exist and that the pictures could be of any country in that area. So the U.S. Ambassador to the United Nations reported to the U.S. Ambassador to Vietnam, who went back to Coleman and said that it was official! The camp did not exist.

Coleman called me in with my team and told us what had happened. He said that since the camp "officially" did not exist, then we were to make it so. What could Cambodia say since they had just told the U.N. that there *was no camp there? They couldn't complain that we had destroyed something that didn't exist.*

This was not the first time we had done something of this nature, so we talked about how to eliminate the villagers. In the past, we just used a force of about 30 of us and went in and killed everything that breathed air. On one mission we cut off the head of the village chief and put an M-16 cleaning rod though his ears to hang it on the village gate with a note telling the villagers that if anyone helped the VC again, we would be back. I'm sure it didn't help a lot because they were more afraid of the VC than of us. The VC would always be there, and we would not.

This particular village had about 1,500 people in it, and it would take too large of a force to just shoot everyone. Plus, we had to be more discreet than the Army since we were in Cambodia and not supposed to be there. Since there could have been a lot of VC living in the village when we got there, Coleman decided that we should use nerve gas. That way, a small force could kill many of the people and be quiet at the same time. It was going to take a lot of gas for a village that size, plus the timing had to be just right. It could not be raining, and we would need a day with a good wind to spread it through the village and have it blow away from us.

We spent a week working on how to accomplish this. We decided to use about 30 guys to insert by boat up the river, with a lead team going in first to check things out. The second team would be waiting at the river to get out fast with the gas if something went wrong. They could deliver the gas and equipment after the first team had everything ready.

We were worried that if something went wrong, we wouldn't be able to get rid of the gas, and that someone would find out we were using it. We needed to be able to get rid of the evidence quickly. Most of the gas came in hard case canisters, so the only way to get rid of it was to pull the pin and let it loose. Even then, you would still have the empty canisters and no way to get rid of them. Fortunately, The Company found some gas in bags. They were double-lined, but still only bags. We would have to be really careful not to kill ourselves. If something went wrong, all we would have to do is cut the bags, dump the gas, and take the bags with us to throw in the river or bury.

It took about two weeks to get the gas in the bags. They came in OD (olive drab) green hard case suitcases with locks. We had gas masks, M-17A1s (telescope and quadrant mount), but we had to figure out how to disperse the gas. Joe came up with the idea to use fans. In the camps, they had fan units to blow tear gas down tunnels. There was a fan in each cage about 18 inches *in diameter. A fan had a shoot on the top to dump the tear gas in, and a gas engine that powered the fan. This seemed like it would work, but we couldn't use the gas engine or it would make too much noise. Joe came up with another solution. We went to the army combat engineers and had them replace the gas engine with the pedal part of a bike so we could just use our hands and peddle and spin the fan. We tried it and it worked.*

We had the engineers build four of them for us and we gave them four AKs and two VC flags in return. In fact some of the units later used this idea so they didn't have to use the heavy gas engine for the tear gas unit. Of course, we told the engineers we needed these to take out to our camps and that our camps were way out from everyone, so we didn't have much to work with. With these we would be able to keep cool and could use them for ventilation when we didn't have electricity or gas power. At least that's what we told them.

Now we were ready. All we had to do was keep checking with the weather guy. We would need the right weather for about a three to five-day window. The weather looked good, and we were ready to go. Most of the boats working the rivers were Navy or Coast Guard, but we were going to use Army boats. There were many Army boats on the river. They seemed to be larger and were used to carry men and equipment up and down the river, whereas, the Navy boats were more like gunboats, and didn't have room for troops and supplies. This boat would carry all 30 of us, plus all of our gear. It was an Army LCU #1577. The captain of the boat was Steve Gross. I stopped to talk to him whenever I saw him because he lived about 25 miles from my home back in Indiana.

We also had three heavily armed Navy swift boats with us for protection. No one on the boats knew who we were, because we wore sterile uniforms with no patches or markings on them, and the gas was in suitcases without markings. If any of us were killed or taken POW, we didn't want the VC to say that we had U.S. troops in Cambodia. For that reason, we made sure no one had anything that would identify them as a U.S. Soldier. We had no papers or anything except our dog tags with the name of someone who had been dead for at least a year. That way, if the VC said they had killed a U.S. Soldier in Cambodia and they had his dog tags, we could say the dog tag was from a guy who was dead and buried a year ago in the States. Of course, it was important not to leave anyone alive so the VC could make him talk or put him on TV. For that reason alone, we had to get all of our men out or make sure they were dead.

The village was about 100 miles up the river from Saigon, and we left at 0800 hours in order to get there at dark. When we arrived, the landing boat was tied off on shore and the three swift boats stayed out in the river to give us cover fire if we needed it. Upstream about five miles on the Vietnamese side of the river, we had a light infantry unit from the 196th spread out and firing. It had the attention of the VC in the area.

We sent 20 of our guys to the village to look things over and see if it was okay for us to come in with the gas. Around 2000 hours, they called to let us know they were in place. They said that things looked good, so I had everyone get some rest.

At 0200 hours, I took the other nine guys, gas, and fans, and headed for the village. We all met up at about 0600 hours. There were not many armed men around but there were a lot of villagers. The wind was from the southwest at about 10 to 15 mph, so we moved to the southwest side of the village. The village was about 1,000 feet wide and 2,000 feet long and had as many as 1,200 people.

It was 0630 hours, and the people in the village were moving around, making fires and mingling. It was just dawn. We took the four fan units and put them about 50 feet apart and told all the men to don their gas masks and put on their gloves. Everyone stayed back who didn't need to work the fan units. The guys manning the units started to paddle and slowly pour the gas into the hopper. It was a fine powder, something like flour. The wind was just right. It blew a cloud of white smoke over most of the village.

About 70 to 80 percent of the village was being hit with the gas. It was chaos in the village, as people just started to drop right where they were standing! Some people ran to see what was wrong with the ones on the ground, and they also fell dead. Some ran into the jungle yelling.

It took us about 15 minutes to empty the gasbags. No one noticed us and no one fired a shot. They didn't know what was going on, they just ran away as fast as they could. I had all but five of our group grab the fans, empty the bags and head back to the river as fast as they could.

The remaining five of us waited for about 20 minutes, until we couldn't see anyone moving or hear any noise coming from the village. We moved into the village and took pictures making notes, then we headed for the river. When we got to the river the men had burned the bags and washed the fan units off in the water. Only then did they take off their masks and gloves. Everything was ready, so we jumped into the boats and got out of there. It was about 1000 hours when we left, and we were back to base by about 2300 hours.

The next day I reported to Coleman. I gave him the film, told him we had terminated about 600 personnel with the gas, and that as far as we could tell, no one had seen us or knew what had happened. The gas had dissipated by the time we had left, and no one would ever know what had happened to the villagers. True to character, he was very pleased!

It all seemed logical at the time. The VC were using the international laws of humanity and technicalities to cross the river and regroup, so they could come back and kill the South Vietnamese and American Soldiers. It didn't seem right that they were abusing humanitarian laws to be able to kill the people of Vietnam. This was the only efficient way had to try to them from butchering more innocent people.

Imagine, what a conflict this was for an Eagle Scout, to have to use such tactics to save lives. Just being there causes PTSD, but it is actions like these that caused Moral Injury to me and so many others, after the war. Actions that seem necessary and right at the time, are in total conflict with our upbringing.

It's now 1985, and I'm back. It's been a long time, but at the same time, it seems like it just happened yesterday.

CHAPTER NINE

To Tây Ninh!

"Bull, how's everything going so far?"

"Good Kurt. We have all the weapons loaded and most of the other supplies."

"Okay, then let's get to the other side of the river as soon as we can."

"Alright, we're ready. I have about six other men waiting on the Vietnamese side of the river with transportation to Tây Ninh," Bull added.

"What kind of transportation?"

"Some old trucks. Let's see, there's you, Ton, Robe, four others, my four guys, and me; that makes 12 of us, plus our stuff. We have three old trucks, but I think we can all get into two of them with our gear. Two trucks won't attract as much attention as three."

This was so strange to me, being back in Nam. It looked just like the other side of the river, but it didn't feel the same. When I looked into the eyes of Bull's men, I saw Song and my other men. It had been years since the war was over when Saigon fell, and yet the look in their eyes was still the same. The war was not over for these guys. There was still an enemy in their country.

It was hot with high humidity. Just being here had changed my mindset. I felt more alert. I wasn't sure just what it was, but I was ready to kill again! It was hot, and my AK was hot. The magazine was hot.

Pull the bolt back and check again. Yeah, a round in the chamber and the mag was locked in.

"How long to Tây Ninh, Bull," I asked impatiently.

"It's about 25 miles, so it should be about two hours at this speed. You can keep the back flap open until we see someone and then close it. I'll ride up front and check out anyone who we pass. It should not be a problem if we see people; the war has been over a long time. No one is looking for Americans or anything like that."

"Okay Bull. By the way what do your men know about all this?"

"Well, they know who you are Kurt, and that you are here to get a Vietnamese friend out who helped you in the war. They don't know who he is. This is a chance for them to get back at the VC a little; anytime they can do anything to hurt the new government they will, no matter how big or small. Most of them have been working on this for almost a year just to get you in and out of here, and they are all willing to die to help with this mission."

"Okay Kurt we're about five miles from Tây Ninh. It's a big place and we are going to meet some of my men just north of the city about a mile or so."

"This is it! Everybody out," Bull ordered.

"Good, I'm glad to get out of that damn, hot truck," I said. "That was a miserable, dirty ride."

"There are three hooches here. Let's keep everyone inside or make sure they keep their weapons out of sight so we don't stand out if someone comes along. Get the gear in one of the hooches."

After a few minutes everything seemed to be in place, and I said, "Okay Bull now how do we get in contact with General Fong?"

"We don't Kurt. I have some of my men working with him, and all we have to do is wait here while they bring him and his family to us. He is in Hồ Chí Minh City."

"Damn, I hate that name! It's still Saigon to me."

"Me, too, Kurt," Bull smiled grimly. "No place for an American. There are a few American businessmen there, but that's about all. My men will get the General here, though, don't worry."

It seemed so peaceful, but it sure wasn't the last time I was here. We were now about five miles from Núi Bà Đen. It wasn't too far from here that I fell into a Punji Pit (booby trapped pit with bamboo spikes). Let's see, it must have been just a little north of this area.

CHAPTER TEN

The Punji Pit

There had been a lot of VC activity around the mountain, so we were going to set up at night and see if we could observe any activity around the base of Núi Bà Đen. We had decided to set up on the southeast side. It was only about four klicks from us, so we walked. I wanted to be in place by dark, so we had to leave at 1500 hours. I took Joe, Ed, Song, and Tuk. This was not going to be an ambush, so even if we saw VC we would not engage them. We were just looking to gather intelligence. We needed to know how many of them there were, what kind of weapons they had, where they came from, and which direction they were going.

It was hot again, 90 degrees and 90-percent humidity, but that was nothing new. It was always hot here. Some days just seemed hotter than others.

Song took the lead with Tuk bringing up the rear. We would have to pass two villages on the way, so we had to be careful and try to make sure no one in the villages saw us. There were some rice paddies we would have to go around, too. We would stand out in there, so we needed to stay in the jungle or brushy areas as much as possible.

Four klicks didn't seem like a lot, only about two and a half miles. You could walk that in about an hour or so back home, but it took us about four hours since we had to move slowly. We were out of range of the base camp, because the PRC-25 only transmitted two miles or so over here. They say it will go five miles or more. Well, maybe on the water or in a desert, but I had never gotten that range over here. Sometimes it did better at night and better when it was overcast. Of course, you could bet it would not go a mile if you were under attack.

We got around the two villages without being seen, and we were on the south base of the mountain. We had to stay off the mountain because it was full of VC. We were going to stay about 200 yards off the base and work around a little to the east. We really needed to move slowly around there because the VC had set up lots of booby traps. I would like to have found a place where it looked like there had been some activity, but the jungle grew so fast you couldn't tell if someone had been there more than a few days ago. The VC knew by then not to use the same trails too often, just as we did.

It was the rainy season and the humidity was really high. It was hard to breathe sometimes and the sweat was running down my neck. It felt like bugs crawling on my skin, and sometimes it was. The mosquitoes were so big and bad. One day I was laying there and three of them were carrying me off when one of them said, "Let's get him out of here before the big ones come and take him away from us. Ha! Just kidding!"

There isn't much you can do about the mosquitoes out there. Back home it was better. The land was more open, and when there was a breeze they were not around as much. You could use repellant. But even if there was a breeze in Nam you didn't get it in the jungle, and you couldn't use repellant. The VC could smell it. In fact you couldn't wear anything out there that smelled like anything but the jungle.

The jungle was wet. That was good and bad. It made it hot and full of bugs, but you didn't make much noise when you moved. When you put your foot down slowly it didn't rustle like when you step on dry leaves. On the other hand you couldn't hear the VC, either.

We started to work ourselves around the base of the mountain to the east. We only moved three steps and then had to stop, look, and listen. Everyone stayed close so we could see each other at all times. That meant in the thick jungle we were close, but as the vegetation got thinner we would spread out.

We came to a place that was not jungle. It had brush about waist high, but no big trees. I would have preferred to stay in the jungle but at this spot, the only jungle was on our left. Moving into the jungle would have put us too close to the mountain. It was completely open to our right, and it was only about a 100 yards across that area before we were back into the jungle. Our plan was to move across the opening to the other side and back into cover.

We had to move slowly, keeping our eyes open because we would be out in the open. There was a quarter moon and just enough light to give us away if someone was out there.

I told Song I would take the lead and he should stay behind me with Joe, Ed, and Tuk staying in the back. I told everyone to stay in my path, that way if there were mines or booby traps and I missed them, so would everyone else. I got low and moved into the brush about five feet. It was a low area with about six inches or so of water. I wanted to keep low, so I was walking like a duck. It was hard to walk like that, and it was especially hard to walk that way and not make noise. But it kept you lower and your head out of sight. I could have crawled, but that would've been too slow. Besides, I really didn't want to get all wet and muddy. That's what would have happened, and then I would have had to spend the night out there soaking wet and miserable.

We moved slowly toward the other side. I stopped and listened but didn't hear anything. I was about two-thirds of the way across when I stopped. I thought I heard something moving in front of me. I had heard something, but it was some kind of animal. I could hear it moving in the water to my left front. It sounded like a bird or lizard or something small. Whatever it was, it was not a man. I looked back at Song and he shrugged his shoulders to say he didn't know what it was and then nodded his head to say, "Let's go."

I had my shotgun with the sling around my neck and the weapon in front of me, my right hand on the grip, and my right index finger over the trigger guard. I looked up and around and didn't see anything, so I pushed up on both knees and bent over. It felt good to bend my legs a little.

I looked up and stepped forward with my right foot. I put my weight on my left foot, but when my right foot touched the water it kept going. My right foot kept going down, and I fell forward. As my left knee hit the water there was no ground there and I kept falling forward. I let go of my weapon to reach out with my right hand in front of me but there was nothing there but water.

My left knee slipped off the ground and I fell into the water. My face went into the water, and I could feel my Boonie hat (soft, camouflage hat) come off. I had put my right foot out to try to stop me when I fell. When I did, I felt a sharp pain in my foot and my right leg! I didn't fall far. The hole was only about four feet deep. When I lifted my head out of the water Song was right there with his hand out.

I had a terrible pain in my foot and I had made a ton of noise. I put my finger up to my lips as I looked at Song and he nodded and looked around. We didn't hear anything. By this time Joe, Ed, and Tuk had caught up to us.

Song, Tuk, and Joe set up in a tight circle around me, and Ed who was the biggest guy there, reached out his hand to help me. I grabbed my shotgun and poured the water out of the barrel, took it off my neck and handed it to Ed, who then passed it over to Song.

The burning pain was in my right leg and foot. I slowly moved my left foot – no pain. When I pulled my right foot up a little, agonizing pain shot from my foot up my leg, all the way to the top of my head! It felt like something had a hold on my foot! The pain was so intense I put my foot back down less than an inch. It took my breath away and I bent my head back and gritted my teeth. I wanted to yell but I didn't dare, the VC might've heard.

I took a breath and looked at Ed. It was an old Punji Pit. I was lucky it was the rainy season, and the pit was full of water. The ground around the spikes was loose and most of the spikes must have fallen over, because I thought I only had one in me. The pits usually had lots of spikes in them.

Well, I couldn't stay in the pit, we had to get out of there. I took my right hand and ran it down my right leg. The water was just above my stomach. I could feel there was a thin piece of bamboo in my knee just to the right of my kneecap. It was running down my leg, and I presumed it was through my foot. I wondered how that could be, since we had steel plates in our boots. I didn't think it could've gone through that.

I told Ed to get behind me. I was going to need someone to help pull me out. I was not going to be able to help much. I told Song we were going to need his help, too. Ed and Song got behind me. I put my hands in the air, and Ed and Song each got a good hold on my hands. I told them when I nodded my head, they were to pull up hard. I picked my foot up a little but it didn't seem to come loose, it just hurt like hell. Well, I didn't know what was going to happen when they pulled me up. Maybe the spike would hold in the ground, and that would pull the spike out of me, or maybe it would come loose from the ground and it would come out of the pit with me still in my leg or a little of both. I didn't like either idea but I had to get out of there. I had to get that spike out of me and get back to the base for help!

I laid my head back and looked up at Ed and Song. I took a deep breath and grabbed their arms. I could feel them tighten up on my arms and I looked Ed in the eyes and then Song. I nodded my head, and up I went.

There was a pain in my leg like I had never felt before! I had been shot and stabbed, but nothing had hurt like this! I gritted my teeth hard, in an effort not to yell.

I felt the spike start to pull out of my foot and leg but then it let loose from

*the ground and out of the pit I came with the spike still in my leg and foot.
The guys pulled me back so I was sitting on the ground in about six inches of
water. I could see the top of my foot but not my leg. I laid back in the water
with both of my elbows on the ground and lifted my right leg up so it was out
of the water. I could see the bamboo coming out of my foot just behind my
toes at the first set of laces. Shit! That's why it had gone through my boot. The
steel plates in our boots only went part way up the foot. It was made to stop
something from going up the heel and into your leg, but not the front part of
your foot. That way it allowed your foot to bend for walking.*

*The stake went back through my pants just above my boot. I couldn't see
it under there, but I could sure feel it in my leg. I laid my leg back down and
took another breath gritting my teeth again and yelled inside. I know they
didn't hear anything but I could! I said we had to get out of there and into
the jungle. The pain was too bad for me to move much and I couldn't stand
up because the spike was still protruding out the bottom of my boot about
five inches with mud on it.*

*Song and Ed grabbed the straps of my web gear at my shoulders and
started to pull me the last 30 or so yards to the jungle. I instantly yelled, "Stop!
Stop!" The pain was too much to take. Again I laid back on the ground. I
said, "Look. Someone has to pull this damn thing out of my foot!" Ed was our
medic, but he said it would be better to let them take it out at the hospital. I
said, "I know that, but I can't stand the pain! If we have to engage the enemy
I can't fight or run with this damn spike in my foot!"*

*Ed said, "Okay, I'll cut the spike off where it comes out of your boot and
pull it out of your foot leaving the rest in your leg. Then you might be able to
stand up and it won't hurt quite so bad. The doctor could pull the rest out
when we get back to the hospital."*

*I thought about this and talked it over with Ed. The problem I saw was
that we didn't know how long it would be until we could get back, so we had
to get all of the spike out, even the piece in my leg. Ed said okay, we would
pull it out. So Song sat down behind me with his legs on both sides of me
and I laid back with my head on his chest. Ed had Joe hold my leg up out of
the water. Ed ran his finger over the bamboo and said it was running up my
shinbone into my knee. Tuk was on his knee keeping a look out. Song put his
arms under my armpits and locked his hands around my chest. I grabbed his
hands with my hands. Ed got down on his right knee with his left foot on the
ground right at the end of my foot. As easy as he could, he cleaned the mud
off the end of the spike that was sticking out of my boot.*

Every time he touched the bamboo I could feel it all the way up my leg to my kneecap! Ed looked at Joe holding my leg up, and then at Song, and then at me. I took a breath and nodded, and he leaned forward. He grabbed the bamboo and pulled hard and fast. The pain was so bad I think I passed out for a second!

It felt like a hot rod was running through my foot. Seconds later, it was like a flow of pain left my body, and the terrible burning stopped. I relaxed in Song's arms, and I could finally relax my leg.

Ed said it would be good to take my boot off and clean the wound on my foot, but he thought it would be best to leave my boot on to hold down the swelling. That way I'd be able to walk better if I had to. My boot was also stopping most of the bleeding. Even if I got an infection, it would take some time for that to happen. We would be back at base by then. He cut my pants up to the knee, cleaned the wound where the spike had entered my leg, and put a bandage on it.

We were still out in the open and had to get to the jungle. Ed and Song pulled me to my feet. My foot and leg hurt, but the pain was nothing I couldn't stand better than having the spike in me. I put my arms around Ed and Song's shoulders and we made it to the jungle. Ed was six feet tall, Song was only five foot five, so Ed got under my right arm to keep my injured foot off the ground. It was like having a pair of crutches with one shorter than the other.

By this time it was dark. Joe got on the radio and tried to contact the base. Song and Tuk set out some Claymores for security. Ed started working on my leg and foot. He cleaned the wound again and put a clean bandage on my leg. He gave me a shot of morphine and a shot of penicillin.

Joe couldn't raise anyone on the radio, because we were out of range. It was too dangerous to move in the dark, so we settled in for the night. We had good luck. We didn't see or hear anything all night.

The next day we started back, heading south, away from the mountain. By now my leg hurt and my foot was swollen so much that it hurt very badly. Ed cut the laces on my boot and that helped some. I was slowing everyone down but we didn't have too far to go, maybe a klick or two until we could make radio contact. Joe kept trying the radio every 15 minutes.

We had been walking about two and a half hours when Joe said he had the base. We weren't far from one of the villages and only about three klicks from the base, about a mile and a half, or so. Within 20 minutes, we were on the chopper. It wasn't long before we arrived back on the base at Tây Ninh.

They pretty much took me straight to the 45th Surgical Hospital. There were a lot of people around. Ed was talking to a nurse telling her what had happened. Before she and the doctor could come over, someone started an IV in my left arm and began cutting my right boot and sock off. About that time the nurse, a redheaded Major, came over and started to examine me. Before I could say anything, she cut my pants and shirt off. That's all I had on. I never wore underwear when we went to the field. We never knew how long we were going to be in the field, and your clothes got dirty in no time.

Well, there I was, naked. She started to look me all over and asked if it hurt here or there. I kept telling her it was my right foot and leg. It was my body, so I knew where I was hurt, but it was as if she didn't even hear me! She just kept right on with what she was doing.

The doctor came over and looked at my foot and leg. He said it needed cleaning and to added penicillin to the IV. One of the nurses started cleaning me all over. She gave me a shot for pain and put a blanket on me. The redheaded nurse brought a tray over and started to work on my foot.

The doctor came over and asked how I was feeling. I said my leg and foot hurt, and I didn't feel very good. It felt like I had a fever. He said I did, and he was worried about me getting an infection, so they had to clean the wounds. He walked away and the redheaded nurse put something in a syringe to kill the pain and started to inject it into the hole in my foot. When she stuck that needle in, I thought she must have gotten her training at Dachau (the first Nazi concentration camp opened in Germany)!

While she was waiting for the Novocain to work, the nurse started to talk to me. The first thing she said was that I was malnourished and she was going to report me. I said, "No shit! Here is how it works, you give me food, and I will eat it. They don't have mess halls in the jungle!"

"By the way," I asked, "why did you cut my clothes off? Those were the only clothes I had." She asked where all the clothes were that the Army had issued me. Unbelievable! I just told her to get on with her job so I could get the hell out of there.

Well . . . then she got out a long thing that looked like my M-16 cleaning rod and brush. She dipped it in some hydrogen peroxide, and ran it through the hole in my foot! If I'd had a weapon at that moment, I would have shot her!

After that, she just walked away. I thought at least that was over, and she either hadn't seen or had forgotten about the hole in my leg where the spike went up my shinbone and into my knee. No such luck. Back she came with some kind of a tool. She put the end into the wound on my shinbone, and *when she squeezed the handles together it opened up the hole in my leg so she could run that same M-16 looking cleaning tool all the way up my shinbone and back out! Now I was sure she got her training at Dachau! I was sure she was a Nazi from WWII hiding here in Vietnam! In spite of the tender care given to me by the redheaded nurse, I survived, and was back to the unit in about two weeks.*

Surviving the Punji Pit

CHAPTER ELEVEN

To Núi Bà Đen

"Hey Kurt. Here comes one of my men who's been working on getting the General out. I'm going to see what he has to say." Bull walked over and was in deep conversation with the man for several minutes.

"Okay," Bull said as he walked back, "It looks like we will have to get the General and his family out at different times. They are watching him, and it would be hard to get to him and his whole family at once. The General said he wouldn't leave until he knows we have his family and they are safe. But it's not a problem, because we have enough men to take them out first and then go back to get him. We're going to get three of his family members out first, his wife and two daughters. The daughters are both grown; one is 21, and the other is 25."

"Doesn't he have a son, too," I asked.

"He does, but the son is an Intelligence Officer in the People's Army and a loyal Communist. He would not leave his country, and he is a problem. We think he would turn his father and family in if he found out what they're doing, so the family has to be careful around him and make sure he doesn't know anything."

"It looks like we have a plan in place to get the family out first in a few days, and then we will work on getting the General. There's a temple on the top of the mountain, and his wife is going to take her two daughters up to see it. When they get there we will rescue them, and then we must get to the General right away, before someone finds out the women are not returning to the city."

"Sounds good to me Bull, but we need to have a closer look at the base of the mountain where we're going to grab the women."

"That's no problem. It's only about two miles away, so we still have time to get there today. At the base of the mountain is a village of about 600 people and the people work the area around the mountain where tourists go up to see the temple. This is a good road (for this far out in the country, anyway) to take to the mountain. I don't see any real problem other than to make sure no one sees an American when we take the women."

"Wow," I thought, "Here we were right at the base of the mountain. It was right over there about 200 yards away where I spent my worst day of the war."

CHAPTER TWELVE

The Bad Day

An Army unit from the 196th had lost some of its men and left some bodies up on the mountain. My group had to go in and get the bodies out.

It was May of 1967, and I was at the Army base camp at Tây Ninh about 60 miles northwest of Saigon. It was hot, in the high 90s and even in the 100s some days. We were a Special team; a small unit assigned to assist the Army units in the Iron Triangle. There were only four of us along with four Vietnamese that we had trained who had been with us for over a year.

There was a lot of VC activity in the area. We were close to Cambodia where many men and lots of material came down the Hồ Chí Minh Trail and across the river into Vietnam. About five miles northeast of the camp was a mountain called Núi Bà Đen or the Black Virgin Mountain. It was about 3,000 feet high and very steep on all sides, 45 to 60 degree angles, and almost impossible to climb. The U.S. controlled the top of the mountain and had a Special Forces communication camp up there.

The U.S. Army patrolled the area around the base, but the VC owned the mountain. They had been there for years, fighting the French and the South Vietnamese and now the U.S. The mountain was full of tunnels and the vegetation was thick. My team had gone up some parts of the mountain, but you could never get a large force up there. Every time a unit would try to go up the mountain, they would be driven back and would take lots of casualties in the process.

We had bombed the mountain with B-52s for years and about every day the artillery would be hitting some part of the mountain. The network of tunnels was very extensive. The tunnels were not only in the mountain, but ran from the mountain to the towns and the areas all around the mountain. In fact, this was the area where most of the VC units came from that hit Saigon during the Tet Offensive. The tunnels ran from this area all the way to Saigon. That's how so many VC got so close to Saigon. They came down the Hồ Chí Minh Trail from North Vietnam to Cambodia, across the river into the Tây Ninh, Củ Chi, and the Núi Bà Đen area, and then used the tunnels to get into Saigon.

The Army would patrol the area around the mountain constantly to try to keep the VC from moving to and from the mountain and the surrounding areas. The SOP (standard operating procedure) for the area around the mountain was to patrol around the base, but to stay off the mountain!

We were back in camp. We had been out on patrol for the last five days just west of here, near Cambodia. We were tired and needed some rest, but Colonel Aims called and wanted me to come over to his HQ. In spite of being tired, I was prepared to assist him in any way possible because he was a man of integrity. This was his third tour in Nam. He was a West Point grad and should make general before he retired. He looked like a poster boy for the Army – tall and fit, and he spoke with confidence and authority. He wasn't an armchair officer; he was out there in the middle of the fighting with his men.

It was 1000 hours. I took my bodyguard Song with me. Colonel Aims said that a patrol was out at the mountain and had been hit. I asked what they were doing on the mountain. None of the patrols are to go on the mountain. He said that I was right; the men were to be working the south base. However, this new Lieutenant thought he would take his platoon up the mountain for some reason, who knows why.

They got hit badly. The Lieutenant was killed, there were four wounded, and they left eight bodies on the mountain. The Colonel went on to say that he'd sent two infantry companies up there. They were set up about 300 yards from where they thought the bodies were. The Colonel said that he was sending up four 155 mm artillery pieces to support them along with six M-48 tanks. He also had helicopter gunships and some F-105s (fighter bomber jets) ready to add support.

This was going to be a mess. The Colonel said he couldn't stand to think about our men lying up there and what the VC were going to do to their bodies. I agreed, but asked what he wanted us to do. Colonel Aims said that *we couldn't leave the bodies up there and the VC knew that. They would be set up and ready for us when we went in to retrieve the bodies, and he wanted us to do it. "Oh, great," I thought.*

He said that our guys had been on the mountain, had worked the area up there, and knew it better than anyone else. He also thought it would be better for a few men to try to find the bodies than for a mass of men, who would make a bigger target. He added that he was hoping the VC would be expecting a large force and not four or five men.

I went back and told the guys we had a job to do. We were going to the mountain to recover eight bodies that were left behind. This was going to be a bitch of a job! The vegetation was thick, and we were going to have to get in close. No one was exactly thrilled with the idea, but they were good Soldiers and didn't complain.

I told them to take whatever they wanted but I was going to take a shotgun. It was going to be hard to see anyone in there. It was going to get up close and personal, so I was going to take my bowie knife, too. We were going to have to drag bodies a long way, in hot weather, under fire, so we didn't want to take anything we really didn't need. I knew it was going to be hot. It must've be in the 90s already, and everyone would still have to wear their steel pots (helmets) and flack vests (body armor).

We got on a slick and went out to the south side of the mountain. I met up with Colonel Aims. He had the platoon sergeant with him, who was with the unit when it was hit. His name was Sergeant Hays and I learned later he was regular Army, only three years to go before he could retire. He had served in Korea before Vietnam. Looking up at him now I guessed him to be about six foot four. He was well built and seemed to be in good physical condition. It looked like he could've used a shave, and his brown eyes had dark circles beneath them. In spite of being tired he looked like he was ready to do this. I knew he must have been from the South as soon as he looked at me and asked, "You-all ready?" Yeah – definitely from the South.

Sergeant Hays and I crawled up on one of the tanks and he tried to point out where he thought their position was when they were hit, but he was not really sure of the spot. The jungle all looked the same, and when you're under fire it's hard to keep track of anything. They were firing and moving the whole time, trying to get everyone out, so he wasn't sure about the exact location.

Sergeant Hays and all the guys from the platoon that got hit, wanted to go in and get their friends' bodies. Colonel Aims said that he didn't think that was a good idea. I said we could use some help, since there were only the four of us plus four Vietnamese to get all eight bodies out. The four Vietnamese were great in the jungle, much better than us, but they each weighed less than 100 pounds and would have a hard time dragging a 200-pound body.

Colonel Aims said we could have as many men as we wanted. I talked it over with my men, including our Vietnamese. They had risked their lives just like us and deserved to have a say. The plan was to have two six-man teams go in and recover the bodies. Two of the Vietnamese would go out in front to try and find the bodies and VC. Two of us would be right behind them to drag the bodies out. We would take two of the men from the platoon that got hit on the mountain with each team as back up to cover us as we carried the bodies out. It would be hard to drag a body, watch for VC, and shoot at the same time.

Colonel Aims said he would have the two infantry companies assault the mountain on each side of the area where we were going to enter to look for the bodies. The 155s would open up at point blank range as would the tanks. They would be firing at a range of 300 to 400 yards. They normally fired at ranges of many miles, so they would be firing level at the mountain.

Both companies would move toward the mountain. The one on the right would move up and to the left, and the one on the left would move up and to the right. We would try to form a "V" with the point of the "V" at the base of the mountain. We hoped we could work inside the "V" and that the VC would have all they could do to deal with the incoming fire. We were counting on the infantry companies drawing the VC's fire.

The 105s would start the offensive by hitting the base of the mountain in front of where we were entering. When the infantry companies went in, the gunships would try to keep the VC's heads down. As soon as all the action started, we would go in and see if we could find the bodies.

Colonel Aims was going to start things off at 1500 hours. I knew the VC could see the 155s and hear us, but we didn't hear or see anything. If I hadn't known better, I would've thought there was no one out there, but I knew they were there – just waiting for us.

It was 1445 hours. It must have been 110 degrees with 90 percent humidity. I don't know why, but I felt like something was wrong, and I was sure this was the day I was going to die. I was tired and scared, but with all that, I didn't think about not doing this. I don't know why but I just didn't.

It was so hot I took off my shirt. I put my helmet and flack vest on. I didn't wear them often, only when we were pretty sure we were going to get hit. The helmet was steel and hot, and the flack vest weighed about 12 pounds and was really hot, too. I had my bowie knife on my right lower leg. I took four M-2 Grenades, two smoke grenades, and put my Kodak instamatic camera in one of my ammo pouches. I slung my PRC-6 over my left shoulder and I put an ammo belt of 12 gauge 00 buck so it was over my left shoulder and under my right arm. I had my 12 gauge Remington Model 10 in my right hand.

Song and Tuk were going out in front of Ed and me. Sergeant Hays and one of his men were going to be right behind us. The other team was ready to go. They were about 50 yards to my right.

The 105s started the air attack a little late. It was about 1510 hours when they opened fire and started to hit the mountain. They continued the attack for about 30 minutes, and then they were gone.

It was quiet. The VC had not fired a shot. I could hear the gunships coming over my left shoulder. They stayed about half a mile back, and the Colonel had the two infantry companies move up. Still not a thing from the VC.

The companies had moved about 100 yards when the whole mountain opened up on them! The fire was coming from a line about 400 yards long and about 100 to 300 yards up on the mountain. Our men opened up and there were bullets coming and going from everywhere. There must have been hundreds of AK-47s. The VC also had larger weapons. It sounded like 50s, and you could see RPGs (rocket propelled grenade launcher) coming at us!

As the infantry companies engaged, they called the gunships in. It was time for us to move up. Song and Tuk were looking at me, waiting for the sign to move. I looked at Song and nodded my head and he and Tuk started forward. We went about 50 yards into the jungle where it got really thick. We had to stay within eye contact of each other so we were all close. Then we came to an area where it was mostly tall grass. Song and Tuk moved up about 25 yards in front of Sergeant Hays and me and the other guy was about 15 yards behind me. Ed was just to my right about 10 yards back.

I looked at Song, and he pointed to his eyes and then to a spot in front of him. He could see one of the bodies. I looked at Ed and he had seen Song and was on his knees working toward him. I got down and crawled in that direction, too. I was about 10 yards from Song when he opened up on someone! Ed was on his knees firing at someone, too. I heard two rounds pass right by my head but I didn't see anything to shoot at. I called and told the Colonel we had found one of the bodies but we needed some air support now!

By this time the infantry was in a massive firefight. The 155s and tanks were pounding the mountain. Even with all this firepower the VC were not letting up at all. The gunships came in and were hitting the position about a hundred yards in front of us with three-inch rockets. There was a lot of smoke. Ed and I had gotten to the body at the same time. The guy had been hit in the face and the top of his head above his right eye was gone. The VC had taken all his gear, but hadn't mutilated him. I grabbed one arm and Ed grabbed the other. Together we started to drag him back. We had gone about 25 yards when I looked up and saw Sergeant Hays stand up and aim right at us. He looked me in the eye and then looked behind me, and I knew he had seen someone in back of us. I hit the ground just as he opened up.

I rolled over and two VC came running at us firing their AKs. I was on my back with my shotgun in my right hand and my left hand still holding the dead guy's arm. I shot at the VC closest to me. He was about 15 feet away when I fired. I hit him in the left leg just above the knee and I could see the blood and flesh fly as it spun him around. He fell onto his back and was yelling and grabbing his leg. I pulled the shotgun across my chest and used my left hand to pump another round into the chamber. Just as the VC who I hit went down I could see the other VC right behind him firing his AK and still running at us. Before I could get off another round, three rounds came out of his chest, and his blood splattered all over me. He fell dead, about 10 feet in front of me. When he went down, there was Song, standing behind him with his 16.

I told Ed to get going and he started dragging the body back. He had only gone about 10 yards when Sergeant Hays and the other guy got to him. They drug him the rest of the way back to our line. By now Song and Tuk were engaged with more VC. Song had stopped and turned around, firing at the jungle. The VC I shot had gotten his AK and was trying to fire at Song or Tuk, I couldn't tell which. I got up on one knee and shot him in the back of the head. It hit him on the left side of his head and blew his skull off.

We all got back to our line, and we sat down to rest. The sweat was running down my face and into my eyes. I was so tired I had to lie there for a few minutes, as did everyone else on the team. I looked up at the beautiful blue sky and then looked around at the jungle. This was a beautiful country and a beautiful day, but people had turned this place into hell. For just a moment, the noise around me seemed to stop. I started to think about Mom and Dad and my little town back in Indiana. Of course, I had thought about them many times before, but this time it was different somehow.

I'd been scared many times, but not like this. Yet, even though I was afraid, I somehow felt at peace. It was not the kind of fear that made you want to run or get out of there. It was as if whatever was going to happen *was the right thing, no matter what it was. I had accepted the fact that I was going to die that day.*

Song grabbed my arm and I came out of my daydream. The noise was loud and the heat intense. The other team had gotten one of the other bodies, and was getting ready to go in again. We used the same plan and headed for the same location. There was a lot of traffic on the radio. The Colonel had called in for more air support, and there were three more infantry companies coming in. The Army was taking a lot of casualties.

We started back into the jungle near where we were the last time. Song and Tuk were in the lead again and we moved a little past where we had found the first body. Song and Tuk were to my left front and Ed was on my left about five yards. I could hear Sergeant Hays and the other guy coming up behind me, when 15 feet in front of me, a hatch opened and a VC popped up! I hadn't seen anything until the VC in the tunnel appeared and opened up on us with an M-2 carbine on full-auto! He fired 15 or 20 rounds and then dropped back into the tunnel and was gone.

It happened so quickly I didn't even have time to return fire. The funny thing was, it seemed like the whole thing was happening in slow motion. I could see his face and it was as if I could see the bullets coming out of the weapon straight at us. One of the rounds hit me in the right chest! I felt it hit me just as I was trying to hit the ground. Thank God, it was a carbine round and it didn't penetrate my vest. It put a pain in my chest and a big bruise to two ribs.

I fell to the ground on my right side and heard someone behind me yell that he was hit. I looked back and could see Sergeant Hays holding his right leg. I looked back to where the VC had popped up but didn't see anyone. I moved to Sergeant Hayes, who was only 20 feet behind me. The other Soldier with Sergeant Hays was down on his right knee, pointing his 16 at the position where the fire had come from. Sergeant Hays said he hadn't seen who was shooting at them. He was lucky, because the round went through the top of his boot and leg without hitting a bone.

By this time Song, Tuk, and Ed had come back to where we were. I picked Sergeant Hays up in a fireman's carry and started back for our line. I only got about 50 feet when I went down on one knee. By this time in the war I had been in Nam for months. I'd gone from 180 pounds down to 160 and had been shot, knifed, and beaten during that time. I had just come off of a five-day mission and was tired from that. At this moment, I just ran out of strength and went down to my knees. There was so much sweat in my eyes I couldn't see. I was so hot, I felt like I had a fever.

Song and Tuk were firing and I could hear bullets flying past us, hitting the grass and dirt all around. Ed put his weapon in his left hand, and with his right hand pulled up on Sergeant Hays who was on my back, and helped me get to my feet. I made it another 100 feet and then fell again to the ground. Hays rolled over my head and onto the ground in front of me. By this time, a group of Soldiers came up and took Hays away and the rest of my men came back. We moved back to a point near an M-48 tank. We were all dead tired. We drank some water and salt tablets, and then rested for 15 minutes.

I said that we needed to deal with the spider hole and the tunnel first before we went back into that area again. So my team moved back to the area where Hays was hit to try to find the hole. Ed, the other Soldier, and I watched for VC while Song and Tuk began to hunt for it. Within 10 minutes Tuk found it, and we all gathered around. Ed and I both pulled the pins on an M-2 Grenade. Song quickly pulled the lid off the hole and Ed dropped his grenade in. Three or four seconds later, I dropped my grenade. Everyone lay down and waited for the grenades to go off.

There was still a lot of firing going on around us, but it didn't seem like it was coming at us. I took off my helmet and vest and laid my weapons and gear on the ground. I'd grabbed a 45 from one of the guys to take with me into the tunnel. The spider hole was about two feet by two feet and four feet deep with a tunnel running to somewhere at the bottom of the hole. The tunnel was about 16 inches wide and about 30 inches high. The top of the tunnel was rounded. The team set up a perimeter around the hole.

I had the 45 in my right hand and a flashlight in my left, as I jumped down into the hole. I was only 160 pounds, but I was tall. I think the average VC was a 100 pounds and five foot three or so. The tunnels were made for them, not someone my size.

I thought I was scared above ground, but now I found myself in a position that made me even more afraid. It was hot, damp, and dark, and I mean dark. I could smell the dirt and explosives from the grenades. My mind flashed back to a time in Indiana when I had to crawl under our house to fix a water leak. I didn't liked that. The dirt was in my hair and face. There had been spiders, rats, and sometimes snakes. I hated snakes even more than I hated the VC. I would rather have fought 10 VC than deal with one snake. I remembered the smell of dirt and that musty smell under the house. How I hated to go under there, but at least there was not much of a chance of being *killed back in Indiana. Here I was with those same smells and fears, plus the possibility of a VC, a poisonous snake, or a booby trap waiting for me.*

The hole was small, and I had a hard time getting down into the tunnel. As soon as I put my head in and moved forward, my body shut off what little light was coming in from the hole behind me. It was hot and the humidity was so high it was almost like breathing water. The tunnel was tall enough that I could crawl on my knees, but I found it was easier to move if I lay down on my stomach. I also made less of a target in the tunnel. By lying down, I didn't block the tunnel so what air there was, was free to move over me.

Both of my arms were rubbing the sides of the tunnel. The sweat was running off me everywhere. The dirt was sticking to my arms and some of the sweat beads were so big they felt like insects crawling on me. I kept my hair really short, and when the sweat mixed with the dirt it was like mud running down my face.

I moved into the tunnel about five feet and stopped listening for any sound. I couldn't hear anything except the sound of my own breathing. Even the sounds of the battle going on outside were barely audible. It was dark and I was so scared I can't describe it. Then my imagination took over and I was worried that right in front of me was a VC lying there ready to kill me, or maybe a snake. I wanted to turn on my flashlight and see what was there but I was worried if I turned on the light, anyone who was there in front of me would see the light and it would give me away. What to do?

I just had to know what was there. I had to turn the light on. I pointed the 45 in front of me. Now came another choice. If someone or something had been there I would've needed to fire quickly, so I would need to cock the hammer on the 45 to fire. But cocking the hammer would make a noise that the enemy would hear for sure.

My heart was beating so hard I was sure anyone in the tunnel could hear it. I had sweat and mud in my eyes. I tried to wipe my eyes with the back of my hand, but there was so much mud and sweat on them it didn't help much. I held my breath and listened. I strained to hear anything, but heard nothing. I took a deep breath and pointed the light in front of me. I used my right thumb and cocked the hammer of the 45. In that tunnel the sound was so loud I thought even the guys outside could've heard it. I quickly turned on the light hoping to let me see, as well as temporarily blind anyone or anything if they were in front of me.

When the light came on there was nothing there, only darkness. I moved forward about 20 feet. The tunnel seemed to end then, but when I got closer to the end of the tunnel I could see there was water there. I had come to a wall with a water trap. This was a wall with a tunnel under the wall filled with water. The water would stop sound from the other side and would also stop gas from moving into the next tunnel.

Well, I had two choices now – go under the water trap and see what was on the other side or blow the tunnel right here. To get to the other side of the tunnel, I would have to roll over onto my back, hold my breath, and go head first and upside down under the wall in the water to come up on the other side, with VC or snakes possibly waiting for me. I was not here to see where this tunnel went, and some of the tunnels we had found around here were miles long. One that I had gone through previously had been five stories deep, plus I was not a tunnel rat. I just needed to clear this tunnel so we could finish our mission of recovering the bodies.

I backed out and had one of the guys go grab five pounds of C-4 (plastic explosive). I went back to where the water trap was, placed the charge at the wall, backed out, and connecting the wires to blow the tunnel. The blast wouldn't destroy the tunnel, but it would block it for now so we didn't have to worry about anyone using it today. That would give us time to finish the mission and evacuate the area.

We moved back from the tunnel entrance and I contacted Aims to see how things were going. He said that all of the bodies except one, had been recovered. He said it looked like most of the VC had moved away from the area where the bodies had been, and were back on the mountain. He was going to keep up the air strikes and the artillery bombardment so we could try to recover the last body.

By this time I was almost too tired to walk. Again, we drank water and took salt tablets. Song came over and said that he and Tuk thought they knew where the last body was. We had a quick meeting and headed for the mountain. We got to within a 100 feet or so of where the body was and stopped. If the VC had gone from this area, you couldn't tell it. The firing was intense – the heat was unbearable. I was so tired, it took everything in me to move forward. I knelt down. Again, I could hear rounds going past my head, and dirt flew up between Ed and me when a round hit the dirt at our feet.

I couldn't believe I had lived this long this day, and I was too tired to think or move. In front of me, there was smoke from all the artillery rounds going off and a lot of small arms fire coming from the jungle to the front of where we were heading. Not only was I tired, but I really thought I was about to die, so I took out my camera, held it out in front of me, and took my own picture. Then I put the camera back into the ammo pouch. For some reason I wanted my Mom and Dad to have a picture of me just before I died.

Even though I was sure I was about to die, I felt calm and could see that everyone on the team was about at the end of their endurance, too. It was as if we were all zombies. I just stood up and started moving forward.

Tuk was to my right front at about 50 feet. I could see he was trying to drag something and I assumed it was the body. I moved in that direction as fast as I could. When I got to within 15 feet of Tuk I could see that he was indeed dragging the body. Ed was right behind me and Song was coming from my left at about 30 feet. Just as I reached down with my left hand to grab the hand of the dead Soldier, a VC came up out of the bushes right behind Tuk!

In my peripheral vision I could see two more coming from my left front, near where Song was! I knew you first take out the closest threat, and that was the one in front of me, right behind Tuk. I had my shotgun in my right hand and pointed it at the VC pulling the trigger. The shot hit him just above the groin and he was knocked backward to the ground. At about the same time Ed opened up on him with his 16 and put six or more rounds into him. I let go of the body with my left hand so I could pump another round into my shotgun, and I turned to help Song.

He had apparently killed one of the VC, because one was lying on the ground not moving. Blood was everywhere. Song was in a hand-to-hand fight with the other VC! I ran over to where they were, and just as I got there, Song and the VC fell to the ground with Song underneath and the VC on top with a knife trying to stab him. Song had a hold of the VC's wrist fighting for the knife.

I was right there but I couldn't shoot and take the chance of hitting Song, so I reached down on my right leg and grabbed my bowie knife. I came up behind the VC who was on top of Song, and with my left hand grabbed the VC's hair pulling his head back with a quick jerk, exposing his neck. Song had the VC's right hand with the knife in it. I came down on the VC's Adams apple with the bowie knife. It cut into his neck about four inches, almost taking his head off. The blood splattered all over my face and eyes, and his body went limp as I pulled him off Song by his hair.

Song just looked at me, smiled, and gave me a "thumbs up." He quickly jumped up, and we pulled the last body back to our line.

I really didn't understand it. We were all safe, tired, and beat - but safe. I had been so sure I was going to die. I was still in a daze from what I had just been through. Colonel Aims came over and said that it was great we had recovered the bodies. In the process, he said we lost 12 men KIA (killed in action) and 23 wounded.

I'm not really sure what I did then. I remember walking around and thinking how crazy this all was. Twelve more men had died to recover eight dead bodies. Song almost died, and I had thought I was going to die. I was really confused. We couldn't leave the bodies there, but how could we let 12 more men die for dead bodies? Somehow both ideas seemed right. I would hope they would never leave my body.

I was just sitting in a daze, and there on the ground right in front of me, was a baby rabbit. All the noise going on and all the men around, and yet here was this little rabbit just sitting there looking at me. I picked him up and he didn't even try to run away. He was so small and soft and he smelled so good. Something in the back of my mind told me that I knew there were no rabbits in Vietnam. There was no explanation for this.

I walked over by one of the tanks and just sat there with the little rabbit. I don't know what it was about holding that rabbit but it seemed to put sanity back into my life that day. I believe God sent the little animal to me to remind me of all the good things there were in the world, and that even in the midst of hell, there was always something good, sweet, and kind.

"Okay, Bull, that's enough talking about the old days," I said gruffly. "Let's get back and get ready to get the girls out of this damn country!"

Rabbit from God

CHAPTER THIRTEEN

Getting the General's Family

"Coconut! My men just told me that the General's wife and two daughters will be at Núi Bà Đen tomorrow at 1100 hours."

"That's great Bull. Do you know how many will be with them?"

"My men tell me a driver and two Soldiers will be there for their protection."

"Right," I thought, "Like they really cared about what happened to the General's family." Núi Bà Đen would only be about 25 miles from Cambodia, and I knew the military just wanted to make sure the women weren't trying to defect.

Bull told me that his men had found out what the women would be wearing. I told him that we couldn't be sure if the guards would go up to the temple with the women or stay with the car, so we'd need to have a plan to get them no matter what the Soldiers did. I asked Bull what he thought the locals would do if they saw what took place. Bull said he thought that most of them wouldn't do anything. He doubted anyone would try to interfere, but it was possible one of the young ones might go get Soldiers at Tây Ninh.

I told Bull that we would need to have his men ready with transportation to get the women back across the river into Cambodia. We'd also need men on top of the mountain to kill the guards if they decided to walk up there. We would need three local women to change places with the General's wife and daughters, and we would have to be down near the car to take out the guard (or guards) and get the women on their way to Cambodia. Two more men had to be on the road from there to Tây Ninh, to stop anyone who headed that direction to get help. If we could, I wanted to leave someone alive to tell what had happened.

"But Coconut, if someone is left alive and tells what went on they'll kill the General."

"No Bull we're going to make it look like someone kidnapped the women. The authorities will think the women were kidnapped, and not trying to defect. If they suspected it was a defection, they would kill the General for sure."

"Okay that sounds good," Bull agreed.

"We'll take the General's wife and daughters away and kidnap the women who are impersonating them. The Soldiers and any locals will see us taking the imposters away in a different direction."

"Sounds like a good plan Coconut. I'll get my men ready and we can brief them tonight."

It was 1000 hours the next morning when we saw two cars heading our way. There was a driver and three women in one, and a driver and two more solders in the other. We could see that one of the Soldiers was going up to the temple with the women, and it looked like the other two were going to stay down with the cars.

Ton was waiting on top of the mountain. He watched until the women entered the temple to see what the guard was going to do. The guard just stood there looking at the spectacular view from the mountaintop. Ton moved closer to the guard and said, "Hey, look at the view from over here! You can see Tây Ninh." The guard's weapon was slung over his shoulder and he was looking down the mountainside.

At that moment Ton's left hand moved over the guard's mouth. With the knife in his right hand, he pointed the sharp edge of the blade to the front and pushed it through from the right side, slicing through the guard's neck, just behind his Adam's apple. Then he ripped it out the front, severing the esophagus and jugulars at the same time. Looking up I saw Ton toss the guard's body over into the jungle.

All six women headed down the mountain. Our plan was to keep the General's family just up the mountain and out of sight. As the three local women came down, we would grab them. We were going to use four guys, having two of them shoot at the guards. I had the guards in my sights. As soon as my men got the General's family into the car and headed down the road to Củ Chi, I would kill the guards. No, I would kill all but one of them, and leave him alive to tell about the women being kidnapped.

"Great going, guys," I thought. "Now it's my turn to deal with the remaining guards." I was about 150 yards away from them. I knew this was too far for the AK, so I had one of the guys bring up the sniper rifle. It was a Remington 700 in .308 with a twelve-power scope. I knew I could make a good shot with it. It was hot and the sweat was running down my face. Damn, this reminded me of the time I took the long shot at a river not far from here back in the war.

CHAPTER FOURTEEN

Long Shot at the River

It was November 1967. I was at Tây Ninh, about 60 miles northwest of Saigon. There was a lot of VC coming down the Hồ Chí Minh Trail and across the border from Cambodia into Vietnam, about 25 miles west of here. It was safe for them if they stayed on the Cambodian side of the border, because we were not allowed to cross over, even if we were taking fire from there. If we chased them to the border and they got across, we still couldn't follow. Northwest of Tây Ninh at the border, there was a river that ran along the border. It was not right on the border, but we called the river the border at that point.

Not crossing the border was the "official" policy, anyway. Of course, we were not official. In fact, we were not even in Vietnam, officially. So how could we do anything against official policy if we weren't even in Vietnam?

One of our teams had been in Cambodia a few days earlier and said there were two camps of VC about three miles inside Cambodia. One was near a small village and the other was camped along a small river. There were about 500 men in the village of Phumi Bat Tras and about 40 or 50 men camped by the river.

Because the VC thought they were safe over there, it was sometimes good to go over and cause a little trouble just to keep them on their toes.

If they sat there with no interference, they could make plans, cross over into Vietnam and wreak havoc, then go back to Cambodia for safety. We couldn't go into Cambodia with a large force or do anything too big, or someone would get word of it. That would have caused problems. But if we could go in with a small force, no one would know, and that was what we were good at – doing things that no one knew about. Or at least they didn't know how we did it.

I felt like it was time to go and do something bad to someone. We couldn't do anything that would make a big difference in the war. If we could go into the Viet Cong's safe area and kill some of them, it might cause them to change plans or set back any plans they had and make them be more cautious. At least that would slow down everything they were doing.

Sometimes we blew things up, set booby traps, or grabbed one and beheaded him to leave him behind to be found. In this case, I thought we would go in and try to kill someone of a high rank by shooting him, so we were going to be snipers. That is not what we were most of the time. Most of the time we were assassins.

There's a big difference between a sniper and an assassin, but most people, including the media, interchange these terms all the time. A sniper's target is a "target of opportunity." The sniper is put in a place where he may or may not know if there is going to be a target available, or he may work himself into an area where he believes there will be targets, but he has not been assigned any one target in particular. Also he may have many targets to choose from and it's up to him to determine which target to engage. He may take many shots, some at a very long range, and miss the target with no consequences to the mission if he misses.

The military sniper tends to set up for long-distance shots. The advantage is that it's harder to see a sniper from a long distance. If he comes under attack, the enemy has a longer distance to cover to try to get to him. Also a sniper can take long shots, and if he misses, he will just try again. Snipers have made record-breaking shots, but they have missed many shots that had no effect on the mission.

An assassin's target on the other hand, is a designated individual. The shooter knows before he goes out who the target is. The media and the public think of an assassin as someone who kills a president or some other famous person, but that's not always true. When you see a SWAT team set up with a shooter who everyone commonly calls a sniper, the shooter is not actually a sniper, but an assassin. He knows who he is going to shoot and is not after a target of opportunity.

It's harder to be an assassin then a sniper. The assassin must make the first shot count, so he must be close to the target. Also, the target may have personal protection. He may have on body armor, have bodyguards, or be in an armored car. It's harder to get near the target, and it's harder to get away.

By Presidential Executive Order #12333, it is illegal for anyone in the U.S. Military or any government agency to assassinate a head of state, but this does not stop them from assassinating high-ranking military personnel.

In Vietnam, Coleman would give us a target and tell us to make sure we "terminated with prejudice." He told us that we should pretend he was standing behind us with a 45 to our heads, and if we missed, he would shoot us. We had to make sure we were close. For this reason, we didn't take long shots. It was hard to get close, but that was what made us good. We tried to get within 100 yards of our target compared to a sniper who likes to set up at 500 to 1,000 yards. Being snipers for the CIA, we were called missionaries for the "Christians in Action" we were making "spirit world referrals."

In this case, we were going to be inside Cambodia and in the VC area with no help, so I was going to try to get a long-range shot. A specific target was not important. I hoped to find an officer, but if not, I would take anyone. Sometimes killing an ordinary Soldier does more psychological damage to the enemy's morale than killing an officer. If you killed an ordinary Soldier it was hard for the officers to get them to go out to engage us, and that gave us time to get away.

I got Ed, Joe, Tuk, and Song, and told them what we were going to do. We would be gone five to seven days with no contact or help, so they could bring whatever they thought they would need for the mission including their sniper rifles.

I went over to the armory and talked to our armor. Since this was going to be a long shot, I grabbed a 30-06 that I had been practicing with. It was a Model 77 Ruger. Since I only used it for long- range, it was zeroed at 600 yards. I was going to use a 165 grain bullet at 2,700 feet per second. Being zeroed at 600 yards, the bullet would strike the target where I placed the cross hairs. I had a chart that told me how much the bullet would rise or fall at *other distances when I was zeroed at 600 yards. I also had to consider any crosswind as can be seen by the chart below:*

Ruger 77 – Rise/Fall Chart

Ruger - Model 77									
30-06 165 Gr. @ 2700 FPS									
Bullet Drop In Inches									
16	28.4	34.1	32.3	21.7	Zero	-33.8	-82.8	-150.6	-239.7
Energy (Muzzle-2720 Ft-Lbs)									
2350	2010	1720	1460	1230	1040	870	730	620	530
Wind Drift (Inches) 10 mph Crosswind									
0.7	3	7.2	13.2	21.4	32.4	45.9	62.4	82.4	105.5

We arrived at the Cambodian side of the river that night at about 2000 hours. The jungle was thick and it was hot. The drops of sweat were so big when they ran down my neck I thought they were bugs crawling on me.

We set up a small perimeter and were only about one mile from the village, so this was a good spot to spend the night. Being on the Cambodian side of the river there should not have been any U.S. forces, and the VC felt safe over there. They didn't have much security out. Nevertheless, we had one man awake at all times; we set four Claymores out in front of us and two behind us.

At 0530 hours we got around and ate something. Even at a mile away, we could smell the smoke from their fires. It was hard to carry enough C-Rations (canned, wet, pre-cooked food) for this long of a mission; it would mean carrying a lot of cans and too much weight. Instead, we had brought K-Rations with us. Being dehydrated food, it didn't weigh much, but then it didn't taste like much, either. Song and Tuk brought rice. They liked it better than the Ks. I think they were right.

I put a small amount of the dehydrated potatoes in my canteen cup, added a little water and waited a few minutes. I added a lot of salt and ate it. It had no flavor and sat in my stomach like a rock. I hated the water, too. I had been drinking this hot, nasty tasting water for two years, and it made me sick to drink it. It was so bad, I had my mom send me the small packages of Kool Aid to put in my canteen. I thought about putting some of the Kool Aid in the potatoes. It couldn't have made them taste any worse.

We moved out at a slow pace; Tuk was up front, with Song bringing up the rear. When we got to within half a mile of the village, we stopped. Song and I moved up to have a closer look. At about a quarter of a mile away we could hear sounds coming from the village. As we came closer we could hear voices. We found a spot about 100 yards from the east edge of the village and looked around. We had left our sniper rifles back with the others. I had my shotgun, and Song had his 16. We all had brought 45s with silencers. All the sniper rifles had silencers, too.

The other team had been right about a large number of VCs being in this village. There were many targets here but there was not a good place to take a shot and still have much cover. Plus, with that many Soldiers we would've had a hard time getting back out of the area, and we didn't have the firepower to engage in a firefight with a force that large. We wanted to take a shot or two and get the hell out. So we went back to where the others were, and told them what we had seen.

I decided to go have a look at the other 40 to 60 VC that the other team had seen near the river about half a mile from here. We got there at 1530 hours and found a spot to make a small base camp. We left Joe at the camp with the food and sniper rifles while Song, Ed, Tuk, and I went to look around by the river. I could hear voices as we approached the water. It must have been 110 degrees, and in the jungle there was no air movement, which made it seem even hotter. I had my shotgun slung over my back, and the ground was wet and full of insects – biting insects, but thank God I didn't see any snakes!

I crawled to the edge of the jungle. The VC all seemed to be on the other side of this river. It was not the big river that was the on border. This was a small stream that ran into the main river. When I heard the voices my heart started pounding. We were in Cambodia where it was against the law to be. No one knew we were there and if anyone did know, no one would have admitted it, and for sure no one would come to help us if we got our asses in a jam.

The jungle on our side of the river was thick, but on the other side where the VC were, there was little or no jungle. I came out of the jungle about 600 yards south of the VC camp. That put the village about half a mile to my left, and the small camp by the river about 100 yards to my right.

It was about an hour until dark, so we laid there and watched the VC camp. From the jungle's edge on our side of the river was about 20 feet of dirt and then the river. The river was flowing to my left. It was about 30 feet wide. The water was not moving very fast, and it didn't look more than a few feet deep. On the other side of the water the dirt was about 30 feet across until it came to the bank. On the other side of the bank it was mostly grass with a few trees. The VC had set up their camp about 50 feet back from the bank. It was stretched out along the river for about 100 yards. There was a large hooch up on a little hill in the middle of the other small hooches. They were all made of mud and straw. The small ones were about 12 feet by 10 feet, and the larger one in the center was about 12 feet by 20 feet. All of them had openings for windows and an opening for a door, but nothing to cover the openings.

There were 36 men moving around the area. They had AK-47s and were in khaki uniforms so they must have been part of an NVA unit. I didn't see anyone who seemed to be in charge. There was a small fenced-in area for the animals and a dozen fires for cooking. About 100 feet behind the large hooch on the hill was a dirt road that ran to the village.

When it got dark, we went back to our camp. Ed and Tuk had returned. They had gone up to the edge of the jungle, but had come out upstream of the camp and us. They said they had seen about the same things we did, but they also had seen what they thought was an officer on the north end of the camp. It was too dark for them to know for sure.

The next morning at first light Song, Joe, and I were back at the edge of the jungle watching the camp. The fires were already going and men were cooking and moving about. I was just about across the river from the big hooch. There were two Soldiers at a fire just to the left of the door of the main hooch and at about 0600 hours, the men stood up at attention. A man came out of the hooch and said something to the two other men. One of the men bent over the fire, picked up a cup, and gave it to the man who had just come out of the hooch. He was a big man. He was more our size than that of a Vietnamese. He had on a khaki uniform with red on the shoulder. He said something to the two men and one of them ran around yelling at all the other men.

Soon they all came running, and lined up near the edge of the river in two lines of 20 facing away from us and toward the big man, who by now was standing about 20 feet in front of them. He stood up the hill so he was above them, facing them and us across the river. There was one other Soldier standing in front of the men and facing the big man. All the men had their backs to us and I could see the big man facing me. He stood there and took his hat out of his pants, putting it on his head. He put his hands on his hips, looked the men over, and yelled at them. I could hear his voice but couldn't tell what he was saying. This went on for about 10 minutes. The man in front of the men saluted the big guy and the big guy saluted him back. Then the big guy turned around and went back into the hooch. The other Soldier turned around and said something to the other men, and they all went back to what they were doing. Not much went on the rest of the day.

The next day the same thing happened, just as it had the day before. Right after the formation broke up, I rounded up all the guys and went back to our camp. I told them this big Soldier was a great target. It looked like he followed this same routine every morning, and that was going to be the death of him. I said I was going to try to find a spot for the kill shot. I told Joe and Ed to find spots where they could fire the "Oh, shit," shots. Song and Tuk were great in the jungle and they were going to set booby traps and Claymores to cover our backs and clear the way for us to evacuate the area.

I found a spot up in a tree about 600 yards from the target where I could take the shot. We brought a pair of pole climbing spikes to help us climb. I got my spot ready and then spent the rest of the day climbing up trees between my shooting spot and the target. I wanted to cut a little vegetation where there was a hole through the trees from my spot, to the target. That way I could see the target, but from their end, they couldn't see anything through all the jungle.

I got up into my nest and pulled up my rifle. I cut limbs until I had a good rest for the weapon and a good place for me so I didn't have to use my muscles to hold myself in the tree. I needed to be able to use my arms solely to control the weapon. I used some straps to help me stay in place without having to use my muscles, and had parachute cord ready to let my rifle down quickly I also had a rope for me to get down in a hurry, too.

I looked though the scope, and every now and then someone would pass by so I could try to get an idea about the range. I had a 4 x 12-power scope. I didn't have a range finder, but we had gotten pretty good at judging distance. I also had become very accurate at judging the distance by the size of the man in the scope. It looked to me as if it was a little over 600 yards, maybe 630 yards. The weapon was zeroed at 600 yards, but at 700 yards the bullet would drop 33 inches. So being off on my distance could make a miss, most likely. If I was right about the distance then the bullet would drop about 10 inches from where I put the crosshairs. I just wanted to make sure I hit him center mass, so I would put the crosshairs right on his neck, just below his Adams apple. That would've been about 10 inches to the center of mass. If it was longer than 630 yards and more drop than 10 inches, I should still hit him in his body. If it was shorter than that I could still hit him in the head, because it should've been about 12 inches to the top of his head.

I was ready, and I checked with Joe and Ed. They had both found good spots to fire the "Oh, shit," shots. Okay, I did things a little differently than most sniper teams. Most snipers fired and then moved out as quickly as they could, but I didn't like that. It made no difference if you were an American, a VC, or anyone else. Everyone reacts the same when they are shot at. As soon as the shot goes off, everyone hits the ground. There is a short pause and everyone opens up in the direction from where they think the shot came from. Then there is another short pause while they got ready to move out and come after you. So you didn't have much time to get away.

We set it up a little differently. We had one man take the kill shot and get down and out of there. Everyone would hit the ground, and after a short pause open up in the direction of the shot. After another short pause they would get organized and start out after us. That's when one of my guys would kill the first man who stepped out, and then that man would get out of there and join the others. The VC would all hit the ground again and after a pause they would return fire. Then there would be another pause and they would start after us again. And again, one of my guys would kill the first man that stepped out, and then he would move out and join us.

Now the VC were saying, "Oh, shit! Did you see that? I'm not going out there!" No one wanted to be the next guy to step out. Then we could move out, because they would now be moving slowly after us.

We also left obvious booby traps, ones that they would find. We wanted them to find them, things like grenades at eye level with a trip wire. We weren't trying to kill them, just slow them down. When they would find a booby trap, they would have to stop and deal with it, which took time. They would also have to move slowly looking for other traps. Every minute they stopped or slowed down allowed us to put more distance between them and us.

The next morning we were all in place. The big man stepped out and put his hands on his hips. This was the shot but I could see the smoke from the fire blowing from his left. It looked like a five to ten mile an hour wind. On the chart I had from the armor, a 10 mph wind at 600 yards would move the bullet about 30 inches. I didn't know if the wind was five mph or 10 mph, so I didn't want to take the shot with the wind. I called the other guys and said to hold and stay in place. If the wind calmed down, and the target came into view, I would take the kill shot.

There was nothing else to do but wait. I made a call to each guy every 30 minutes. We sat all day but never got the shot. We had been out there for three days and were tired and hungry. It didn't take long to get tired of K-Rations.

On day four, the wind was blowing harder than it had the day before. It was about 1500 hours when the wind calmed down, but the target was not in sight. I was so tired of sitting in that tree, I had to move my legs a little to keep them from going to sleep but I had to keep an eye in the scope, continually looking for the target. The headband I had on was soaked, and the bugs were everywhere. If I had been home in Indiana I could've used bug spray, but then if I had been back home, I wouldn't have been sitting up in a tree all day waiting to kill someone. Not what an Eagle Scout does.

I wondered for the 100th time why I was here. The answer was really dumb – it was because I wanted to be here. No one had sent me here; it was my idea to go on this mission. Here I was, scared, hot, and dirty, and I could've been in a safe place – well, safer than here. How dumb was that? I had been shot, stabbed, beaten and didn't have to be here, yet here I was.

This was a long way from my little town back in Indiana. No one ever died there, at least not from guns, or anything like that. Just a few years before, I hadn't even known there was a country named Vietnam, let alone where it was. Now, here I was, waiting in a tree to kill someone. Not only would I not have been in a tree back home, but even if I was, I would be deer hunting and I would only have lasted an hour. I had no patience then and couldn't sit anywhere longer than that. Here I was, sitting in a tree in Cambodia waiting to shoot someone I didn't even know. More than that, I had been sitting in this tree for two days.

Most of my friends were back home riding around and going swimming. In their letters, their big problems were what beer to buy and how to have *sex with some girl. Right now, I didn't know how I felt. I envied my friends in some ways, having food and a girl, or going swimming at Lake James, but most of all I envied them for not knowing how it felt to kill someone. They would never know how lucky they were to never have killed. On the other hand I was glad I was here. I had saved many poor, innocent people from the VC, and helped lots of little kids who might have died if I hadn't been here, but I was paying a big price. I knew I would never be that good Eagle Scout again. I couldn't change things; I just needed to make this shot.*

It was day five at 0555 hours. All he needed to do, was come out of the hooch. The smoke from the fire was going straight up, no wind. And then suddenly there he was. "That's it," I thought, "Drink whatever it is. Okay, now move up. That's right."

I needed to close my eyes for a second. Okay, I was ready for the shot. The rifle was steady, and I was ready. The barrel was resting on a limb; my left hand was around the back sling loop holding the weapon up, tight into my right shoulder, with my right hand resting on my knee. The men were lining up, and here he came. He put his hat on – time to put my right index finger in the trigger and my thumb behind the trigger guard. "Okay, big guy, stand up tall and put your hands on your hips. Great. Now I take a breath and let some out and hold it. Crosshair's on the neck about six inches below his Adam's apple, now pinch the trigger."

At 2,700 feet per second and the target a little more than 1,800 feet away, it took less than a second for the bullet to get to the target. It seemed like a minute. I was right on target when I squeezed the trigger. It was 600 yards and not more than that, because the round hit right where the crosshairs were, just below his Adam's apple. It looked like it took his head off! I could see all the Soldiers who were in the line in front of him hit the ground.

I tied the parachute cord onto the front sling loop and lowered the weapon to the ground. This kept the barrel pointed up so it didn't get dirt in it when it hit the ground. I had my shotgun slung over my back and grabbed the rope and went down to the ground quickly. Just as I started down the rope I could hear the sound of AKs and rounds going through the trees. Then there was a pause, then a single shot, another dead VC. I hit the ground and grabbed my weapon running for our camp. Again, I heard the sound of AKs. I got to where Song and Tuk were and gave them the "thumbs up." They went right to picking up the Claymores and our other gear. We had left a lot of booby traps around, meant to slow the VC down.

Then the sound of the last "Oh, shit," shot could be heard. That meant that Joe and Ed would be on their way here, so we set up a line in case someone was right behind them. Soon we could hear the AKs again. Within a minute Ed and Joe showed up. They gave the "thumbs up," and we put the sniper rifles in cases and headed out. We made it to the river in about 90 minutes and were across, and back in Vietnam in less than two hours from the last shot. By that night, we were back at our base camp at Tây Ninh.

We had a debriefing and Song said he thought the big guy was a Chinese advisor. I don't know if that was true, but it did make sense.

Well so much for that old shot. That was long ago, and now it's 1985 – time to concentrate on this long shot at the guard.

The guard is moving a lot so here it goes! This first shot is just going to be center of mass and that would put him down for a good kill shot, I thought.

"Damn, he keeps moving! That's it," I thought to myself, "Stop and look up the mountain! Now! Crosshairs are center of his back between his shoulder blades. Pinch the trigger. There!" It entered his back just right of his shoulder blade. It drove him into the car, and I could see the blood splatter on the window. That might've killed him, but he was still moving his left leg.

"This next shot is for all my men you bastards killed!" My cross hairs were just above his left ear. That blew off the whole right side of his head. Now for the other one. Too bad I needed him alive. "That's it! Check your buddy." The others had stopped firing now.

I needed him alive but I couldn't let him be a problem for us. This was a good angle. He turned 45 degrees from me. My crosshairs were on the back of his knee and in the center. This should've taken out his whole kneecap. I held my breath and pinched the trigger. It hit a little to the left but took his whole knee and maybe his leg off. Shit! He was going to bleed out and die! I yelled at Bull to get one of his men out there to help him and make sure he lived to tell someone the women had been kidnapped.

All the locals had run away and were hiding. We had to get the girls in the truck and get them to Cambodia. We would keep them there in the safe house until we got back with the General. If we got the General out, we would go down river and out into the Gulf of Thailand and meet up with a U.S. ship, but they couldn't get on the ship without Robe or me. If something went wrong, and we didn't get there in 72 hours, then Bull and his men would take them on to Bangkok to Ron. He would take care of them.

No, wait! I had it! I told Robe that he had to go with the girls and then if we didn't make it out he could meet the ship and get the girls out.

"No, Kurt," Robe objected, "This is the first time I have had a chance to be on a mission, and I love it! I finally feel like a warrior and I am going to act like one. I am not going to leave you or anyone behind. We all make it or we all die . . . please, Kurt. I need to do this." I could see the desperation and sincerity in his eyes.

"I understand Robe," I told him. "Okay, Bull tell your men to stick to the first plan and wait 72 hours, then get the women to Ron in Bangkok. You both got it?" As always, Bull quickly agreed, and Robe nodded with relief on his face.

I thought, "Now, what about the General? We will get word to him within two hours that we have his family. After that, we will work on having him in position to be able to get him out."

CHAPTER FIFTEEN

The Medal of Honor

We were back at our camp just north of Tây Ninh. Bull had taken two men and gone into Tây Ninh to get any Intel he could about what the local police and military were thinking and doing following the firefight and kidnapping.

Robe thought we should all get medals for this, but of course this was his first time on a mission. There wasn't a chance of that happening. Even if we pulled this off, no one would ever know we were here. We were in a country we should not be in, and we were killing their people. I didn't think anyone was ever going to hear anything about this – not and live.

I always got a big laugh when I thought of how the military gives out medals. Not to make fun of the medal; most of the guys should have gotten more and better ones than they did. But sometimes they gave out medals just because it was good publicity, and other times they didn't give medals when the guys earned them.

"Robe, I remember one time when I had it worked out how to win the Medal of Honor. I think it was back in '66 or '67."

We were sitting around the village of An Lộc south of Da Nang. It was Joe, Ron, Song, Tuk, two other Vietnamese bodyguards, and me. I don't remember the bodyguard's names. "How sad," I thought. They had given their lives for us, but I can't remember their names. It was at times like this that I didn't think much of myself; I got upset when people didn't remember

*what all the men who gave their lives, did for us. I said I would never forget,
and I did. I really hated myself for that.*

*Someone from the Public Affairs office had been in the village last week
to take pictures and write about us, and all the good we were doing while
living in the village. We were a little bit of good news with regard to what
was going on in Vietnam. We were getting great Intel and killing a lot of VC,
but more than that, we were really helping the villagers. We protected them;
we taught them about hygiene, how to produce more food on their land, and
saved many lives with our medical skills. We were their friends, and they
were our friends.*

*After a mission I would write an after-action report. I hated doing that.
My reports were short and to the point. They went something like this: 'We
entered village, killed VC, and returned to camp.'*

*Well, the public relations people wanted something better to put in the
papers, so they sent someone to go on a mission with us. We took him on a
short mission to search a village about four klicks away, where we thought
VC might be living. Song was in front. It was only Ron, Song, Tuk, the PR guy,
and myself. When we got about 100 yards from the village, we started to take
fire. It was only one guy with an AK. He didn't hit anyone, and we hit the
ground returning fire. In about five minutes the incoming fire stopped. This
was not uncommon. What this meant was that we had come upon the VC
in the village, and this guy was supposed to slow us down so that the other
VC could "đi đi mau."(Get the hell out of there).*

*We were a small force and were out there to get Intel. So the VC knew that
we would not follow them to engage and they could get away. This happened
a lot. We would then enter the village, talk to the people and see what we
could learn about the VC who had been there. We would search the homes
for paperwork, ammo, or anything we could find, and then report what we
had seen. This would give us a picture of what the VC were doing in the area.*

*On this day we did just that. We spent about an hour there talking to the
village chief and the people, and searching the place. We didn't find much,
and as usual, all the villagers were afraid to tell us anything. As soon as we
would leave, the VC would come back and kill them if they had cooperated
with us.*

*We got back to our village and a slick came and took the PR guy back to
Da Nang. We didn't hear anything for about a week. Then one day we got a
call from HQ saying that they were sending a chopper for us to come to Da
Nang. They said they only needed Ron and me, but we never went anywhere*

without Song and Tuk, so we took them both with us. When we got there, a Colonel came out to meet us and shook our hands. Cameramen were taking pictures, and reporters were there from the Stars and Stripes.

The Colonel took us to a building where there were 20 or so people waiting. A congressman from Ohio was even there. Everyone was shaking our hands and congratulating us. We of course had no idea what was going on. We were really uncomfortable with the whole situation . For one thing, everyone there was wearing nice uniforms, but we were wearing rags covered with blood. One of my boots had the sole coming off, and I had commo (communications) wire around it to keep it from flapping when I walked. Thank God we had not brought any of the dried ears that we put on our belts sometimes to scare the villagers! I am sure that would not have gone over well with the Congressman!

The Colonel said it was time for the ceremony, and he had Ron and me stand up front between the American and South Vietnamese flags. The Colonel stood in front of us and read from the certificate. It went on and on about us – how with disregard for our lives and under fire, we had entered a village and routed 20 VC, saving the villagers and collecting vital Intel. Then he pinned Bronze Stars for valor on both of us. We looked at each other with dumb looks on our faces. We just stood there with everyone shaking our hands and patting us on the back; everyone wanted to have their picture taken with us, even the Congressman.

We were sure we were going to be in big trouble because they must have had the wrong guys. We couldn't think of the time when all that was said about us had happened. We had done a lot of things like that, but we couldn't think of this one in particular. As for the date of about a week ago, the only mission we had been on was when we went out with the PR guy.

We went to the mess hall and had a hot meal. At this point, we didn't care if what they said about us was true or not; it was worth coming here just for the food. About an hour later I saw the PR guy who had been with us on the mission and asked him what this was all about. He said it was for the mission that he went on with us. He said, "It's all in how you write up the after-action report." He went on to say that he had turned this one in for us, and this would really help the Army's image and make everyone look good. I asked if the medals were really for Ron and me, and he said, "Yes, you're heroes." I told him if he thought this was worth a medal, he should come with us on a real mission; if he would write up the reports, we would get the

Medal of Honor. Ha! We ate some more and told the Congressman lots of war stories. Afterwards, we got on the chopper and went back to the village.

The next day, I got to thinking how we had done all those dangerous things and never got any medals for them; the only thing we got was tired and shot. Yet when we did something easy, we got a medal just because of the way it was written up. I started to think of how I could fake something and win the Medal of Honor. That way, I would get to go home, stand next to the President, have him hang it on me, and receive money each month for the rest of my life. What a deal! But when I talked it over with the other guys and we tried to think of how we could be sure to win it, the only thing we could come up with was to throw ourselves on a grenade and have it go off. We knew it must go off, because we had two guys who had thrown themselves on a grenade to save a buddy, but the grenade didn't go off and the guys only received a Silver Star.

Well I kept thinking about how I could do it and make it work. We had a lot of VIP coming out here, and we would be their bodyguards and guides. I thought I would wait until a VIP came and have our Vietnamese bodyguards shoot at us. I could have the VIPs hit the ground, throw a grenade beside one of them, jump on it, and save them to win the Medal of Honor. Of course, the only problem is how to survive the grenade blast.

I started to work out how I could do this. All the guys thought I was crazy, but it would be great to do if we could make it work. They were all thinking and helping, too. First we took an M2 grenade since that was all we had, and tried some experiments with it, but it was way too powerful. It had a spring inside for shrapnel, and we couldn't get it out and still make the grenade work. Then I remembered that the Marines used a lot of the old WWII pineapple grenades. They don't have any shrapnel inside; the outside breaks apart so you don't have as much shrapnel to deal with. It's filled with flaked TNT, and that's not as powerful as the M2, because it has plastic explosives in it. I realized you could easily take out some of the TNT. I went up near Da Nang to a Marine camp and traded them some Claymore mines for pineapple grenades. Now we were set to try this and see how things would work.

First I took a grenade, removed some of the TNT, and set it off. I kept taking more and more TNT out until the grenade was as weak as it could be and still sound like a grenade. Then all I had to do was take my helmet and jump on the grenade with the helmet covering the grenade! I knew I would have my flack vest on so it should only throw me up into the air and maybe break a rib or two. This was not too much of a price to pay to win the Medal of Honor.

Okay now I was ready; all I needed to do was make up a grenade and put some tape around it so I would know which one to use. We picked a place that would work for the firefight, and Song and Tuk practiced what they were going to do, and how to get out of there and not get hurt. All we had to do was wait until a VIP came out here again.

A few days went by, and Joe said we should do a test run to be sure that it would work. I said, "Okay," and started to think how we could test it. I had an idea. I didn't say it was a good idea. We went out into a field and I drove a stake into the ground; I wired one of the grenades that I had made, to the stake with a string on it. Then I put my helmet over it, my flack vest, and three big sandbags on top of that. I set this up just like it would have been if I had jumped on the grenade wearing my helmet and flack vest.

We all sat down about 50 yards away to see what would happen. I pulled the string, and the grenade went off. The helmet, the flack vest, and the sandbags went about 100 feet into the air, and then sand and pieces of helmet and vest rained down on top of us. We all just looked at each other; no one said anything.

We got up and walked back to the village. No one ever said a thing about it again. It was as though it had never happened, and it was washed out of our minds.

I told Robe this was 1985 now, and that there was no way to win a medal on this mission, any more than there was a chance my friends and I were going to receive the Medal of Honor back then. I told him even if he died here, no one would ever know or care.

CHAPTER SIXTEEN

They Get Bull!

Robe shouted that there was a truck coming up the road fast, and he could see men and weapons. I told Robe and the men to stay out of sight and see if they passed us by. If the men stopped and got out, they should wait until I fired and then open up on them.

The truck came to a sliding halt, and two men with AKs jumped out and stood there. I took the safety off my weapon and put the sights on the center of the chest of the one closest to me. He was in the dirt street about 100 feet from me. I was in the hooch, so he couldn't see me. He was Vietnamese, and holding his AK in his right hand. It was down by his side, not the way you would hold your weapon if you were going to engage someone.

Then as I have always done, I took a deep breath and had one more look around to see if everyone was ready, or if there was something that had changed before I fired. Everything looked good. I turned back to my weapon and started to pull the trigger, when the one guy yelled in English, "Coconut! Coconut!"

I froze. "Oh my God! This must be one of Bull's men; but where was Bull?"

I came out of the hooch, and he ran over to me. He said that the police had stopped Bull and were holding him! They said he didn't have the right paperwork to be here.

Well I knew we would have to do something quick.

I wondered if this guy knew how close he had come to dying. It wasn't his fault; it was mine. It had been a long time since I'd been on a mission, and I'd been missing things that I wouldn't have missed if I'd been in combat all this time. I should've made a point to shake hands and look each of Bull's men in the face so I would recognize them. Damn! A mistake like that could have cost a good man his life!

I remembered a time that a dead battery almost got a lot of people killed, too. But again, it wasn't the battery, but me, who screwed up.

It was back in May of 1967, and I was in my hooch in the village of Lây Túy. It was about 0400 hours, and everyone was asleep but me. There were a few villagers up and about, but for the most part the village was quiet. I was going to make a trip around the village and check the gates. There were seven gates in the village and we closed and locked them from 1900 to 0600 hours each day.

I stepped out of our hooch and looked to the left where I could see the main gate to the village. It was about 100 feet from us, and opened up to allow people into the main street of the village; it went right past the front of our hooch. Our hooch was just mud and straw with a layer of sandbags around the inside and screen over the window openings to keep anyone from throwing something inside. There was no door on the front so the villagers could walk in and talk to us.

The street widened and went up a small hill for about a quarter of a mile, to a height of 300 feet. There was an Army Infantry Company located at the top. We received our logistical and combat support from them if we got hit or needed any other kind of help. Between each of the seven gates there was a fence about 10 feet high, then a ditch in the form of a "V" about 10 feet wide with cacti inside. This was followed by another 10 feet high bamboo fence. These seven gates were our weak points, so we had to check them every hour all through the night.

That night I checked the gates and came back to the hooch.

We had to call in a situation report every hour on the hour. We were supposed to call in like this:

"Charlie Base, this is O P Black."

"O P Black, this is Charlie Base."

"Charlie Base, situation report is negative."

"Roger, O P Black, understand your situation report is negative."

"That's correct, O P Black. Out."

We got tired of going through all that so I picked up the microphone on the PRC-25 and said,

"Charlie Base, OP Black. SIT-REP negative." I didn't wait for a reply. Normally, all they do on the other end is key the mic two times which means they received the transmission. What I didn't know was that the radio battery was dead, and that the Army Company up on the hill didn't hear my transmission. Up on the hill the RTO told the Sergeant of the Guard that we had not called in at 0400 hours. The Sergeant got the 1st Sergeant up and told him that we had not called in, and that they could not raise us on the radio.

The 1st Sergeant was a friend of mine named, Chuck Extram. His code name was DBB. He went back to the radio tent and they tried to contact us again. When they got no response, he went to the perimeter nearest our village and listened to see if he could hear anything unusual. He couldn't hear anything out of the ordinary so he rounded up about 20 men and gave the guys on the perimeter a quick briefing on what they were going to do. They were going down to the village to check on us.

I was unaware that anything was wrong, but if I had listened to the radio I would have heard or in this case not heard, Charlie Base respond and would have checked the battery . . . but I didn't.

DBB and his men started down the hill. There was a road from the hill right to the front gate of the village. Because I was worried about being attacked from there, I had the villagers build a fence on both sides of the road. The first fence was 200 feet from the gate so that if anyone would attack us from there, they would be inside a funnel right up to the gate and couldn't get to us. We could concentrate our fire on them. On that night, this would have been a great maneuver if it was the VC coming to our gate, but it was our own men.

Chuck and his men came down right up to the gate. They were on each side of the road but couldn't really get in a good position to take cover, because the fences kept them in the road with very little protection.

DBB and the guys sat and listened. Then they moved up to the gate and sat and listened again. The men were being as quiet as they could, but on my side of the gate I could hear men and movement. I got Song, Ed, Tuk, and Joe up, and told them I thought there was someone outside the front gate.

We were ready for this kind of thing. First, we had buried Claymore mines along the sides of the road, so Ed and Tuk went to the spot where we had the wires for the Claymores and attached the plungers, waiting for me to give them the sign to set off the charges. Joe set the M-60 up so that it was *pointing at the gate and would eat up anyone trapped in the road between the fences. Song and I moved up near the gate to listen. I was on one side of the gate and Song was on the other side.*

I could hear the sound of people and weapons. I thought this was going to be easy. There was no place for them to run or hide. I had told my men I was going to throw a grenade, and that would be the signal to set off the Claymores and open up with the M-60. I pulled out a grenade and put it in my right hand. I had my right thumb over the grenade strap. I put my left index finger in the ring and my left thumb on the grenade ready to pull the pin and throw it.

I could hear someone near the gate. I looked to see if everyone was ready. Ed and Tuk were there with the plungers for the Claymores; Joe was on the M-60 and ready to go. I looked at Song; he had a grenade in his hand and was ready to throw it. I took a deep breath and put my arms up to my chest to pull the pin. Just then I heard someone push on the gate.

The gate had a chain and a lock on it. Someone pushed against the gate until the chain was tight. It's important to know that grenade pins don't pull like they do on TV, and it's for sure you can't pull it with your teeth or you would lose your teeth. I used my thumb to push on the grenade as I pulled the pin with my finger. The pin was out; I put my right hand with the grenade in it low on my right side and stood up. I planted my right leg back a little and was about to throw the grenade when I heard someone in a low voice say, "Coconut, Coconut." I recognized that unmistakable gruff voice with the New Jersey accent. It was Chuck!

A chill came over me. I suddenly felt light-headed. Time seemed to stand still when I realized I had only been a moment away from killing my friends!

I was worried about saying anything right then; my men were ready and might open up if I yelled anything at all. So I moved out and walked right up to the front of the gate, so I was in clear view of all my men. I turned so my men could see me and held my hand up and made a fist, the signal for them to hold their positions. I said, "DBB, is that you? It's Coconut!"

Chuck said, "What the hell's going on? Why didn't you answer the radio?"

I had Song unlock the gate.

I still had a grenade with the pin pulled in my hand. It would have been easy to throw it but we were in the village. It would have scared the villagers, so Joe came over with a light and a pair of pinchers. We were able to get the pin back in and bent it over so the grenade was safe again.

Chuck came back to the hooch and I told him that we didn't hear anything on the radio. I picked up the mic and tried to call, but it was dead. Joe grabbed a fresh battery and put it in and I tried a second time. Then you could hear that the radio was working, and we got a response from Charlie Base. I told them everything was "okay."

We all sat and talked about what had just happened, and then we got some sleep. In the morning we went over what had happened again. We showed the men where we had the Claymores and the M-60 and they could see that they wouldn't have had a chance if we'd opened up. I was so scared thinking about how close I'd come to killing our own men. It would have been my fault because of a dead battery, but most of all because I didn't wait to hear back from Charlie Base on the radio. I took a shortcut from procedure. From that time on, neither the men up on the hill nor I ever took shortcuts on the radio again. Plus we always kept two radios in the hooch.

CHAPTER SEVENTEEN

Worried About Bull

It's 1985, and this had turned into a really bad situation with Bull being captured. We needed to prepare to get the General out within the next 24 hours, and now we had to rescue Bull, too!

Back in the old days I was six foot and 180 pounds. I was down to 160 at one point, but now I'm 190 pounds. I couldn't pass for a local, so I can't get involved in the rescue or it could jeopardize the entire mission. Bull may have to take his chances, at least until we get the General out. Once I had the General in Cambodia, then I would stay and die if I needed to, in order to get Bull back. But we can't risk the mission for him, me, or anyone else. The mission must come first, and Bull knows that.

I didn't want to think about what they were doing to Bull. I hoped he could hold on until we got the General out and could help him. It's so easy to say that the mission comes first and everyone knows the risk, but the mission is just a mission. Bull was a living breathing person. This was the shit I hated, and no one who has never had to make this call will ever understand.

I sent two of Bull's men back to stay close to him and see if they could find out where he was being kept. They needed to get all the information they could about how many were holding him. We needed to know where he was, and anything that would help us get him back. We also had to watch and see if the police moved him. That would be the best for us;

it would be easier to take him back if they moved him. It's hard to take a building in a big city and get out, but on the road, we could kill the enemy quickly and get the hell out of there.

It was so hard to sit there and not act. I couldn't help but think about Commander Thomas.

CHAPTER EIGHTEEN

The Torture of Commander Thomas, POW

It was in '66, and my team and I were in Da Nang. It was a hot, hot day. So what else was new? It was always hot. It was 1245 hours and I had just gotten a call from Marine HQ. One of the Navy pilots had been shot down just south of Hue. He was hit by a SAM (surface-to-air missile) while flying as close air support for a Marine unit near Hue. They had sent the pararescue team to try to get to him.

Anytime one of the planes got shot down, we went on alert. Ninety-nine percent of the time the pararescue guys went in and got the pilots out right away. If something went wrong and they couldn't find them, or the enemy got to them before the pararescue team did, we went in to try to locate and rescue them.

We had interviewed many POWs and VC, and knew what the VC would do if they caught a pilot. We were an Army team. First Corp was made up mostly of Marines. Our primary mission was to gather Intel for The Company. We were part of a detachment that worked for William Coleman, the CIA Station Chief in Vietnam. However, we also helped with POW recovery when the military in this area needed us.

It was now 1630 hours, and the pararescue team was back. They said they had gone in with two Jolly Greens (search and rescue helicopter) and were on site within 20 minutes. They found the plane and were on site for 30 minutes. The plane was an F-4 Phantom II (fighter jet). It had both a pilot and a WSO (weapons system officer). *The pararescue team found the WSO dead, about 200 yards from the plane. He had punched out and survived the landing but was shot and killed on the ground, still in his chute.*

They found the pilot's chute about 300 yards away from the WSO's chute, but no sign of him. Since the WSO was shot as soon as he was on the ground, we knew most likely the VC were right on the spot and got to the pilot as soon as he hit the ground. There was always the chance he had gotten away and was still in the area, but doubtful. The pararescue team didn't leave the immediate area to hunt for the pilots. So now it was our job to go out to see what we could find and follow trails, hoping to find the pilot and bring him back.

I got Song, Tuk, Ed, Joe, and three of the other guys. We grabbed our gear and got over to the chopper pad as soon as we could. Time was the big enemy for us. The VC would try to get the pilot out of the vicinity and into a safe area for them as quickly as they could so we had to go now – right now. Every minute was putting more ground between the pilot and us.

The pararescue team was going to take us to the spot where the plane went down and they had found the WSO and the pilot's chute. The wind was from the north, so we took off on runway 35L and were heading north right away. The pararescue team gave us all the information they had on the mission. The pilot was Lieutenant Commander Thomas, USN. This was his 14 mission. He was 31 years old, and married with two little boys back home. This all helped. He should have been in good physical shape, unless he was hurt when he bailed out or by the VC. Being married and having the boys back home would help him want to live and fight to stay alive.

It only took about 25 minutes to get on site. Our Jolly Green landed while the other one provided cover for us. Just as we exited the chopper, I could hear gunfire. It was one of the Jollys. He was taking fire and returning fire about 300 yards west of us. The Marine unit that the F4 was supporting was still engaged north of us. That meant there were a lot of enemy around here. This was bad for us in one way, because we would be right in among them. On the other hand, if they thought they were in a safe area with a lot of VC around, they might not take Thomas too far away this first day.

We were going to have to move fast. The VC would try to get all pilots to Hanoi as soon as they could. They used to keep POWs somewhere in the area of where they captured them and then move them up to North Vietnam at a later time, but not into Hanoi. At this point in the war, they took them right to Hanoi as soon as they could.

One of the parajumpers took us to the pilot's chute, then they got back on the Jolly and "*đi đi mau'ed.*" We set up a perimeter; Song and Tuk looked around. They were great trackers as well as good warriors and good friends. They found a little blood, a lot of tracks, some empty AK-47 cases and two .38 special cases. That could be from the pilot's revolver, but since it was a revolver it did not eject the used casing when it was fired. You had to open the cylinder and eject the cases. I didn't think Thomas would have opened it until it was empty so he could reload. It held six rounds. That told me that the VC had him, and one of them had opened the weapon and emptied the two spent .38 cases.

Song thought there were about eight VC and they had headed northwest. Normally when you were in an area where you knew there were a lot of VC, you moved really slowly and took your time, but we didn't have time if we wanted to find Thomas. Whenever we were trying to find and rescue a POW, we liked to talk about him and use his name. This kept us all remembering what we were doing, not just out on a mission, but trying to rescue a person, not just a Soldier or pilot, but a real guy.

It was almost dark and I hated to stop moving. We had night vision, and I was sure the VC would stop for the night and we could gain on them. The problem was that we didn't know where they were going and we couldn't follow their trail in the dark. With all the VC in the area, it was too dangerous. We couldn't help Thomas if we were dead, and I was not really keen on dying right now.

We had grabbed some K-Rations, so we set up a perimeter and started to eat and drink. We kept two people awake at all times until dawn. It was hard for me to sleep. We could hear the fighting going on with the Marines about half a mile away. There were a lot of airplanes and choppers flying overhead, and every now and then you could hear an AK going off somewhere near us.

We were too far out for a PRC-25 to reach base, but a chopper came over every three hours to relay our radio traffic for us. They had air support ready to give us cover if we needed it and the Jolly Greens were standing by to extract us. We also had our own Mike Force (Mobile Strike Force) standing by. The Mike Forces were under control of each detachment. They were mostly used for reinforcement of camps under attack, but also conducted their own operations, gathering intelligence, disrupting/eradicating VC/NVA activities in remote areas. On some occasions they also conducted U.S. and allied personnel recovery.

The bugs were eating me up! I was tired and hungry, but first thing in *the morning we moved out. There was a little bit of every kind of terrain here in the area – some jungle, rice paddies, and fields. We formed a box-shaped formation, two men on each side with Song and Tuk out front. We kept our eyes open hoping for the best and moving as fast as Song and Tuk could keep on the trail. With eight VC and a POW, the trail was easy to follow. Every now and then we would find a little blood telling us that Thomas was still bleeding, but also telling us he was still alive. We found where they had sat, ate, and slept. It didn't look like they were trying to hide their trail, so they didn't think anyone was after them. That was good for us and bad for them. The trail ran right into a small village. I am not sure you could have called it a village. It only had four mud and straw hooches with a dirt trail in and out of the area. The hooches were about 50 yards away from the jungle.*

We were still heading northwest. We needed to know if they had stopped here, were still here, or if they had moved on. We had to get close to the hooches and have a look. Song and I moved around so we were on the north side of the hooches where the trail left the village. We went north and waited. Tuk, Ed, and Joe set up on the west side and the other guys stayed on the south side where the trail went into the village. We had a good view of all the hooches. I couldn't see anyone that looked like Soldiers or a POW.

I was just about to send Song back to tell everyone to bypass the village and get back on the trail, when a man with an AK walked out from behind one of the hooches and was about 10 feet from Ed. Before the VC could fire, Tuk opened up on him and down he went. It was time to do something; we couldn't allow anyone here to stay alive to tell that we had been here. Everyone on the team knew that once a fight started under circumstances like this, we must kill everyone.

I stood up and headed for the hooches. I heard M-16 fire and saw two guys running out of the village into the field headed for the jungle. One looked like he had a weapon but he was not doing anything but running. I didn't see a weapon on the other guy. They were only about 50 yards away from me running hard for the jungle.

I pulled up and aimed for the center of the back of the one with the weapon and fired. I hit him high and to the right in his right shoulder and he went down. The other guy stopped, looked down and then back in my direction. I didn't see any weapon, but before he could turn and run I fired at him. I hit him in the right hip, and I saw the blood fly. He went down. I took a quick look around and not seeing any more threats, I moved toward them. I got to them just as Song, Tuk, and Ed got there. Ed put his foot on the AK that had fallen about two feet from the one VC, and said they had gotten six remaining in the village. Everyone was dead.

I nodded and looked at the two on the ground. One was on his right side holding his right hip and crying, and the other one was still face down and not moving but making a moaning sound. I told them to go get everyone over here – we needed to get going and get out of there. Tuk and Ed turned and headed back into the village to get the guys.

I looked at Song and then at the two VC and nodded my head. He looked at me and nodded. Song took his 16 and put it about six inches away from the head of the VC who was lying on his face and pulled the trigger. His head exploded. I pointed my 16 at the young man who was crying and holding his leg. You could see the fear in his eyes. I thought to myself, "You are crying now and scared, but you would not be if you had me." I thought about Thomas and how we couldn't leave anyone to tell them we were coming, so I pulled the trigger. I hit him above the right eye blowing the top of his head off. By this time all the guys were there and it was time to go. We trailed them all that day, and most of the next day.

At about 1500 hours we came upon another small village. At this point, we had gone about 20 miles from where we had started. As we neared the village we could hear voices and see smoke coming from the campfires. This village had seven hooches. There was a main street with four hooches on one side, and three on the other. The hooches had windows and door openings but nothing covering them. There were no guards set out anywhere. I counted 14 men. All had weapons.

We sat for about an hour, but we didn't see or hear anything that would tell us Thomas was there. Some of the men would go in and out of the hooches. There were two fires, and most of the men were setting or standing around them. Five of them had on some kind of uniform, and they looked more like NVA than VC.

One man came out of one of the hooches and everyone stood up and looked at him. He said something and then went back into the hooch. We didn't see Thomas, but Song and I were sure these were the guys we had been trailing. Tuk went all around the village and said it didn't look like anyone had come out of the village and for sure the guys we were trailing had gone into it. Well, if those were the guys we had been trailing, then where was Thomas? Maybe we had lost them or they had met someone and had passed him off to someone else. I didn't think so. I was going to bet these were our guys and that Thomas was in one of the hooches. The problem was that we could kill them all for sure, but could we kill them before they killed Thomas? We didn't even know where he was even if he was here.

We watched for two more hours. The men went in and out of all the hooches except one. That one, they would only go look into every 30 minutes or so. I was sure that was where Thomas was being kept.

Most of the time they would leave one man to guard the POW. We always brought a Remington model 700 in .223 with armor piercing rounds with us. We would try to get one man in close to fire the first shot and stop the guard from killing the POW, then everyone else would take out the rest of them. We worked with doctors to try and determine where to shoot the guard so he couldn't get a shot off and kill the POW. What we found out was that you couldn't be sure the guard won't get a shot off before he dies no matter where you hit him. Sometimes his weapon goes off as he falls or as it hits the ground. So we got with the armor and worked with all the different weapons the VC used. We decided we would shoot the weapon in a spot that would render it useless, rather than shooting the guard on the first round. This way the guard can't get a shot off. The next shot is for him.

In this case it looked like there was no one guarding Thomas for some reason. Maybe, he was inside the hooch, and we couldn't see him. We had to go with another plan.

We pulled back about 500 feet; I left Tuk to watch the camp. I made a plan –I didn't say it was a good plan – just a plan. Song and I were going to work in close to the hooch where we thought Thomas was, and everyone else was going to engage the main party when we took the hooch.

We had to wait until 0100 hours for the plane to come over to relay our message to the base. I told them where we were, that we thought we had found Thomas, and at 0300 hours they were to have an air strike two klicks north of our position. At that time, we were going to hit the camp. They were to give us 30 minutes, then have the Jollys come in and get us. They said they would have a plane overhead from then on to keep in contact with us.

We went back to the village and looked around again – still no guards. There were four of the men still up and sitting around one of the fires. We all moved up to the village from the west side. Song and I were on either side of the hooch we thought Thomas was in and the other six guys were around the other hooches on this side of the village. The fire was in front of one of the hooches on the east side of the street with the other three hooches. The fire was great because it lit up the village so we could see. Ed was going to start the thing off by throwing a grenade into the fire or as close as he could right after the air strike started.

At about 0303 hours the air strike started. It was far enough away that the men didn't get excited and grab their weapons, but they did stand up and looked in that direction. The head man came out of his hooch and looked to see what was going on. By this time, five other men came out to see and hear what was going on. So we had four men at the fire, the main man, and five others for a total of ten men standing right in the light. The head man said it was too far away for them to worry about and for everyone to go back to sleep. He could not have been more wrong; in fact, he was dead wrong. Ed pulled the pin on the grenade and let the handle go into his other hand so it didn't make a springing sound. He held it for about three seconds and threw it at the fire. It landed about 50 feet from Ed.

I couldn't believe it, but the sound of the air strike and the men talking must have covered the sound of the grenade. No one seemed to notice! It landed about two feet behind the men around the fire. They were standing and looking away from where the grenade came from in the direction of the air strike. The main man was about 10 feet to their right looking up at the sky. At that moment Tuk and Joe threw two more grenades into the street. Everyone else picked a target and opened up.

Just as the grenades went off, Song and I ran into the hooch. It was dark and I didn't see or hear anything. I said, "Thomas! We are Americans; we are here to get you out." Still nothing, not a sound. Outside there was a lot of firing, and then it stopped.

After the noise of the grenades and firing, the quiet was very strange. Then I heard Tuk and Ed say, "Coconut, it's okay out here. They're all dead, and we're all okay. Did you find Thomas?"

Well if there had been a VC in there I was sure he would have fired by now, so I turned on my flashlight. I had a red lens in it; I could read a map but not send out a beam showing where I was. It gave off an eerie glow. I could see what looked like a man standing in the middle of the hooch. Ed was at the door and asked again if I had Thomas? I said I thought so.

Ed could tell from my tone that something was wrong. I took the red lens off my light so I could see. I really didn't want to see. I was sure it was Thomas, and I was sure he was dead. He was hanging by his hands in the middle of the hooch with his feet about a foot off the floor. He was covered with blood from his neck down. All I could think of right then was, "Who is going to tell his wife and sons?"

When I shined the light on him, it was as if I had failed him. I guess I had. I didn't get to him in time. Maybe if I had moved faster or kept going through the night, I could have gotten to him sooner. I don't know. All I knew was that I didn't get here in time.

Ed and Joe were in the doorway and said we only had about 10 minutes until the chopper was going to be in the area. I told Joe to go find an LZ, call in the chopper, and to set up a perimeter in case any VC in the area came by. Song and I would cut Thomas down to bring him out.

I looked at Song and we went over to where Thomas was hanging. Song pulled out his knife to cut him down. I grabbed Thomas around the waist to hold him up, but when I grabbed him he moaned and jerked.

Oh my God, he was alive!

Song pulled out his poncho and spread it out on the ground. Then he cut the ropes and we laid Thomas on his back on the ground. I called for someone to bring the medical bag. Ed our medic came in and opened the medical bag. Song held the light. Thomas was barely alive.

I started cleaning the blood off his chest. As I looked at his chest I stopped and couldn't believe what I was seeing! I looked at Song and he had a look of horror on his face. He looked into my eyes and it was as if he was saying what can we do? The VC had hung Thomas up and then taken a razor blade and cut him starting at his neck going down to his belly, not deep, maybe a quarter of an inch deep. They had cut him about every inch or so from the neck to his belly. Then they had used something to grab the skin at the top and peel his skin off in one-inch strips all over his chest. It was not just blood but body fluids. This was like having third degree burns all over your body! There was no place to touch him, and nothing we could do for him even if we were in a hospital right now. The choppers were coming in. I couldn't leave him, and we couldn't stay there much longer or we would all die.

I told everyone to get ready to leave and that Song and I would be along in a minute. Ed asked, "What about Thomas?" I said that Song and I would take care of him. I looked at Song again. He looked into my eyes, and I saw a tear run down his cheek. He knew what I had to do. He looked at me and nodded. Then he stood up and went to the door and told everyone to get back and get ready to get on the chopper. I knew what I had to do, but I didn't know if I could do it. I looked into Thomas's eyes. I don't know what I was looking for, maybe just a look to let me know it was okay like in the movies when the guy says, "It's okay, I understand." But his eyes were blank. I said, "Okay, God! This is it. With all I have seen and all the hard things I have had to do,

I have never asked anything of You. Mom always said You would be with me over here, and my minister says this is Your world, we are Your children and our lives are in Your hands. It's time for you to take Thomas, right now!"

I waited for a minute. Song yelled that it was time to go. I looked at Thomas and touched his hand; he was still alive. "God, please don't make me do this!"

Song said, "It's time, it's time!" Then a dreaded feeling came over me – maybe because of what I had to do, or maybe because I knew there was no God. If He was there He didn't answer prayers. I told myself that there was no point in ever praying again. If God would not answer this prayer, then how could I pray for things like a car, a job, or all the things you were supposed to pray about?

I talked to Thomas and told him how sorry I was, and that I didn't expect him to forgive me - I understood. Here I was again, in a position where I felt it would be better to die for my country than to have to kill for it. How could I ever face anyone back home again if I did this? I could never tell anyone, and I didn't know if I could live with it. Maybe that was the answer. If things went right, maybe I would be killed over here, and that would make everything all right. I knew if I didn't die here, then I would never find anyone to love someone like me who could do what I was about to do. I knew I didn't deserve to ever be loved from this day on. I didn't even know Thomas, but I did love him.

Song told me I had to hurry – that the choppers were here. I nodded. I grabbed the morphine. I kept injecting Thomas until he stopped breathing. I almost couldn't see to do it, I was crying so hard. I looked at Song; he was standing in the doorway so no one could see. I looked at Thomas and I really wanted to push the morphine into myself so my pain would go away, too. Just then Ed and Joe came in and said we had to go now! They grabbed Thomas, and out they went. Song came over and grabbed me by my arm pulling me up.

I don't remember going back to the base, I just remember taking the sleeping pills in the medical bag when we got back to camp. I took a lot of them. I slept a long time, but not long enough. I remember lying on my bunk and seeing Jesus on the cross and God's face. He was crying. He had the power, but not the right to save his Son. Then I knew! God was there, but the only way for us to be judged fairly was for God to put us there and not interfere and see what we would do. Right or wrong, and I had done wrong – the big wrong – I am sure God was crying for me, too. I could never pay enough for what I did. Never. I must help others and never be loved. It would not be fair to be loved again.

That was a long time ago; I had to concentrate now on rescuing Bull. I pushed thoughts of Thomas out of my mind. I had to get my act together; we had to make plans to get the General into Cambodia and then into the hands of the U.S. Military, then we could get Bull out. I would get him out or I would die here; I knew I couldn't leave another man in Nam.

CHAPTER NINETEEN

Word about the General!

We spent a long night without much sleep. I kept worrying about Bull and I kept thinking there would be hundreds of Soldiers here, soon. At least the women were okay for now.

Robe had been playing radioman. He said the General's family was in Cambodia and should be safe for a day or two. There were 10 men with them for protection. The boat was going to leave in 72 hours with or without us, so we couldn't just wait. I had to put a plan together, and I needed to keep in mind that the war was over. It was odd, because some ways it was just like it was back then, yet different.

As I stood there in the doorway and looked out, everything appeared the same. There were as many water buffalo on the roads as there were cars or trucks. Everyone dressed like they did back then, and the hooches hadn't changed. Kids were still hitting water buffalo with sticks to move them along. Most of the hooches had window openings, but no windows and most didn't have a real door, just an opening. The heat was intense. It was still hard for me to get into my mind that it never got cold here, ever. The roads were no more than dirt trails. But there were big differences. The main thing was that with the war over; there were no large army forces around, only a few Soldiers in the towns. With no war going on and no insurgents, the only use for the army was to act as a police force to see that the people stayed in line. Some of the bigger towns had a police force, but out here in the countryside there was not much need for the police or the army.

I hoped the authorities thought a gang just wanting money, kidnapped the women. If they found out there were Americans here, it would be like the war. The place would be filled with Soldiers.

The people were not allowed to have weapons; only gangs and bandits had weapons, and most of them lived in the hills or over in Cambodia or Laos. So the local police and Soldiers didn't think they were going to face much of a force. This would give us a big advantage, but we would have to kill everyone, so there was no one left to tell anyone about Americans being in the country. That was another reason we needed to be very careful that a local villager didn't see Robe or me. As much as I would hate it, we would have to kill anyone who saw us.

Robe came in to tell me that the U.S. Navy ship was in place off shore south of Vietnam just outside of Vietnam territorial waters. This was good news. All we needed to do was take the General from them and make it 25 miles to Cambodia and then down the river and out to sea. Sounded easy . . .

One of Bull's men came and told us that it seemed like the government believed the disappearance of the General's wife and daughters had been a kidnapping. Good. It looked like they were going to bring the General out here sometime today and talk to anyone who might have seen anything. That should help us. The locals only saw what looked like a kidnapping and the thugs driving off in the direction of Củ Chi. Củ Chi was east of here and the General's wife and daughters had gone west to Cambodia. All we could do now was wait.

This was one of those missions when you didn't need to use a sophisticated plan, just remember, KISS (keep it simple stupid). We had a big advantage, because they didn't know we were here or about the firepower we had. The plan was to wait until the General was somewhere with only a few police or Soldiers around, 10 or less, I hoped. We would attack and kill them all quickly, and head for Cambodia in a hurry.

There was no one around here right now, but Robe and I needed to stay hidden in the hooch in case a local came by. Before long, one of the guys showed up with some food, so now I knew that the food hadn't changed, either. He brought some rice and a banana. I remembered when we were here before fighting NVA all day; we actually had to steal food from our own Army Supply just to get by. Hard to believe.

Back in 1967, Song and I were at the main military base in Da Nang trying to pick up supplies. We picked up some C4 and Claymore mines from the ammo dump. Most of the time we had no problem getting ammo, but this time we also needed boots, so we went to Supply.

Trying to get something from Supply was harder than pulling teeth; you would think that the Supply Sergeant owned everything himself. Of course, you could trade the supply workers for anything, but it took a pile of paper work to get something through channels. This time we traded an AK for the boots. Then we asked if we could get some canned fruit. The supply guy actually laughed at us. He told us we couldn't get any but he would trade for some. What a great guy!

"Well," I thought, "I could sneak up on the VC so why couldn't I sneak up on this supply lot and steal canned fruit?"

Song and I started walking around and looked over the Supply Depot. There was a building at which to pick up supplies and a back lot behind that. The lot was fenced in and would be hard to get into, plus there were a lot of people standing around. Walking around the camp we found that about half a mile away from the supply building was the main supply lot. There were many more supplies there than at the supply building. We watched awhile and saw that the supply workers would move things from this lot to the supply building as needed.

This lot had a 10-foot high fence around it and only one entrance. I was sure we could penetrate it, but it was so big we would never find anything. If we were spotted, someone could get hurt; we sure didn't want to get hurt or hurt one of our own, just for some food. So we sat and watched for a while.

I saw two different types of people going in and out with supplies. One group was guys who worked for Supply and were moving things from the main lot to the supply building. The second group were people from units who were picking supplies up at the main lot for their unit. The guys who worked for Supply had trucks, but the guys from the units just used jeeps most of the time. Usually, they had two people in the jeeps and drove up to the gate. There was a guard at the gate who would talk to them and check their paperwork. The guard at the gate was an E-4 (a military pay grade). I had a plan so we went back to our village about eight miles south of there.

Back at the village we were only about half a mile from an infantry unit where we got supplies and worked with them on Intel and missions. I was good friends with the 1st Sergeant. I told Chuck about my plan and that I needed a jeep, a driver, a clipboard, and a new uniform with Captain bars.

I told him I would share what I got with him. Chuck was glad to help. He gave me a supply requisition form and I forged a name on it. Now I was ready to go.

I decided to use Ron as the driver because he had a lot of guts, and I thought he would do a better job than one of Chuck's men. Off we went to the Supply Depot in Da Nang. We drove right up to the gate. Now it was up to us to be good actors. Most of this was going to just take nerve more than anything.

The guard put his hand up for us to stop. We did, but before he could do much I got out of the jeep and walked over to him. He saluted, and I returned it. Before he could say anything I started to look him over; I stared at his boots and then looked up and down at his uniform very slowly. By this time he was starting to look at his boots that were in bad shape and not shined. I asked him where the boots were and then looked down at my clipboard as if I was checking it. Then I asked where the canned food was located. By this time, I was right on top of him looking him straight in the eyes. Before he could say anything, I said, "Well, I can't stand here all day. Where the hell is the stuff?" He stepped back, pointed and said the boots were third row down on the left and the canned food fifth row on the right. I thanked him and started to salute. He quickly came to attention and saluted. I turned and started to return to the jeep, but just before I got back there, I turned and looked at him and asked what unit he was with. He told me and I looked at his boots again and asked what his commander's name was. I asked him if that was that how his commander shined his boots, and then I got into the jeep.

Ron and I went right to the canned food and loaded up the jeep. We covered the cases with a tarp and started back to the gate. The guard was supposed to check what you have to your list but after what I'd done and the way I had acted, I was hoping he didn't want to talk to me again. We approached the gate and slowed down; as we got close the guard was on my side of the jeep; I started to salute. He again quickly returned my salute, but instead of putting his hand up for us to stop he raised his hand and waved us on. This was just what I was hoping for.

Off we went to the village with a jeep full of canned fruit. All we had to do was act like we knew what we were doing and we got what we wanted. Sad, but we had to steal food from our own supply. It was fun though, and that was not the last time we did it. It worked so well we kept doing it the entire time I was there. It got even better because the guard didn't even stop us going in when he saw it was Ron and me. He was just glad to see us go away each time.

Here in 1985, there is no U.S. Army supply depot to steal food from, so this rice and banana would have to do. It wasn't too bad, because we wouldn't be here long. I knew I could go without food, or eat bad food for days, on a short mission.

I had to get back inside because there was a local and his son coming up the road with a water buffalo going right past the hooch. It always amazed me how a little boy could control a big animal like that. I can't remember a time when I ever saw a water buffalo cause any villager a problem. Can't say the same for me.

CHAPTER TWENTY

The World's Biggest Water Buffalo

Sometime in 1966, we were on our way to a village located about five miles from our village of An Lộc, south of Da Nang. It was a small village with about 200 or 300 people. Some locals had told us that they thought there was some VC activity there. I was with Ron, Song, and four PFs (Pacification Force). There were seven of us.

When we got within half a mile of the village, we started to move more slowly and stayed in the jungle as much as we could, so the VC in the area couldn't see us coming. We got to within 100 yards of the village and stopped. There was dense foliage right to the edge of the village, so we couldn't see much. I decided to sit and watch for a while.

We separated and sat watching for about an hour. Villagers came and went but we didn't see anything that looked out of place. We didn't see anyone with a weapon, so we moved around to the other side of the village where we could see a different part of the village. Again, we waited for about 30 more minutes.

One of the PFs about 50 yards from my position moved up to me and said he had seen a man with an AK-47. I followed him back to where he had been to see if I could see the man. I told everyone else to be on their toes.

At first we didn't see the guy, but in about five minutes he moved into view. He had his AK slung over his shoulder and was talking to a villager. We waited about 30 minutes more, but didn't see anyone else with a weapon.

I told Ron to stay there and keep an eye on the guy with the AK. The rest of us moved around the area to try and get a look at all parts of the village. We agreed to meet back here in an hour. After an hour, everyone came back and reported that they hadn't seen anyone else with a weapon except the one man.

Most of the time you didn't see just one armed VC anywhere, and since he had his weapon slung and was talking to the villagers and didn't seem to be threatening them, I thought maybe he was from this village and was here visiting someone. If this was the case, I thought this might be a chance to grab him and gain some Intel about the unit he was from.

I told everyone what I wanted to do and asked what they thought; everyone agreed. It's always dangerous when you try to take someone alive. It's always easier to kill them than it is to grab them. You have to get close, which gives him a better chance to kill you, and since he will try anything to get away, I always talked it over with everyone before we tried something like this. If the person you are after is important, then it may be worth the risk of harm to you and your men to get him. In this case, I had no reason to believe this man was really important. I told everyone not to take any chances; if they were in danger, they should just kill him.

Since this plan was my idea I told everyone to move around the village and stay just outside. Song and I would go into the village and try to grab the guy. If he ran, one of the other guys could grab him or shoot him in the leg – not kill him. That would be up to whoever was there; it was their life, and only they could decide if they wanted to risk their life to grab this guy. All my men knew that my first concern was for them, and that I supported them in whatever decision they made.

Song and I waited 30 minutes so that everyone could get into place, and then we entered the village. Song took one side of the street and I took the other. We moved from one house to another trying to stay out of sight until we could get close to the VC. It was hard to move from house to house going around behind them, because most of them had fences in the back. The fences were to protect their gardens and to keep the livestock in; some had cows and pigs, and there were a lot of people around. I didn't know about Song at this point, but five or six villagers had seen me. Each time, I had put my finger to my lips for them to be quiet and so far, none of them had said anything. They didn't know what was going on but they knew if we were here that it could be dangerous for them. They all disappeared into the village. They were right to be quiet, because if any of them had alerted the VC, most likely there would have been shooting right there in their village; some of the villagers could get hurt.

I hoped that the VC was not paying attention to this part of the village, because as we moved toward him, all the villagers disappeared. There was no one on the street. Song was across the street from me and we were both about 50 yards away from the VC, who was standing on my side of the street talking to two men. I could see it was going to be hard to get closer than this, without him seeing us. I looked at Song and he looked at me shrugging his shoulders as if to say, "What do we do?"

I pointed at him and pointed at my M-16, indicating that we would jump out, point our weapons at the guy and yell at him to give up. Song nodded. I was thinking of all the things that could happen now, and how to respond in each case. Hopefully this guy would just put his hands up and we would have him. His weapon was still slung on his shoulder so it would take some time for him to make his weapon ready. This would make it hard for him to fire before Song or I could fire. I was worried he would grab one of the men with him using them as a shield, and since we didn't know if they were friendly or bad guys, he could just run.

What if there were more VC in the village that we had not seen, or in a hooch where we couldn't see them? Did some of the villagers who had seen us go to get weapons or tell other VC? There was just no way to know and I was really scared. I could feel my heart pounding in my chest. I was just hoping the guy didn't shoot or we would have to kill him before he could hurt us or one of the villagers.

It was hot and I stopped to wipe my hands on my pants. I wet my lips with my tongue and took a deep breath looking at Song who was staring at me, waiting for my signal. I nodded my head, and Song and I jumped out and pointed our weapons at the VC. Song and I both yelled, "Chu loi, chu loi, give up!"

I kept both eyes open so I could keep the VC in my sight and still see what was going on around me, just in case someone would step out of a hooch with a weapon. The two men with the VC turned quickly to look at us and then took off into the village.

The VC, who was facing away from us when we stepped out, turned and looked at us. He was young, maybe 18 and his eyes were open wide. He was wearing a light-colored thin shirt, shorts and sandals, no hat, just an AK slung over his shoulder. He looked scared. He started to pull his weapon off his shoulder but Song yelled something and he stopped. He looked around and let his AK fall to the ground and looked around again.

Song and I started to move toward him but he turned and ran up the street. We started after him and Song stopped and picked up the AK. I called the other guys and told them he was on the run, but didn't have a weapon. Just up the street about a 100 feet, he turned and ran into a hooch. Song and I got to the hooch and positioned ourselves on each side of the door. I knew I had to be careful here. Did he have a weapon in there; were there other people inside and if so, were they good or bad guys? Did they have weapons?

It was daylight, so our eyes would not adjust quickly to the darkness of the hooch when we stepped through the doorway. I would not be able to see and at the same time I would be a silhouette in the doorway making an easy target. Song yelled for him to come out and told him we would not hurt him.

We heard what sounded like someone running out the back door. I signaled for Song to go around the hooch, and I jumped into the hooch quickly stepping to the right so I would not be a target in the doorway. I heard Song yell that the VC was out back but had jumped the fence and was running for the jungle. I could see out the back door where there was a gate and I could see a bamboo fence about six feet tall. I looked around and didn't see or hear anyone in the hooch. I moved through the back door, opened the gate, and ran up to the fence to see if I could see him. I could hear Song running and yelling at the VC, and since I was not about to try to get over a six-foot fence, I turned to go back into the hooch and out the front door.

When I turned around there was the world's biggest water buffalo standing between the door and me! I started to move slowly along the fence toward the door, but the buffalo stomped his front hoof and moved until he was about 20 feet away, blocking my path! I moved back to the corner of the fence, putting myself 30 feet or so away from him.

About this time I heard Song, Ron, and some of the PFs coming back on the other side of the fence. I yelled at them to come get me out of there! They had captured the VC and had him secured. Song and Ron came over and started to laugh. I said it was not a laughing matter and to get the owner to come get the damn thing!

By this time there were a lot of villagers standing around, as well as my guys. Song and Ron beat on the fence trying to get the buffalo to move away from the door, but he didn't move. He just kept his eyes on me. One of the kids took a stick and stuck it between the bamboo slats stabbing the buffalo but all that did was piss him off. So he rammed the fence! When he did that,

I tried to move toward the door. The buffalo quickly moved back in my way and dug at the ground with his hoofs throwing dirt in the air.

All this time I had been pointing my 16 at the buffalo in case I had to shoot it, but I knew that the buffalo was more than just an animal to those people; this is how they plowed the rice fields and grew food for their family, and we were here to help the people. I didn't want to kill the buffalo if I didn't have to.

By now, this was "the big thing" going on in the village, and I think everyone was there. The owner came into the hooch and was at the back door with a stick hitting the buffalo on the back. He yelled something at it but the buffalo just turned and charged him. He jumped back and closed the gate. Now I didn't even have a way out.

All of the kids were laughing at me. You would think that my guys would be worried about me, but no. Ron said, "If I you're a big, brave VC killer, then how can you be scared of an itsy bitsy buffalo?" Song asked if I needed a saddle so I could ride it out! All I could think about was, here I am in Vietnam and have been in a lot of firefights. How humiliating it would be, to die being killed by a water buffalo.

Well it had been about 30 minutes and I was tired, scared, and had enough of everyone laughing at me. I didn't want to, but the only way I could see to get out of here was to shoot the buffalo. I had a full magazine. We had 20 round mags, but we only put 16 or 18 rounds in because 20 rounds would wear out the spring. I also had an additional six mags with me. The buffalo had big horns and having seen the skulls of dead buffalo I knew they were thick and hard so I aimed at his chest and fired five rounds.

A little blood run out of the wounds, but the buffalo didn't do anything but dig in the dirt again. At this point I decided that I should just kill it because once I shot it, it would die anyway. There was no reason to mess around, so I pulled up and aimed at his chest again firing all thirteen rounds into him.

Now there were a lot of holes with blood coming out of them, but to my surprise all the buffalo did was charge me! I jumped to the side, quickly loaded another mag in my 16, hit the slide release, and sent a round home. The buffalo was still on his feet, and I was really scared now.

Ron yelled, "Hey that big of a target and that close and you still can't hit it? Ha! Ha!"

This time I aimed at the buffalo's leg right at the joint. I started shooting and must have hit it ten times or so when the buffalo fell down. He was not dead and was really pissed off now, but with him down I was able to get out of there – no thanks to my friends. I use the term loosely.

I felt really bad about killing the villager's buffalo. A buffalo cost about $20, so I gave him $50 and the villagers cut it up. We all ate the buffalo that night. That was the most expensive steak I have ever eaten, but we got the VC and everyone had some fun – at my expense.

Local Loving and "Friendly" Water Buffalo

No buffalo was charging me here in 1985, Thank God!

Just then Bull's man told us he had just received word that the General was on the way, and he was going to the mountain to see where his wife and two daughters had been kidnapped. The General had been told about our plan and that we would be waiting to retrieve him at the base of the mountain, so he had demanded to be taken to the mountain.

It was time to go get in place and wait.

CHAPTER TWENTY-ONE

Brutality in Củ Chi

We had to get in position at the mountain to take the General. Robe said that the General's wife and daughters were in Cambodia, safe now. Ten of our men had come back across the river to the Vietnamese side to and cover us when we arrived in case someone had followed us.

The women who played the part of the General's wife and daughters lived about a 50 miles north of here. They abandoned the car outside of Củ Chi and should have been back to their homes, by now.

We had to get the General out and then come back and get Bull. Only then could we go home. Right now I wasn't sure I was going to make it home. I thought we could get the General out, but after we did that everyone here would be after us. Coming back to get Bull might be the end of us. I knew that the General and his family had to get out, but the world would not miss me if I didn't come back.

One of the men came to tell me that the Soldiers and police were in Củ Chi and had found the car we used. They were beating the villagers and being cruel to many of them in an attempt to find out what had happened.

I thought it would be okay because our people would have been gone before the police got there, but I underestimated the Communists. How could I have forgotten how cruel that government was, and still is! People

in the States never really heard much about the ruthless brutality of the VC. This reminded me of when they cut off that little girl's arm . . .

We were at Tây Ninh, and it was getting near the time for the elections in the fall of 1967. The VC were working hard to see that no one voted. If the villages were near or had regular contact with the U.S. or South Vietnamese troops, they were less likely to have trouble. But in the villages that were out away from us, or over near Cambodia, the VC had more control over the people than we did. They may not have had all the money and resources we had, but they knew how to terrorize and control the people. They had all the patience in the world, and that meant a lot over here.

One time when we were set up in an area outside of our base camp they hit us with about 300 men, but only about half of them had weapons. After the battle, I was checking bodies and pulled one of them off the concertina wire (razor wire) who was still alive. He didn't have any weapons and I asked him what his job was at this battle. He said he had to walk here, which was about 25 miles, and when the battle started his job was to throw his body on the concertina wire so the men with the weapons could step on his back and get over the wire to get to us. He had walked for three days to get here with only a little water and rice to eat each day. He was a thin little man with weary eyes, no shirt and a pair of raggedy pants and worn out sandals.

We talked for a while and I asked why he would throw his life away like this. I told him that we had so much firepower that they could never win a battle based on firepower alone. So why do it? He said that this was his land and the land of his father, and his father's, father. He said that we were just one of many that had come and gone fighting in their land, and that a thousand years from now his people would still be here. We on the other hand, would be long gone.

I walked away and I remember thinking that he was right; we want things done right away. I knew right then we could not win this war without killing all of them. How could you defeat someone who is thinking a thousand years down the road, when we were only planning for next year? They can put someone on a trail with a weapon and wait until someone comes along. They will wait for days and then fire one shot and run. I couldn't get my men to sit still for one hour. For every one we killed, we fired 30,000 rounds, but the VC killed one of us for every three rounds they fired.

I realized that they were in this for the long run and we were not. This is why the outer villages were under the control of the VC. They knew that we would come and go, but the VC would always be here. The best we could do was to try to help them, and try to show them that life would be better in a free country than under communism. Sometimes this worked, but sometimes it backfired on us.

About six months earlier we had gone out to a village about half a mile from Cambodia to spend the day talking with the villagers and providing medical care for the people. We took six Vietnamese trained to talk to the villagers about government programs, and we supplied the medical personnel. We treated many people that day for everything you could think of. One of the things we did was to vaccinate about a dozen kids. Things went well, or so we thought. About a week later Song came to me and said we needed to get back to that village; something bad had happened. I took Song, Tuk, Ed and Joe with me and went back to the village.

When we got there, we found eight dead kids and four barely alive. We were told that when the VC heard we had been to the village, they came and shot the village chief and four other men. Then they took all the little kids we had vaccinated and hacked off their arms that had the vaccination, leaving them for dead. They told the villagers not to have any dealings with the U.S. or South Vietnamese government, or they would be back.

This may have been cruel, but it worked, and it didn't cost the VC anything. The most important thing to them, was that we had nothing to offer that would win them over, nothing that would be worth it to them, considering the consequences. The only way we could control and protect all the people in South Vietnam would have been to occupy the whole country, and that would have taken a lot more men than the United States was willing to commit to this war. That was the big problem here, how did we win the hearts and minds of the people with the limited personnel and resources we had?

It was close to Election Day and we were going out again to two small villages near the Cambodian border. It wasn't far from the village where the VC had killed and cut off the arms of the little kids. I took Joe, Ed, Song, Tuk, and five Vietnamese from the government Pacification Team. Because this was a hostile area, I also took a 10-man Army squad for more firepower. The village was about 25 miles west of Tây Ninh. My guys and I got on one slick, the 10-man squad got on another one, and we headed out. There were two villages in the area we were headed and they were only about two klicks apart. We were going to set down at one and walk to the other.

We arrived at 0830 hours approaching from the west, and flew over the village one time to take a look. We didn't see anything unusual. There were *no armed men or anyone in uniforms in the village that we could see, but if they heard us coming they could have hidden in one of the hooches, so we still had to be careful. We had reports that both of these villages had a lot of VC in them; we had to treat them as hostile, and at the same time try to leave the villagers with a positive impression. This was tricky. It was too dangerous to let our guard down, but we didn't want to look too scary and frighten the villagers. After all, we really were there to help them.*

The slicks landed about 300 feet from the west edge of the village. The choppers stayed operational and ready to go until we checked the village out. The door gunners stayed ready. The five Vietnamese from the Pacification Team went in with Song, Tuk, Ed, Joe, and me. The 10 Army guys came up behind us.

Song and the PF men started to talk to some of the villagers, but after a few minutes Song came over and said there was something wrong. Some VC had just been in the village about two hours ago but the village chief said that they were all gone now. This was one of the times that our safety was more important than the mission. The villagers might have been telling the truth or they might have been lying because they were afraid of the VC. They knew when we left, they would be at their mercy.

It was time to turn this mission into an Intel and combat operation instead of a public relations mission. I told Song and Tuk to have the village chief get all the villagers out into the street and then take them out into the field by the choppers. There were about 150 villagers. I had the pilots shut down the choppers and told the door gunners to help keep an eye and weapons on the villagers along with five of the Army guys.

It was time to check the hooches. I told Song to get out the shotgun and tape. It was a hot, bright day. If someone was in one of the hooches, you would make a great target when you stepped into the doorway. It was dark inside, and your eyes couldn't see anything when you first entered the hooch. If there was a booby trap in there you'd be dead. So when I was searching hooches in a village where there was a high threat, I searched using the village chief. Song, Tuk, Ed, and Joe would keep close to me when I entered the hooches. I had the Army guys stay on the street and keep ready.

Song came over with the village chief. I asked him one more time if there were any VC or any weapons in the village. He still said, "No." I turned him around so he faced away from me. I used a model 10 Remington 12 gauge with the barrel cut down to 14 inches and the handle cut off to make a pistol grip. I put the shotgun in my left hand and put the barrel up to the back of the chief's neck. Song took tape and wrapped it around the barrel and then around the chief's neck. I took my 16 and put it in my right hand. Song and I headed for the first hooch. I kept the chief in front of me and using the shotgun pushed him into the doorway – if he didn't want to go into the hooch then I was sure I didn't want to, either. If we took fire or if anything happened, all I had to do was pull the trigger on the shotgun. That would blow the chief's head off and I would be free of him.

We searched all the hooches in the village and the Pacification Team talked to the villagers who were in the field. We didn't find anything wrong in the village. Song and Tuk talked to the members of the Pacification Team. They said that the VC had been there and were all over the area telling everyone not to vote. They thought that the VC had gone to the next village about two klicks away. That was the other village we were planning to visit next.

I left the Pacification Team, who was well armed and trained, and five of the Army guys with the choppers there to watch the villagers, and took the other five Army guys with Song, Tuk, Ed, and Joe with me. We headed for the next village to see if we could see any sign of the VC. We only wanted to look. There were not enough of us to engage a big force.

It was a little over a mile to the next village. We had to move slowly and tried to stay out of sight, yet still keeping an eye open for VC. It took about 50 minutes until we got close to the village. We moved into a grove of trees and sat there to see what was going on. It was a small village of about 100 people. The village was not very wide and it ran north and south for about a thousand feet. We were on the south edge of the village. No one moved in or out of the village the entire time that we sat there, around 30 minutes. We didn't see or hear anyone in the village, and that was strange. It was midday and there should have been a lot of activity at this time of day.

We could hear what sounded like voices at the other end of the village. I took Song and three of the Army guys and started up the eastside of the village to the north. I sent Tuk, Ed, Joe, and the other two Army guys up the west side to the north. On the eastside where we were, there was a hill that ran along side of the village. It was about 50 feet or so high and full of trees, so we moved up into the trees and then moved slowly north.

As soon as we moved up the hill about 25 feet, we could see that the villagers were gathered in a group at the north end of the village. There were about 25 VC in uniforms surrounding them with three of them out in front talking to the villagers.

Ed and the other guys were on the west side of the village and they didn't *have as much cover over there as we had. I called Ed and told him what I had seen and that they should stay where they were. We were going to try to get closer and see what was going on. They were to cover us in case a fight started and we had to get out of there fast.*

We slowly moved north on the side of the hill until we got to within about 200 feet of where the villagers were. I could see that the men standing in front of the villagers were officers with the NVA. The man in the middle was Colonel Nguyen Van Trang of the 48th NVA Battalion. I could understand Vietnamese pretty well, but I couldn't make out what he was saying; he was talking too fast. Song said he was warning the villagers not to vote in the upcoming elections. They were not to cooperate with the U.S. at all. Then he went over to a man in the group, grabbed a little girl who looked to be 10 or so years old, and pulled her up in front with him. He reached over to the Soldier on his right and grabbed his machete, then he grabbed the little girl's right hand. With one swing of the machete, he cut off the little girl's right arm! He waved it in the air and yelled that if anyone voted he would be back to kill them all!

A man ran to the little girl and I could see blood flying everywhere! All I could think of, was we have to get to that child. I looked at Song and his eyes were as big as mine were. I looked back at the three Soldiers and they had shock and horror on their faces. They didn't say anything, but I could see they wanted to do something. I looked at Song again. In his eyes I could see he wanted to get down there; I am sure it brought back old memories to him. He was only 19, but had lived a long life and was an "old man" in many ways.

This act of brutality had happened so quickly that I didn't have time to stop it or even think about what to do. There were only five of us and over 20 of them, but I didn't care at this point. There was a rage inside me like I had never felt; I didn't think, I just stood up and got one of the men up front in my sights and pulled the trigger. I didn't see where I hit him, but I saw him drop.

Then all hell broke loose! The villagers ran for the village and the NVA took cover starting to return fire. Everyone with me must have been thinking the same thing I was, because I just got my shot off when everyone around me opened fire at the same time. I didn't even think about the fact I was standing up and making a good target. I just kept looking for targets and firing as I started down the hill towards the NVA. I would stop every few feet and look for another target and fire. We had no plan, just kill them all and get to that little girl. We had no coordination we were all just acting on our own.

We had taken the NVA by surprise, and they were all over the place just trying to get out of there. I kept looking for Colonel Trang but never saw him. We were coming down the hill from the east and about 10 of the NVA moved away from us to the west. I was in such a rage I didn't even think to call Ed and the guys on the west side of the village, but being the great Soldiers they were, they didn't need an invitation to the fight.

As soon as they heard the firing they moved up to support us and were in just the right spot when the NVA moved to the west. Ed, Tuk, Joe, and the three Soldiers opened up on them, and it was all over in less than a minute. The VC were all dead. We had killed six or so, and our 10 other guys had the NVA down to a few men, who ran off to the north of the village. I'm sure all the NVA we shot didn't die right away but when it was over, all the ones who had been hit died right there.

Song and I got to the little girl. She turned out to be the village chief's daughter. Her right arm was cut off just above the elbow. Her father had gotten to her and had put his shirt on the end of the arm and had stopped enough of the bleeding to keep her alive until we got there. I put a tourniquet on to stop the bleeding. She was in shock and was limp in my arms. She had the darkest eyes I have ever seen. Blood covered her body and her long black hair was sticky with it. Her eyes were fixed and I got no response from her. At least she was still breathing.

Ed brought up the medical bag and started an IV. Her father just kept wiping the blood from her face and crying. I looked at him and told him she was going to be okay. I wasn't sure of that, but what else could I say?

I called back to the choppers and told everyone to get over there fast. We worked on the little girl and the other guys were helping some of the villagers who had been hit in the firefight. There was no clear place for the choppers at this end of the village, so they had to land at the south end. By the time we got the villagers and the little girl stabilized, the choppers were coming in. I had them put the injured villagers, the little girl, and her father on one of the choppers along with three of our guys, and sent them back to Tây Ninh. When the other chopper was airborne, they called the base camp to give them a report of what had occurred.

We were too far out for our PRC-25 to reach the camp from the ground. Within an hour, three more choppers were on site. We talked to the villagers and checked the dead NVA for papers. Ed, Joe, Song, Tuk, and I stayed in the village that night and I sent everyone else back. We spent three more days in the village and then an additional five more days trying to track down Colonel Trang, but never found him. We returned to Tây Ninh. We did keep returning to the two villages from time to time and the Vietnamese Pacification Team helped them, supplying food and water for the village. I am sure the villagers were grateful for our help, but they still had to be loyal to the VC. Unless we moved into the village and stayed, they were still at their mercy.

About three months later, I received a call to go to Củ Chi. Ed, Song, and I got on a chopper and went there. When we got there, I was told that the 25th Infantry had engaged a VC unit three days ago, and had taken five POWs. The Military Police (MPs) and Military Intelligence had interrogated them and had not gotten much information. They wanted us to have a try.

I went to the stockade. There were three of the VC there. They were all young; I would guess from 18 to 25 – it was hard to tell. I didn't get anything out of them, either, but being so young I didn't think they knew much. I am sure they could have told us what unit they were with and so on, but nothing that would be good now. The other two were in the hospital so I went over to the 7th Surgical Hospital.

Both men were in a separate area from the U.S. guys with two guards. The one was also young like the others. He had been hit in the leg, and it was in a cast, being held up and in traction. He, like the others, could not speak English, or at least they acted like they couldn't, but I could speak pretty good Vietnamese. Even so, he didn't respond. Every time I asked him something he would look at the VC in the bed next to him. The beds were kept about 15 feet apart so I didn't think the other VC could hear me, but he sure put the fear into this young kid.

The other VC had a lot of bandages and IVs in him and I went over and talked to the doctor to see what was wrong with him. The doctor said he had been hit in the lung, and it had collapsed. He also had a round go through his intestines and they had to remove some. The doctor didn't think he would die from either of those wounds, but that he did have a bad infection that they were having a hard time controlling. He had a high fever at this time. He said the guy spoke very good English and was very polite. I asked him how old he thought he was, and he said in his 40s or 50s.

I went back in to talk to the older VC. I grabbed a chair, set it down by his bed, and sat down. He was watching me as I walked over to him. He had a bandage on his head and an IV in both arms. There was a bandage on his stomach with a tube running down the side of the bed into a glass jar. It had brownish red liquid dripping out the tube.

I looked into his eyes to see if I could get some sense of who this man was.

His eyes were blood-shot and his face haggard, but as he looked at me, he smiled and said, "Hello, Coconut."

I was stunned! I didn't know what to say. That was my code name; how could he know it? If he knew it, who else knew it? I'm sure the shock and consternation showed plainly in my face.

After what seemed like five minutes, because I didn't know what else to say, I said, "What did you say?" I didn't want to say, "Hello." That would have confirmed he was right, and that I was Coconut.

"It's okay," he said, very matter-of-factly, "I know who you are. I have seen you many times, and we have been adversaries for a long time."

I looked into his eyes and tried to think back to where I had seen him – then it hit me! It was in that village where the little girl had her arm cut off. This was Colonel Trang, the Commander of the 48th NVA unit. This was the man who had cut off that little girl's arm, the arms of the kids we had vaccinated, and had killed many of the villagers in this area! I just sat there in silence for a minute not knowing what to do or say.

A thousand thoughts ran though my head. I had wanted to have my hands on this man for a long time. Now here he was, and I was not sure what to do. I couldn't think, I was so full of emotion. I looked him in the eye again and walking out of the room. I was standing outside when the doctor came up to me to ask if anything was wrong. He said that I was white as a ghost, and he thought I was sick.

I turned to him and said, "Doctor, do you know who that is in there?"

"No, I don't. Is he someone important?"

I glared at him and said, "I don't know if he's important, but he is a butchering bastard!"

I was enraged. *I had my shotgun slung over my right shoulder. The barrel was pointed up; I grabbed the butt with my right hand swinging the shotgun off my shoulder, and grabbed the forearm with my left hand. It was a model 10 Remington 12 gauge. I took my right forefinger and pushed in the button that unlocked the chamber. Using my left hand, I pulled the forearm back a little so I could see into the chamber to make sure there was a round inside. There was. I pushed the forearm forward, and the chamber slammed closed. I took my right thumb and pushed the safety forward into the fire position. The sound of the shotgun's chamber going shut was a sound that everyone in a war zone knew. I started to move toward the VC but the doctor, in alarm, grabbed my right arm and shouted, "Wait! You can't kill him!"*

"Oh, yes I can," I shouted back, "I have to, for a lot of people!" I jerked my arm loose from him.

By this time one of the guards had come to see what was going on and was standing right in front of me with his 16 across his chest. He was an MP and only an E-4, very young. I doubt if he had ever fired his weapon in anger. His eyes were jumping from side to side looking at me - then at the doctor - then for someone to come and help him. He had been trained to follow orders, not to think. I'm sure no one ever covered this situation with him. He was probably thinking, "I can't kill an American to save a damn VC, but I can't let him kill the VC, either!" His wide eyes said he was not angry, just scared.

I turned to him and ordered, "Get out of my way, Soldier!"

He looked down at my shotgun - then back over his shoulder at the VC - then back at me again. He licked his dry lips and said, "You can't do this." I could almost hear pleading in his voice.

I looked him straight in the eyes and said, "Get out of my way. Move, or I will move you! The only way you are going to stop me, is to kill me. He needs to die right now!"

By then, the other guard was up there. I could see that both of the young Soldiers were scared and didn't know what to do. I was certain from the look on their faces, they were afraid of me. I doubt if they had fired a shot in this war and they knew who we were, even if they didn't know exactly who I was.

Before I could move, I could hear someone coming from behind calling out, "Coconut, Coconut!" It was Ed and Song. I turned around to face them. They asked what was going on. They said, "People outside said someone in here was going to kill one the POWs."

I said. "They're right. It's me! Colonel Trang is in there."

"Who?"

"Colonel Trang, and he needs to die!"

Ed grabbed my face with both of his hands and pulling me close he said, "Look me in the eyes, Kurt! I understand he needs to die, but not now, not this way! We need to learn anything we can from him."

I stared into Ed's eyes, and the rage slowly left me. "What if they let him go or send him to one of the rehabilitation camps?"

Ed said, "That won't happen, but what if it does? Okay, look, if they don't prosecute him or it looks like they're going to let him go, I will help you kill him. Alright, Kurt?"

I turned to look at Song. He had more of a reason to hate this man then I did. He looked past me at the VC and then looked around at all the people, doctors, nurses, and guards. They were all scared and didn't know what to do. Then he looked back at me and slowly shook his head, "No."

The rage was gone. Looking around the hospital room I started to feel bad; these were the good guys and I had them all scared. I didn't know what they would have done, had I gone through with it. I'm glad I didn't have to find out.

By now I was scared, too. I could have hurt one of our own people. The poor guards wouldn't have had a chance if I'd wanted to get to Trang. How bad would that have been? I would have thrown away all that I was, and all the good I had ever done over here. Thank God, for Ed and Song!

I looked at the doctor and told him I was sorry I had scared him. I turned around and told the MP I was sorry I had scared him, too, and then I pointed the shotgun at the ground, put the safety on, and handed it to the guard. I asked him if he would hold it for me. He took the weapon, looked at me gratefully, and said he would really, really be glad to. He looked at the other guard as the second guard wiped the sweat from his forehead and breathed a sigh of relief. Something like a smile came to his face as he looked at me.

I needed to clear my mind before I went back and talked to Colonel Trang, so I went outside and sat at a table where the hospital personnel took breaks. Looking around, I asked myself who I was, and what the hell I was doing here? Just five years earlier, I was graduating from high school in a small town in Indiana. I had 20 kids in my class, and in all the history of the town, we had never had a murder. I couldn't remember one violent crime. Until I joined the Army four months after I graduated, I had never been more than 100 miles from home. Now five years later, I had lived two lifetimes.

How did I get to the point where I was ready to kill a wounded man as he lay in a bed? What would my minister, and my mother and father think of me? I realized that I didn't get to this point in one big leap. I got here a little at a time, day by day. People back home were protesting this war and that was okay, they had the right, but they were looking at the political part of it and whether we should be in Vietnam or not. I could see that. But I didn't understand why they protested the Soldiers; we didn't make policies. We were just doing a hard job under hard conditions.

There was a song – I think the name was "WAR." The guy sang, **"War, what is it good for, absolutely nothing!"** But he was wrong! If we had not been here, the Communists would have been killing even more people than they were now, and they wanted to take away the freedoms that the people had. The protestors thought they were being good guys but their protesting *just encouraged the VC, and in no way helped to free the people of Vietnam. Their protesting didn't help that little girl, I did! Yet the protestors thought they were better than us and were the peace lovers.*

No one knows what it is to love peace until you have been to war. It's so easy to sit in the United States and talk, but if they really wanted to help these people they would have been here, or at least supporting those of us who were. The only people the protestors were helping were the people who would kill and take away the freedoms of people around the world. If we didn't help these people, who would? The politics of this war didn't mean anything to us who were here. The poor grunt that got sent here was only worried about staying alive 365 days so he could go home. Each day he made it through, was a day he could cross out on the calendar, and that was one less day here, and one day closer to going home.

We didn't sit around, debating the political aspects of being involved in Vietnam. The only thing that counted was staying alive one more day and doing our job the best we could. If we did survive and made it home, we were treated badly by people who had done absolutely nothing to help these people. Instead, their actions aided the enemy.

It was so hard to take when we got back home. Sometimes I hated the protestors and draft dodgers more than the VC. They were my fellow Americans, and they were leaving us there to die. They didn't care about us. They had done more for the bad guys than for us. It has been 10 years now since the war had been over, and I think the hostility between the protestors and the Vietnam Veterans is more intense now than when the war was on. The protestors say we should get over it, it was a long time ago, and that it's over. Well, for them it's over. But it was just something to do at the time for them. Carrying a sign and yelling profanities didn't cause them suffering and trauma or have any lifelong impact on them. So for them it is over. But for the Vietnam Veteran it is not over and never will be until the day he dies! We lived through hell, seeing our friends die. We suffered trauma, both physical and mental, with lifelong consequences. The protestors were wrong to take it out on the Soldiers. They are still, even to this day, our enemy.

I couldn't think about whether or not we should be there; I could only see and think about that little girl whose arm, Colonel Trang had cut off. That was reality, and there was nothing that the protestors or draft dodgers could have done to help her. It had been up to me, and yet I was sure they would have seen me as a bad guy. But I didn't care about that, because her father and mother had given me a hug and with tears in their eyes, they thanked me. It was things like that I would have to think about when I got back home and was treated badly by my fellow Americans.

I knew then that I couldn't talk to anyone about my experiences in Vietnam. They would never understand if they had not been there. They thought we were just killers, but we had given up a lot for our country and for the Vietnamese people. I could never be that naive Eagle Scout again. I might have been right or I might have been wrong, but at least I tried to help these people, which is more than the protesters could say.

One thing I do know, is I will never be the same again; once you have killed, you lose something inside you and don't feel right around other people who have never had to do that. Once you cross that line in life, you can never go back. The innocence is lost. Even if you killed to save someone else, you will never be the same. That is a big price to pay to help someone – something the protestors and draft dodgers will never feel or understand. They were taking the easy way out. We didn't have that option, and even if I did, I wouldn't change anything. Every time I looked into the eyes of a little child or a mother I saved, it made all the hard and terrible things I had to do, worth it. My hope came from something I read somewhere, "and this, too, shall pass."

I was sure I would never get anything of military value out of Colonel Trang, but I just wanted to ask him why he had cut that little girl's arm off – just why? I went back into the hospital and sat down with him. He of course had seen and heard everything that had just happened. After a moment of silence he said, "You are right, you know."

I said, "About what?"

"Killing me. That would be the right thing to do. If I had you in my control I would kill you, Coconut."

"Why do you hate me so much and want to kill me," I asked.

"Oh, I don't hate you, in fact, I admire you as a fellow warrior. That is why I would have to kill you. You are a threat to my cause and to me, just as I am a threat to you and your mission. The only way to stop either one of us, is for one of us to kill the other."

"Maybe," I said, "but I'm not like you – I don't kill innocent people and children to complete my mission. They are the ones I'm trying to save from people like you."

"Look Coconut, a Soldier has to use every weapon he has. Look at what you have to fight this war with. You have men, weapons, food, radios, helicopters, and all of the Soldiers that you want or need. I don't have any *of that, and I must fight you. I hate the things I had to do, but we both want to control the people."*

"No! That's not right! You may want to control them, we don't. We want to set them free."

"Look," he continued, "We both know that to win this war, you must have the people on your side or control them, whatever you want to call it. I have to use the tools or weapons I have. I don't do all those things to be mean; it's just practical. You on the other hand, can go into a village and provide the people with food and all kinds of support. When it comes to fighting us, you have so many more assets like air support, all the ammo you want, helicopters, and radios. You live well at your base camps and have great medical care. You get to go home after a year. We don't have any of that. This is our home, and we can't go anywhere; we must win or die. I went to school in the United States, and I know how you live. You think that I am a monster because I cut off that little girl's arm. Well, maybe I am, but it is the best weapon I had. Think about it. You have money and support all the time. Think about the money and energy you spent to get the people of that village to vote. All I had to do was to cut off the arm of one little girl and I controlled them all. They didn't vote. I hated doing it, but it cost nothing and was the only tool I had to work with."

We talked a little while longer and then I left. I'm not sure just what I thought about him. I still hated the things he had done, but I somehow didn't hate him anymore. I think I had been in a war zone too long, because on one level I could understand what he did and why. It almost seemed to make sense.

Sometime the following week I received word that Colonel Trang had died from the infection in his intestines.

Brutality again in 1985, and somehow I feel responsible for all of it. I can't stop it this time. This is one of many reasons we should never have left without winning. Our government should have been held accountable for abandoning the Vietnamese. They should have told the people of the United States about the atrocities of Hồ Chí Minh. He killed and abused his people just like Stalin. When we left, he killed, tortured, and imprisoned tens of thousands of people in South Vietnam. It really upsets me every time I read in a paper, and I mean an American paper, something about the reunited Vietnam. It was not reunited! The South was a free and independent country that was attacked, and is now occupied by the Communists. All the pain and suffering of the people

of South Vietnam since the time of the war, now and to come, is the responsibility of the U.S.! Every single day someone there is suffering and no one in the States even thinks about these people anymore. How sad for a country as great as ours to start this, and then leave and abandon these people.

Well I couldn't do anything about all that now. It was in the past. All I could do was get the General and his family out of there, and that would be a small but important victory for me.

CHAPTER TWENTY-TWO

Taking the General

The temple sat on the top of the mountain. We set up at the base of the mountain where we could park. We couldn't get in close; there was too much open area. There was one road coming in and one going out. We needed to set up on the south side of the parking lot where there was some concealment, but there was no real cover, nothing that would stop a round of ammo.

Ton took Robe and went up on the mountain a little way, so they would be up there in case someone tried to evade us by running up the mountain. Ton and Robe were located to the left of where the General and anyone with him should be. We would not be firing at them when we opened up, but we still had to be careful when we fired.

Some vehicles were coming; I hoped it was the General. It looked like it. There was a small truck with a driver, a co-driver, and three men in the back. There was a car following them. I thought it must have the General inside. It had a driver, a co-driver, and two men in the back seat. Behind them was a smaller truck with a driver, a co-driver, and four Soldiers in the back. We didn't think there would be that many of them. Fortunately, they stopped more to our right, and Ton and Robe were hidden way over to our left and up the mountain.

The driver and co-driver of the car got out and opened the back doors to let the men out of the back. I saw a man sitting on the far side of the car who was not in uniform, and he looked older. That must have been the General. The Soldier who came out of the back on our side of the car had a pistol and looked like an officer. The driver and co-driver had AKs, as did all the other Soldiers. I didn't recognize the uniforms. They were a little different than when I was here in the war.

The officer went to the front truck and said something to the driver, who then drove off toward Tây Ninh. He motioned to the Soldiers in the back truck and they came up around the car. The next thing I know, there's a car coming with two men from the direction of Tây Ninh. They both got out to talk to the officer and were wearing police uniforms.

Ton and Robe were near the path up the mountain, toward the temple. There were no locals around; they would always try to stay clear of the police and Soldiers if they could. We had sent the message to the General to walk up the path toward the temple – we would grab him there. He was heading that way, and that should have kept him out of the line of fire when we opened up. That was all he knew. Ton and Robe knew that they must get to him and keep him out of danger. If we allowed General Fong to be killed, our mission would have failed.

I looked at my men. It was time to fire when I fired. As I looked at each one of them, one by one they all gave me a head nod so I knew they were ready. It was a go. We were all ready, and when I looked back, the officer was walking up to the General, talking to him. They were about 50 yards away and heading for the path up the mountain. The only thing we could do at that point was to open up on the others and let Ton and Robe take out the officer and get the General to safety.

Since this was not a war zone none of the Soldiers or policemen had their weapons at the ready. The only problem we would have would be if two of them were on the other side of the car from us and had some cover.

I looked around and didn't see any locals. That was good, because we were going to have to kill everyone. We couldn't let anyone see or know that there were Americans here, and it would give us a little time before anyone would be after us. It was only 25 miles to Cambodia, so with any luck, we would be in or close to Cambodia before anyone followed us.

I was going to take the Soldier to my left and behind the General about 20 yards, who was about 75 yards from the trucks and about 50 yards from where Ton and Robe stood. I took one more look around; everyone looked ready and there were still no locals. I took a breath and slowly breathed out. The Soldier was looking in the direction of the

General and they were both at about a 45 degree angle from me, but facing away. The Soldier was only about 75 or 80 yards from me – an easy shot.

I put my sight between his shoulder blades and squeezed the trigger. He lurched forward like someone hit him in the back with a ball swinging from a crane! My men opened up on the rest of the Soldiers and in just a few seconds all the bad guys were down except one man behind the car.

Suddenly the officer with the General grabbed him and was running for the mountain. It looked like he was trying to protect him, so that meant he didn't realize the General was in on this. He was looking back at us as we ran up to the men who were down.

My men were going around making sure all the Soldiers were dead, and if not, killing them. The Soldier behind the car ran about 10 yards and turned around throwing his weapon down. One of Bull's men went up to him and put a round in his head. I heard him say, "This is for Bull and all the innocent people the VC have killed."

Ton and Robe jumped out about 10 yards behind General Fong and rushed the officer, but they didn't have a sure shot and couldn't take a chance of hitting the General. Ton was only a few steps away when the officer turned around, saw him, and fired. Ton was hit in his right hip! I saw him go down. Robe, who was only two steps behind Ton, tripped over him and went down, too. I took aim at the officer. It was about 150 yards but the General and the officer were moving. I couldn't get a clear shot.

The officer was aiming his pistol at Robe and Ton when he just froze. He didn't fire. I think he realized then that he was looking at an American, and he stopped just for a second in surprise. Then he stepped up to Robe and aimed his pistol at him!

I thought, "Shoot, Robe! Shoot!" But Robe had never been in a situation like that before and he was just staring at the officer. Besides, he had dropped his AK when he fell.

I was going to have to take the shot even if the General was in the way. I was here to get the General out and the mission came first. I couldn't let Robe die; I just couldn't. Before the officer could shoot, General Fong reached out and grabbed his arm and turned him around so they were facing each other. I started to move toward them closing the distance, I was ready to kneel down and shoot if I had to. To my surprise the officer didn't pull away and go back to shooting Robe and Ton. I could see the officer yelling at the General and the General pointing and yelling at the officer. Then the officer looked back at Robe, yanked his arm loose from the General, and then pointed the pistol at the General. He must have caught on that the General was in on this and was now going to kill him!

I immediately knelt to take a shot when I saw General Fong look at Robe and put his hands up as if to say, "Stop!" In the next moment, Robe grabbed his AK off the ground and fired, and his round went through the back of the officer coming out the front splattering blood all over the General! The officer fell into the General's arms.

I shouted for the men to get the trucks up here, that I was going to get General Fong, Ton and Robe. But when I got to the General, he was still holding the officer in his arms, crying. By this time Robe was helping Ton to his feet and down the path to the trucks. I asked the General if he was alright and he murmured, "Yes," as he held the officer tightly in his arms.

"General," I said grabbing his sleeve, "we have to go now!" He just looked at me and I could see there was something really wrong. I asked him what it was; what was wrong? He looked at me and called my name.

"Coconut," he looked down at the officer, "This is my son!"

His voice broke and he began to cry again. I was stunned! I sat down beside him and I started to cry, too, because I could see the hurt in his eyes. I told him I was sorry – that we didn't know. He had saved Robe and it had cost him his son's life!

The General said it wouldn't have made any difference. "My son would have killed me without a second thought and then everyone would have died for nothing. It's not my son's fault, either, though; it's this damn Communist government! They turn families into enemies – I lost my son many years ago to them," he said, shaking his head back and forth.

"Coconut," the General whispered moments later, "you have lost a lot of people you loved and have risked your life for my family and for me. Let's go; staying will only cost more lives."

I walked the General down to the middle truck and helped him inside. I told him that Robe and I would be with him in a minute. We could see that Ton was going to be okay even though he had lost a lot of blood, but we knew if we could get back to Cambodia quickly we could take good care of him. In minutes, everyone was in the trucks and we were on the way to the border.

Traveling down the road I glanced at General Fong's face now and then. It was not hard to see the deep hurt in his eyes over his son's death. I could empathize with him. I knew it was not quite the same, but the worst thing a Soldier can do is to have to kill a fellow Soldier.

I remembered the hurt and confusion I felt when I was on Operation Oak in 1967.

CHAPTER TWENTY-THREE

Operation Oak

Operation Oak was set up to terminate U.S. and allied personal who were providing aid to the enemy. One of the teams was taking out people working the black market. We were not policeman, and didn't care about anyone in the black market business unless they were somehow aiding the enemy. Anyone aiding the enemy would be terminated with prejudice! "Terminate with prejudice," was the CIAs terminology meaning, "to kill." Other teams also took out personnel who were aiding the VC in any way. Some personnel were just unthinkingly giving their girlfriends information about their unit, but some were actually selling information.

I was called in by Coleman and given a briefing on three incidents that had happened in War Zone C. All three incidents involved helicopters and U.S. Soldiers. There were three times when a helicopter was flying over and the crew spotted a Soldier all alone, waving at them. Two times the chopper landed and picked up the Soldier and everything went okay. Both Soldiers had been separated from their unit during a battle and had been listed as missing in action. But on one occasion when the chopper landed, it was ambushed, and we lost the chopper and four men. After the battle the Soldier who they had gone down to rescue was nowhere around. No one had seen what happened to him.

General Westmoreland and others were worried that the VC were using POWs to get choppers to land so they could ambush our men. It was tricky, because they were worried about having the choppers ambushed but they were also worried about the POWs. Westmoreland put Colonel Nelson of the 3rd Rangers in charge of the problem.

Nelson put a platoon of his Rangers on 24-hour standby, and trained them intensively to be able to react quickly to rescue the POW. He set it up so that if any chopper in War Zone C spotted a Soldier alone waving at the chopper, the chopper would drop a note telling the Soldier that they were low on fuel and would be back for him. The chopper would then notify Colonel Nelson. Nelson would quickly get the Rangers into the area to set up so that when the chopper came back, if it was an ambush the Rangers would ambush the VC's ambush, and rescue the POW. The Colonel also sent choppers out every day flying low just looking for any lone Soldier.

That all sounded good, but Coleman was worried that the Soldier might not be a POW but a VC sympathizer. If this was the case, then even if the Rangers rescued him he would be telling the press about why he was helping the VC – saying some kind of shit about how we were bombing and killing civilians, or something like that. What we didn't need was another Wanda Lane. With all the protesting and other anti-war activities going on back in the States, the last thing we needed was a Soldier saying this sort of thing to the press.

The fact was that Colonel Nelson worked for The Company. Coleman set it up so that if someone contacted Nelson, he would put the Rangers in place, and the Rangers didn't know anything except that they were to rescue the POW. At the same time Nelson contacted the Rangers, he would also contact us. We would put our plan into action.

Coleman had decided that we couldn't take the chance of the Soldier being a sympathizer so he would have to be terminated. He had me put a team together to take out the Soldier. I assembled a four-man team. To make sure we would kill the Soldier, I was going to use two shooters. I designated both Ed and myself as the shooters, with two other guys for security to make up the team.

Up until now, when The Company wanted someone terminated, we knew when and where we were going to take the shot. This operation would be different. We wouldn't know until we got there what the terrain would be like or how long the shot would be. Since we didn't know how close we would be able to get to the target, we had to do a lot of shooting at longer ranges than we were used to. That's why I decided to use two shooters to increase our chances to make the kill. We all talked it over and decided that if it was in a location where the VC could pull off an ambush because there was jungle or some cover for them to hide in, then that meant there should be cover for us. Therefore, we should be able to get within 500 yards of the target. For this reason, we only practiced shots up to 500 yards.

The Company armor gave us two Ruger Model 77s in 30-06 caliber. The load we found to be the most accurate was a 168 GR bullet, 46.5 GR of H4895 powder, at 2650 FPS. With this round we zeroed at 500 yards. The drop for this round was +16 inches at 100 yards, + 29 inches at 200 yards, + 34 inches at 300 yards, + 32 inches at 400 yards, + 21 inches at 500 yards.

About 10 days after we started to train, a call came in that there was a chopper going to pick up a lone Soldier about 35 miles southwest of us. Colonel Nelson had notified Coleman and Coleman filled us in on where the pickup was going to take place, and where the Rangers were going to set up.

We picked a spot that we thought would give us cover and a good shot. We got in place just in time. We had only been there about four minutes when the chopper came in. I just had time to find a spot to take a shot. I could see the Soldier in the brush waiting for the chopper. The rangefinder said he was at 458 yards from me. I didn't see any VC in the area.

The chopper circled and the Soldier ran out into the clearing waving his arms. He was now 432 yards from me. I looked at Ed and he had the Soldier in his sights. I knew I would have about a three-inch rise at 432 yards. So I put the crosshairs on the center of his chest. The chopper landed, the Soldier ran up and jumped in, and off the chopper went. No ambush. Great! Another Soldier rescued.

When I got back, I told Coleman that we needed to make sure we were in place before the chopper came in because we almost hadn't had time to get in place to make the shot on last one. So he set it up where we would call him when we were in place. Then he would call Nelson, and he would notify the chopper that it was okay to land.

About two weeks later we got another call from Nelson that a chopper had spotted a lone GI, 20 miles southeast of Tây Ninh. That only put him about 40 miles from us. We jumped on the chopper, looked at the map and talked to Nelson on the way. He told us where the Rangers were going to land and set up. We picked a spot to land about 500 yards away and quickly got into position. We were on the ground before the Rangers got there. We had to move fast, and that was not a safe way to move in VC area, but we had no choice.

I didn't like this operation from the start. We didn't know if there were

VC out there, and if there were, we didn't have any idea where they were. The Rangers didn't know we were here and we were concerned they would target us, as well as the VC. We had to move too fast and didn't have time to make a good plan. What was funny, was that we really didn't have a plan, good or bad. We were just moving and hoping for the best. Hell, we didn't even know if this guy was a good guy or a bad guy. Even if there was an ambush, that didn't mean the GI was a bad guy; he might be a POW being used to bring the chopper down.

The whole thing sucked. I didn't like it and Ed didn't, either. There had been a lot of things I didn't like in this war, but what is there to like in a war? Not much, maybe going home and the war ending. I knew that in this moment, the only thing that counted was surviving this mission and this day, and hopefully taking out some bad guys.

We got to the spot where the chopper saw the GI. There was a field about 100 yards long and 200 yards wide. It had grass about knee high with brush here and there. There was heavy jungle on the north side, and that was where we thought the VC would be if there were any around. The west and south side had jungle, but it was thin. The east side also had a thin jungle about 300 yards deep and an open field behind it.

The Rangers had come in from the southeast and set up in the jungle on the south and east sides of the field. We set up on the west side in the thin jungle. Ed and I found trees that were suitable for climbing and would be a good location for the shot. We had pole-climbing spikes with us to help climb the trees. I moved up the tree about 35 feet and found a spot from where I could see most of the clearing. We also had pole-climber safety belts. I found a spot where I could strap myself in, so I could use both hands for the shot.

I could see the Rangers moving into position on the southeast side of the clearing, and the GI on the north side of the clearing near the edge of the jungle. He was kneeling on his right knee looking at the clearing and up into the air for the chopper. He was only about 355 yards from me. I looked into the jungle behind him with my binoculars. I could see men! I could not see a whole man but I could see movement and an arm or head now and then.

Well, it looked as though this was going to be an ambush. I didn't think the Rangers could see the VC from where they were located. I was ready, Ed was ready and the Rangers were in position. I called Nelson and told him I thought it was an ambush, we were ready, and the Rangers were in position. I looked back at the GI. He was turning around and talking to someone behind him.

"How did I get here and why am I here," I thought. It was hot and the sweat was running down my face. I had on a green bandana. I took it off, wrung the sweat out, and put it back on. My heart was pounding. There were so many thoughts going on in my head. I wanted to contact the Rangers so they would know the VC were there, but they weren't supposed to know we were there. Hopefully Nelson had warned them.

In times like this, I often thought about my mother. She was so loving and caring and loved me so much. She always worried about me. What would she think if she knew what I was about to do? Killing the enemy was no problem and I would have no problem killing the GI if I knew he was a traitor, but I didn't know for sure. In that moment, I thought, "What am I doing in a jungle 12,000 miles from Indiana, about to kill another American? The world was so simple back home, and war should be, also. Kill the bad guys, but who are the bad guys? And who decides who are the bad guys, and by what measure? Today I decide, but I don't want to be the one to decide."

Before I could think about anything else, the GI stood up and walked out into the clearing. I could hear the chopper coming in to my left – it was headed straight for the Soldier and then flared at about 100 feet in front of the GI slowly lowering the skids to the ground. The GI was waving his arms until the chopper's skids touched the ground and then he ran to his right and hit the ground.

At that moment the jungle opened up with small arm fire on the chopper! I would guess about 50 men were shooting at the chopper. A line of fire about a 100 yards long was coming from the jungle. The chopper was taking a lot of rounds and was about to lift off, when the Rangers opened up on the VC. This pulled most of the fire away from the chopper, which then pulled up and banked hard to the left, disappearing over the jungle to the south. It was obvious that the VC were surprised. They were taking a lot of casualties. Most of the fire coming from them had stopped.

I brought my mind back to what I was there for, and pulled the rifle up, looking for the GI in the scope. I scanned the area where he had hit the ground. He was lying alongside a tree stump that looked to be about eighteen inches in diameter. The log was between him and the fire coming from the Rangers, but the Rangers were there to save him, so they were not shooting at him. He was lying on his belly with his head on his right arm looking to the left in my direction. The rangefinder showed he was 345 yards away. This made it a short shot. He didn't have a weapon that I could see.

I put the crosshairs on his body. He looked scared but what was he scared *of, the VC because he was a POW and they had forced him to do this? If so, he must be praying that the Rangers would kill the VC and he would soon be free and on his way home.*

Home, I wondered where that was for him. Was he married? Did he have kids? Or was he scared because he was a traitor and that the Rangers would soon have him? Even if he was a traitor, the Rangers wouldn't know that, and he would still be safe and on his way back to the States. If that was the case, he could be a big problem for us and could do a lot of psychological damage to our war effort.

I knew right then, whatever I did, my life would never be the same. No one would ever understand our doing this and I would have to live with it the rest of my life. I looked at Ed who was in a tree just to my right. He was looking at me; he was not to shoot until I did, unless I missed or was killed.

The look in his eyes seemed to say, "What are you waiting for?" I looked at him and nodded my head and turned back to the scope. The GI still hadn't moved but by now the VC were retreating back through the jungle to the north. There was not much firing going on. If I was going to do this, I needed to fire now while there was still the sound of shooting to cover my shot. We had suppressors but I didn't want anyone to see the GI get hit. I wanted them to believe that he was hit in the firefight.

I looked to my left and I could see four or five Rangers standing up and walking toward the GI. I again put the crosshairs on him. I had a lump in my throat so large I couldn't swallow my own spit. It was now or never, and that's when it hit me, I can't go back and tell them I had the shot and didn't take it!

I pinched the trigger and saw his head explode. I glanced to my right and saw Ed give me the thumbs up. He didn't fire; he could see he didn't need to shoot. The Soldier was dead.

We called in the chopper after the Rangers had moved out carrying the body of the dead GI. I didn't talk all the way back.

Coleman was happy with the operation, but he could tell by my silence and the expression on my face that I had a problem with the mission. Fortunately, he never had me go on any more of those missions; we never talked about it again.

Afterwards it was a big story over there as well as in the States, how the Rangers had tried and almost rescued a POW. The GI was sent home a hero. But he did not go home alive because of me. The Rangers never knew that they never had a chance to save him.

CHAPTER TWENTY-FOUR

The General into Cambodia

I knew that for the General this must be both the best and worst of times. It looked like he was going to get out of here but he had to leave his dead son and this country he loved so much, behind. What he really wanted was for his people to be free and living in peace. At least he, his wife, and two daughters would live free, but only if we could get him out of here.

It was only 25 miles to the Cambodian border and even with the bad dirt roads we should be there in an hour or so. We were lucky this wasn't a war zone; there were not many Soldiers around, and right now they thought what had just happened was only a kidnapping. If they knew that there were Americans here, it would turn into a war zone very quickly! The countryside would be filled with Soldiers.

Fortunately, it was too late for them now. By the time they figured it out, the General would be in Cambodia and on his way to freedom. The problem would be coming back to get Bull. The police would be waiting for us and they would be on high alert. It was not going to be easy to get Bull and then make it back into Cambodia.

We came to the end of the road, and we had about a mile of jungle to walk through to get to the river. There was a place on down the road where we could drive right up to the water, but so could the police and Soldiers. I felt more at ease in the jungle. As strange as it may sound, most of the locals didn't like to live in, or even go into the jungle. The VC had gotten good at using it, but they didn't really like it, either.

The boat that was going to pick us up would not be noticed near the jungle like it would if it came to the ramp on down the way. There was always the chance that there would be locals at the normal access place. Most of them used it to push off into the river.

Everyone was out of the trucks, and Bull's five men were there waiting to guide us back to the river. I had Robe call the men who had the women on the Cambodian side of the river, and tell them to be ready to send the boat over for us when we got there. He contacted them and let them know where we were.

Three of Bull's men drove the trucks away and went to hide them. They would come back for us after General Fong was safe and we came back to get Bull. Robe told Bull's men not to send the boat until we called and were at the river's edge. The Vietnamese may have been patrolling the river and we didn't want to be in the river any longer than we had to.

It was hot and dark in the jungle, but it was safer moving through it. We had to go slow because we are carrying Ton. He was okay for now, but he would need blood soon. We didn't have blood with us but we did have plasma. That would keep him alive until we got him out of there. We had morphine for the pain and he had almost stopped bleeding. There shouldn't have been anyone out there in the jungle, but we couldn't take that chance, and had to move slowly just like back in the war. I had a point man, two flank men, and two men covering our backs. Twenty minutes later, it was time for a break. We should have been about halfway to the river.

Nothing had changed about the jungle. It was hot, dark, and there were bugs – big bugs. I was going to sit between our team and the road and lean up against a tree so I could watch behind us.

Oh, shit! There was a snake not two feet from me!

It was just lying there looking at me, and I didn't know what kind it was and didn't care. It wasn't really big, maybe three feet long, but I didn't know if it was poisonous or not. Any snake is deadly to me; it makes my heart beat so hard I think I'm going to have a heart attack! Back home in Indiana I would have just shot it, but we had to stay quiet, so I couldn't shoot. I decided to lean my AK on a tree and get out my knife. I hated this. I would love to have just thrown the knife, but if I missed, or if it didn't hit blade first, then I wouldn't have my knife. I didn't want to get close enough to just stab the snake.

I broke out in a sweat when I realized this was like the time back in the war when I faced the world's biggest snake up in the tree.

CHAPTER TWENTY-FIVE

Vietnam Snake-Eaters

It was March of '67, and we were out there in the jungle; the problem was that I wasn't sure just where "there" was. I asked Ron, "How long we have we been out here?" He didn't know, but thought it had been about 20 days.

This was a big operation; they were calling it Operation Junction City. It started in February and lasted about 90 days. It was March, but I'm not sure what day – a day was a day here. They were all the same, SSDD (same shit, different day).

We started out the operation by working with a regular army unit, so we had been eating with them. We had Cs (C-rations, wet food in cans) and some hand-prepared hot meals, but for the last 10 days or so, the six of us had been out here on our own doing recon. We hadn't had much to eat and very little sleep. I'm not sure just where we were because the maps sucked. I wasn't sure where all the other army units were, either. We had to be really careful to not get hit by one of our own units.

We saw many signs of VC but had only engaged two small units of six or so men. We had only killed two; the rest had gotten away. We were finding lots of tunnels, weapons, rice, and documents. It was the rainy season, and it was hot. I was hot, dirty, and really hungry. We had been living off the land, but that was hard here, because the jungle grows many things – just not much that we could eat. We had some rice that we found and we did have some Ks with us.

It's always important to hydrate the Ks before eating and not drink water after chewing down dehydrated food – I tried that the first time I had Ks. I thought, "Why bother with adding the water and then eating it?" I ate the dehydrated rice and then drank the water. Bad idea, really bad idea! My stomach swelled up until I thought it was going to burst; must be what it feels like to deliver a baby. The pain was so intense I thought I would die; I hoped I would die! Now I add the water first and then eat the Ks.

We had come upon an army unit four days earlier, and had gotten some Cs and picked up some more Ks. It was hard to get water as far out as we were, and we didn't get re-supplied every day like the line unit (an Army infantry unit that does most of the grunt work). There was a lot of water around, but it was bad. It was hot, and we had to get it out of holes in the ground full of bugs and dirt. It tasted like shit and smelled so bad, I knew I was never going to drink water again when I got back in the world (meaning to be back in the States). I was really craving protein, too. We could never seem to get enough meat.

Now we were working our way into an area where we had taken fire two days earlier, so we had to move slowly and be very quiet. The jungle was really thick and I couldn't see more than two or three feet in front of me. I was sure the mosquitoes had sucked all the blood out of me by now.

Joe was on point and he gave me the sign to stop; he wanted me to come up and look at something.

Great! He had found a snake – a big one! It was in a tree stretched out on a limb about six feet off the ground. It must have been 10 feet long and six inches in diameter. I hated the heat, the smell, and a lot of things over here, but snakes were the things I hated the most. I have hated snakes all my life. Back home even a Garter Snake scared me. Everyone said that they wouldn't hurt you, but anything that made my heart beat so hard it hurt was scary to me.

So here we were with this big snake and Joe and Ron thought we should kill it and have it for a meal. I hated snakes, but they are full of protein and I was hungry.

Joe knew I hated snakes so he said that he would climb up the tree and throw the snake down to me. Yeah right! Fat chance! If he thought I was going to stand there and catch a ten-foot snake, he must've gone crazy from heat and hunger.

Meanwhile, the snake was stretched out on the limb with his head away from the tree trunk, so I said I would climb the tree and throw the snake down to them. I started to climb up the tree, but I would've liked it better if I was going to throw a VC with a knife out of the tree, rather than a snake!

It was so hot I had sweat in my eyes, and my hands were slippery. I was hanging onto the tree with my right hand and reached around the tree with my left hand to grab the snake. My head was about level with the snake. Its tail was about six inches from the trunk of the tree, and I thought if I grabbed the tail and gave a big pull to my left, the snake would fall off the tree and down into Joe's and Ron's arms. But of course I was worried that the snake could bite me before I could throw it off the limb.

I had seen a lot of snakes over there; as a rule, the smaller the snake the faster it is, and the larger the snake the slower it is. If that held true, then this snake should be slow, as big as it was. It was 10 feet long and the head was 10 feet away from me.

I grabbed hold of the tree and reached out holding my left hand right over the tail. I took a deep breath and grabbed the tail. In a split second, before I could even think about throwing the snake off the limb, the snake's head was right in my face, mouth wide open and hissing loudly! He was so close that I feel his hot breath!

So much for my theory about big snakes being slow. I was so scared and shook up that I let go of the tree and fell the six feet to the ground onto my back. I had my 16 slung over my back and it knocked the breath out of me when I hit the ground.

Now I was pissed.

I got up and pulled my 16 around in front and aimed at the snake. Joe and Ron both yelled for me to stop. I did and looked at them and asked why? They said the VC might hear us; we were right in the middle of the bad guys. I took a minute and thought about it but I was so mad, I didn't care about the VC. I opened up on the snake and shot the shit out of it! Down it came.

Well Song cut off the head and the small part of the snake. That left about a four-foot hunk. Song grabbed it and we moved about a klick away, dug in and waited to see if there were any VC coming after us. While we waited, Song and Tuk skinned the snake and cut out all the edible meat.

About an hour later we determined that we had not been followed and the area was clear of VC. We took my steel helmet and put in some dehydrated rice, the pieces of snake meat, water, and some salt, and used a small piece of C-4 about the size of your thumbnail to heat up the snake soup. We ate it – it was not good but we desperately needed the protein.

Dinner anyone?

CHAPTER TWENTY-SIX

❧

The VC Walked Right Over Us

That was a big snake back then and at least this was a smaller snake now. The damn thing was moving away; maybe now I could catch my breath and my heart would slow down from 1000 beats per minute.

In no time, we were on the move again. I could hear the river now, so it must have been just ahead of us. Everyone got down and stayed a few yards in the jungle while I went to check out the river's edge. It was the dry season and the river was low. There was about 10 feet of mud from the jungle to the water. I was going down to see how soft the mud was. It was very soft; I sank in almost to my knees. Everyone would have to be careful getting into the boat and it would be even harder to carry Ton into the boat. I had the guys cut some branches, and we made a litter (make-shift stretcher) so we didn't have to carry him on our backs. I don't think he would have survived that.

I was just about to tell Robe to call for the boat when I heard another boat coming up the river. When it came into sight, I could see it was a Vietnamese patrol boat. It wasn't a big one, only about 30 feet long with four Soldiers on deck. This would not be a problem unless they had a radio. If they did, they could quickly call and give us away.

I was sure we could kill them, but the way it was, no one knew we were here and we needed to use the river to get everyone back to the ship.

If the Vietnamese found us they would have boats all up and down the river. The best thing was to hide and hope they would just go away.

I told everyone but four of Bull's men to back up into the jungle about 50 yards and hide. I spread the four men out on the bank, but told them not to fire unless I fired. They kept back into the jungle a little, and I found a place about 15 feet from the bank, covered with a lot of foliage. I could see the river right at the spot where the boat should pass directly in front of me.

The boat came by slowly but kept moving. Suddenly, one of the Soldiers was yelling something and pointing at the bank. They were too far out in the river and I couldn't tell what they were saying, but they were coming over to the bank and pointing!

Oh shit, I had really screwed up! They had seen my tracks from when I went down to check the mud. I thought, "Twenty years ago I would have deliberately left these tracks to draw the VC in for an ambush. I guess I'll have to tell the guys that this is what I did here, so they won't know I screwed up."

It was time to take the safety off my AK. As much as I wanted to shoot, I had to lie there hoping they wouldn't see us. Even if they did, we would have the advantage.

Damn! There was an insect biting my leg! Still, this was better than the time during the war when I had to hide, knowing if the VC found us we would be dead for sure.

It was in War Zone C during 1966. It all started with Ed calling my name.

"Hey, Coconut! You in there?"

"Yeah, Ed what do you need?"

"Captain Hawks wants to see you over at Military Intelligence, G-2."

I went to see what he wanted. I hoped he had something for us. We had been sitting around there for four or five days. Most of the time when Intel wants to see you, they have something they want you to do.

"What can we do for you, Captain Hawk?"

"It's good to see you, Kurt. We need you to take a team and do a little recon for us."

"Sure, what's going on," I asked.

"One of our platoons from the 196th got hit yesterday about four klicks northwest of Tây Ninh.

My first thoughts were, "Did they take any casualties? When did they get hit? How many VC were there? What types of weapons were used? Did they kill any VC?"

The Captain went on to say that they had one KIA and two wounded. They didn't find any dead VC, but their Soldiers could have taken the dead back with them. It was like most of the firefights. The VC opened up for about five minutes, broke contact, and was gone into the jungle. Our guys returned fire but were not sure if they hit anyone.

The CO (commanding officer) said he thought there were 15 to 20 VC and they had automatic weapons – sounded like AKs – but they didn't see anyone. It was about 1630 hours, they had called the choppers in and got everyone back to Tây Ninh. We had been getting hit a lot around that area, and we thought there was a large force and camp somewhere nearby.

"What would you like us to do, Captain?"

"I need you to take a team and see if you can find anything out there."

No problem, sir. I'll get a team around and go have a look."

Since we were just going to look and not engage, I didn't want a big force. It was just going to be Joe, Ed, Song, Tuk, and me. Captain Hawk said he would have a slick ready for us at the pad in about an hour at 0830. I told him we would be there, ready to go.

I told the guys, "Saddle up, we're on! There's been another group hit northwest of Tây Ninh and G-2 wanted us to go have a look around. They think there is a large force out there somewhere."

I thought we would give it four or five days, so I grabbed the K-Rations. It was too long of a trip to carry Cs with us. It was heavy jungle, so I grabbed some shotguns as well as the 16s. I also brought two AKs, just in case we needed to fool the VC. An AK sounds different than an M-16, so when we shot the AK, the VC thought it was one of their own and not U.S. forces.

We would be too far out for constant radio contact. The radios at that time didn't go very far in the jungle, so we would be out of radio range. G-2 would send an O-2 Skymaster (small two-place Cessna) over the area twice a day, and that would be the only radio contact we would have. We would be on our own most of the time.

I set up an extraction point. We would set points and times for a chopper to pick us up, and establish more than one extraction point and time. If we couldn't make one, we would try to make the next pick-up on the next day. We had to be sure we had our smoke grenades so the chopper could find us.

I told the men to remember that we were going out there to look, not fight. We would go heavy on food and meds, not ammo. If we got hit we would have to split up and "*đi đi mau.*" I had to remind Ed that this meant he couldn't kill everyone he sees, because we didn't want them to see us . . .

We all looked at the map to see where we were going to insert northwest of Tây Ninh, not far from Núi Ba Din, the Black Virgin Mountain. We needed to stay clear of the mountain; we knew it was full of VC, but we were going to search to the north and west of it.

This was War Zone C. The VC had been building tunnels here for many years to fight the French and there could be a large force there and we wouldn't even see them. We could miss them very easily, so we had to move slowly. After all, this war was not going anywhere; we had lots of time. We just needed to go look and return safely.

"Everyone ready? Joe? Ed? Song? Okay, Tuk? Then, let's go."

We were on the ground in no time. Damn, it was hot. I gave Song, point (first, and most exposed position). Ed watched our asses. We proceeded slowly and easy; we were not in a race. I told Joe to look – there was a well-worn path. Since the VC were good at moving in the jungle without leaving much of a sign, there must be a lot of them to have made a path this visible.

Two days had passed and we still had no contact, but had seen many signs. I thought G-2 was right about a big force, but we had not seen one VC.

Day four came and we would be out of here tomorrow. I was hot, tired, hungry, and scared. We were a long way out with no radio contact, so if we got hit we couldn't call for air support or for a dust off (a medical chopper). I thought how glad I would be when this was all over. There was still no real sign of any force, big or small, just a lot of trails that seemed to go nowhere. I was sick of the damn K-Rations. What I would have given for some real food right then. I was tired; we had been walking 14 hours a day and only getting four hours sleep at night.

I knew this mission was about over, but I sure wished we had found something. I wasn't sure if there were many VC out here, but they had been hitting our units a lot. They were so good at hit-and-run. They would hit, and were gone before we could hit them back. If we could just find them in a big unit so we could use our superior firepower, we could do a lot of damage. But damn, they were hard to find; they could find us, we just couldn't find them.

I told Joe we were going to head to the pickup point for extraction. I wanted to get close that night so we could check it out before the chopper came in tomorrow at 1400 hours. We had to be sure it was the place, because the maps were horrible.

"Coconut," Joe called, "This is the extraction point if the map is right, and that would be the first time."

Joe was right – we were here; there was the clearing and the landing zone.

We decided to settle in just inside the jungle and wait until morning. The chopper would be here today at 1400 hours, so we wanted to use the daylight to check out this whole area and make sure it was safe for the pickup. Song and I would look on this side of the clearing. Joe, Ed, and Tuk would go around the clearing and check out the jungle on the other side.

I told Tuk and Ed to keep their eyes open so we could eat and check our weapons and then they would have a chance to do the same. It was early and we had until 1400 hours to get ready – did I say something to eat? I forgot all we had were K-Rations and you couldn't really call that food.

Suddenly someone was coming out of the jungle from the other side! We were about to see who they were and how many now. Shit, here we were, just hours from the pickup time and at the pickup spot, and now we had found the VC, or they were finding us! No good, either way. Here they came, one, two, three, four, five, and a sixth one. They had AKs and were in khaki uniforms; they must have been NVA.

It was only about 150 yards across the clearing; we didn't have time to get out of there and there was no place to go but walk all the way back to the camp. No way could we get that far. We didn't have much food and we were tired. It was hot but that's not why I was sweating.

I looked at Joe and Ed. They were checking their 16s and watching the men as they came closer. I looked at Song and Tuk. Song was only 16, but a hardened warrior. To the rest of us this was a war and the VC were the enemy. To Song, who had seen his mother and father killed by the VC, this was personal. His shirt was open and I could see some of his tattoo. It read, "I eat the heart out of VC," and he literally did.

Song looked into the clearing and then back at me, and pulled his finger across his throat. I knew what he meant; we should take them. Like I said, there was no place to run and no time. There were six of them and five of us. I went to each man and assigned a man for them to take out. They were to fire when I fired, then anyone who could, should take the sixth man. If we waited until they were about 50 yards out the one who was left would have to make about 50 yards across the open clearing and he would never make that.

As many times as I had been in this position, I still got scared. I checked the safety on my 16 for the 10th time. I looked at the guys and then back at the men coming toward us. It seemed like we were in a good position, but we were so far out that if they got one good round off and hit just one of us, it could be a real mess. We only had one chance to make the chopper at this point, and that wouldn't be here for hours. If we missed it then we had to make another point about four klicks away, to try again tomorrow. Problem was, if someone got hit he might not last that long and there would be nothing I could do about it.

The NVAs were moving very slowly across the field. They were about halfway across when Ed touched my left shoulder. When I looked at him, his eyes were really big and he took his two fingers and pointed to his eyes and then pointed to the clearing. This meant he had seen something he didn't like.

I couldn't see anything but the six men so I held up six fingers and the "okay" sign to him, but he shook he head and pointed to the clearing again. I still didn't see anything but the six men, so I moved a little to my right and then I could see what he had seen!

Coming out of the jungle was a large body of men! I turned to the guys and held up my hand in a fist; that was the signal to stop and hold just as they were. Holy shit, we had found the large force that G-2 thought was here, or in this case they had found us. Well they hadn't found us yet, but in a minute or two they would!

I could see there were hundreds of them, maybe more. There was a lot of movement in the jungle. My God, this force was so big it had a six-man point. When you moved, you would put a man out front and he is called a point man; you also put one to the right and left and they were called flank men. The one bringing up the back is called the rear guard. All of them were to stay in sight of the main body, and you only had one man or two out front unless you had a big force and needed to cover a large area.

We were just out there looking; we were not a big enough force to deal with a large force like this. We didn't have much ammo, because we didn't come out here to fight, just to look. This looked like an impossible situation.

By this time the six men were almost across the clearing. I gave the hand sign for my men to move back into the jungle behind us. The VC had not seen us and I was sure they didn't expect anyone out that far. I didn't think we could get out of there; we were too tired and would have to keep going fast to stay ahead of them. We sure wouldn't last long in a firefight so what was there to do? I looked at each of my men; I knew them really well. I wanted to find out what they were thinking. We moved back another 50 yards or so.

Joe and Ed thought we might be able to split up and make for the camp. We had done that before, but we were not this far out and hadn't had as *many bad guys after us. Plus, we had been out here for days. We were hungry and tired and we had been in Nam a long time. We had gained a lot of experience, but I had lost 30 pounds myself. We were all in poor health from too much time in the jungle and not enough food. If the VC would pass on by us, we thought we still might be able to make it to the chopper that would be here in about four hours. The VC should be gone by then.*

I told everyone to spread out in the jungle and try to blend in so the VC might pass us by. I could see no one was really hot on this idea, but I remembered in the past, anytime I told the guys I had an idea they would all say, "But Kurt, you didn't say it was a good idea." Well I was with them this time; this was not a good idea but it was the best chance we had. Sometimes there were no good options – only the best one at the time. This was one of those times.

Song didn't like it; he wanted to kill as many VC as we could and then split and take our chances. My gut said the same thing. At least you have a fighting chance, but I didn't think we could get out of this situation that way and we would all die. So I said, "No, everyone find a spot and get ready."

I moved over to a place where there was a log with a lot of brush and a big "wait-a-minute" bush, covered with lots of long sharp thorns. I hoped that the VC would not want to walk though there. I got down alongside the log; it was about two feet thick. I put my weapons under the edge of the log, and tried to become a part of that log. I pulled lots of vines and leaves around me. We were wearing tiger fatigues and they blended in really well in the jungle. I was worried about my hands and face, so I worked my hands into the dirt and put my face into a space between the log, and where it laid on the ground.

It must have been 115 degrees in the jungle that day, and with my face buried in the dirt, I was sweating so hard from the heat being scared that the dirt was turning into mud on my face. I was well camouflaged, but the bad thing - and I mean the really bad thing, was that I couldn't see anything. All I could do was hear what was going on. I was so scared I was sure they could hear my heart pounding!

Everything was crawling all over me and it was hard to not reach for them. I don't know if they were ants or what, but something was biting my legs. It was all I could do to not yell and scratch. I knew if anyone saw me I would be dead. What could I do? Even if I jumped up and started firing I'd be in the middle of 100s of enemy Soldiers, and I was not going to let them take me prisoner. I remembered how Commander Thomas had been captured and how the VC had skinned him alive before we could get to him.

Well it was too late now to do anything different; I could hear them coming and they were close. I was worried about the other guys. We hadn't had time to talk over what we would do if they found one of us; do you just stay put and hope they don't find you, too, or do we all jump up and kill as many as we can? If we did that, we were all dead for sure. I kept thinking over and over about what to do. I knew that if they found me, I would just try to kill as many as I could and go down fighting.

As they got closer my heart began beating so hard it hurt. Thank God they didn't like thorn bushes any more than we did, so they didn't step on me. One of them stopped within a foot of my head. He stood there for what seemed like an hour. I was sure he saw me and was using his hands to call some of the others over. I could picture them pointing their AKs right at me and about to shoot. It was more than I could take; it would've been better to jump up and fight than to just lay there and let them shoot me. Just as I was about to jump up, I heard someone come over to the VC and say something about being hungry and they were going to eat soon, so I just stayed where I was.

There must have been 500 or 600 of them, because it took about 20 minutes for them to completely pass by us. Even after they were gone and I couldn't hear them anymore, I was worried that they had left someone behind to secure their back. My fear overrode my desire to get up out of that miserable spot, so I waited for about another hour and then slowly moved my head to see a little and hear better. When I didn't hear or see anything I slowly moved and got my weapon out and ready.

It looked like the plan had worked but my heart was still pounding. I didn't know where the other guys were so I just moved around slowly and whistled very softly. Soon, all the team was back together. We all told each other about what had happened to us. Ironically, we all had the same thoughts and feelings; we had never been so scared and we all agreed that it was harder to just lay there than to fight.

The chopper came over and the pilot said throw smoke, so we threw a green smoke grenade. The pilot said, "I see green." and I said, "Come get us." When we got back we had to debrief and get some food. Talking late, we all agreed that this had taken more out of us than a firefight.

We were so tired that we slept for the next 24 hours straight.

Well I survived back then in 1966, but this is 1985. The men from the patrol boat were now so close I could hear what they were saying. They were trying to figure out who made the tracks. I had my sights on the one

in the front of the boat. It was like so many times in the past. He didn't even know I was there or that what he did in the next couple of minutes would determine if he lived or died. I sometimes wondered if over the years I had been in someone's sights and for some reason he didn't fire. I guess I'll never know the answer to that question.

The men could see that whoever it was that left the prints went into the mud and then back into the jungle, but they didn't seem to want to get into the mud just to check it out. If this was a time of war they would have come looking immediately, but there was nothing important going on now. It didn't look like they knew about us and didn't appear to be searching for anyone.

They kept moving on down the river and were soon out of sight. Robe called for the boat and we got on. In about 20 minutes we were all safe in Cambodia.

We started an IV on Ton, and then everyone tried to get some sleep. In the morning I told Robe to take the General and his family, Ton, and six of the men, and head down the river to the safe house on the coast. Once they were there, they would call the Navy ship and get the General and his family on it. I told Robe I was taking 10 men and going back into Vietnam to get Bull.

Robe wanted to go with me, but I told him that he had gone on this mission. He was a true warrior now. I was proud of him, but now it was time for him to go. It would take either him or me to get General Fong on the Navy ship, and I might not make it back. He had to see this through without me or the mission would be a failure. He didn't like it, but he could see that I was right.

I took the satellite phone that they had at the camp so I could keep in touch with Robe. I told them they were not to wait for me. It was more important to get the General out than me.

I had the boat take the 10 men and me to the Vietnamese side of the river where we came out of the jungle. We waited until the boat launched and we could see it heading back down river. As soon as they were on their way, we turned and headed back to the road to rescue Bull.

CHAPTER TWENTY-SEVEN

Going to Get Bull

We headed back to the little village where we'd been before. It was about a mile north of Tây Ninh. The first thing we needed was Intel about Bull. When we got back to the camp, two of Bull's men were there waiting. They said that no one had heard anything about Bull, but that they had men watching the police station and knew the police hadn't moved him yet.

I needed a plan. I needed to look at all of our options, and list the advantages disadvantages. The positives were that the police were not looking for us. They still thought what had happened at the temple was a kidnapping and that the kidnappers headed north. They didn't know Americans were here. They figured the primary thing for the bandits was to get away, and they would not be expecting us to attack. We would have the advantage of surprise, and we had more firepower than they did.

The main disadvantage was that we didn't have much time. We needed to get Bull and get back to Cambodia to the Navy ship within the next 48 hours, or the ship would leave without us. We would be on our own. We could survive and work ourselves back to Bangkok and then Ron could get us out of there. Bad thing was – that could take weeks.

No matter what, we knew we had to make something happen now. We needed a plan to take Bull from the police station and another plan to take him if they tried to move him. They could do that at any time.

If they got him to old Saigon, we wouldn't have much of a chance to get him back. I needed to make a plan quickly; I had been thinking about it all the way back here.

We had two men watching the station. If they moved Bull, one would come and tell us right away. If they did move him, most likely they would be heading east to old Saigon, now Hồ Chí Minh City, and there was only one main road there. The road went right through an old French rubber plantation, and that was the best place for an ambush. During the war the VC loved to hit us when we went through rubber plantations. The trees were all planted in a row and when you passed by a row, they would shoot. Problem was, you didn't have time to fire back.

I couldn't be in both places at once and I didn't have Bull, Ton, or Robe. I didn't know any of Bull's men well enough to know how good they were, and at what. Trang seemed to be the man Bull left in charge so I had to rely on him and what he knew about his men. Trang was Bull's number one man and had been with him for the last few years of the war, and ever since. Best of all, the men seemed to have confidence in Trang and listened to him, doing whatever he said, just as if he was Bull.

We needed to get someone in place on the road right away, in case they moved Bull before we were ready to take him from the station. Trang said all his men were well trained and willing to die to get Bull out. I told him we were going to send 10 of the men to set up the ambush on the road. We had Claymores and a lot of firepower. My worry was to stop the vehicles and get Bull before they could kill him. We couldn't just blow up the vehicles without knowing Bull's location. I walked outside to sit under a tree to think.

Okay, our advantage was that they would not be expecting an attack. Suddenly I had it! "Trang, send your men to a spot they think would be a good place for the ambush. Then get a cart, break a wheel and put it in the road to stop the vehicles. We will have at least three of your men dressed like the local villagers with their long weapons in the cart. We have lots of 45s and four silencers. Give two of the silencers to the men who will be in the road with the cart. If the police move Bull, their vehicles will stop and some of their men will get out to yell at the "locals" to move the cart. You need to have five more of your men just standing around acting like locals trying to see what's going on. Whoever gets out of the vehicles will go to the cart, then you will have your other men circle the vehicles. I can't get any more detailed than that; at that point your men will just have to kill as many as quickly as they can and take Bull. If they take Bull out of the station and your man gets to us in time, we will be there, too. But there's no way we can count on being there in time, so we have to trust your men to do the job."

"Make sure they kill everyone, Trang," I continued, "We can't have anyone left alive to talk about your men having silencers or anything that might give us away, so kill them all. No one is to be left alive!"

That was going to be our backup plan to be used only if they moved Bull before we could go in and get him. Now for the plan to take him out of the police station – it was going to be harder and a bigger risk to take him, right in downtown Tây Ninh with so many people around. The boat would be leaving, so we couldn't wait and hope they took him to Saigon the next day. We had to do whatever we were going to do right now.

I knew I was going to be the biggest problem; I was too big and would never pass as a Vietnamese. The right thing to do would be for me to stay there and let Trang and the men go get Bull, but I couldn't do that. I had to help rescue Bull. I needed to be there in case something went wrong. Besides, if the men didn't make it and were killed or caught, then I would be out here alone and in big trouble anyway.

We were going to have to do this at first light in the morning. The men watching the station said there were anywhere from four to six men there most of the time with a few others who came and went. We had to get in, get Bull, and get out and back to Cambodia. I was sure we could get in and get Bull; I was not sure if we could get out or back to Cambodia.

At the first sign of trouble the locals should hide as usual, and the only people with weapons would be the police and Soldiers. Most of them were out in the villages talking to the villagers trying to get information about the kidnapping.

There was a roving patrol of Soldiers around Tây Ninh. They were in trucks with four to six men in each truck. I thought that our biggest advantage was that the war has been over long enough so most of the Soldiers were young and had never been in combat. They were in for one hell of a surprise! I was sure they'd only dealt with locals or bandits and no one who had ever fought back. We were going to bring hell into their lives and then take their lives just like they took the lives of my men.

Good news – I just got a call from Robe and they were back to the coast and safe. Robe sent the boat back up the river so it would be waiting for us.

It was 0600 hours. Bull had not been moved, so we sent a man to the ambush site to call it off and bring the team to Tây Ninh to help us. Trang had his men drive past the station and around the roads near there; there was not much activity. We had three trucks and 14 men in place on the streets around the station. I was in the back of one of the trucks with two men and Trang. We were now parked about 50 feet east across from the station.

This was different than being in a village. There were no mud and straw hooches and dirt streets. In the city, the buildings were mostly brick covered with stucco. They had real windows and doors. The streets had hard-packed surfaces.

The police station had a steel door and windows with bars. The walls looked thick enough to take a round and provide some protection. It would have been hard to take it with firepower only. Hopefully the deception in the street would bring everyone in the police station out into the street. Plus the policemen are not in war mode and most likely would leave the door open so we could enter and take the jail. Once inside, it would be a better place to take rounds if someone shot at us.

Just like in the war, somehow the locals knew when something was going to happen. You would look around and all of a sudden there would be no one there. That's how it was right now. There had been people on the street minutes ago, but now there was no one in sight.

Here we go. Two of our men were in the middle of the street yelling at each other. Here came two, no three men out of the police station to see what was going on. Two more of Trang's men were going up to them like they just wanted to see what was happening. The policemen were laughing, so they wouldn't be ready for anything like what was about to take place.

I didn't know why but I wasn't scared right then. In fact I was just hyped. My mind was clear, and it was time to act!

I was dressed as much like a local as a 190-pound American could be. This was going to be a big surprise for them. I was out of the truck and walking up to the men in the street. Three of the men were right outside the door of the station, and two men were standing near the door. No one was looking at Trang or me as we walked up to the crowd. I was wearing one of those pointed hats, and I kept my head down.

Two of the policemen were holding the two men who were fighting and one of them was about 10 feet in front of me yelling at them to shut up. I had the 45 in my right hand; I used my right thumb to push the safety down and it was ready to fire. I was right behind him. All I had to do was pull the trigger but I wanted him to know what was going on, if only for a second.

I put my left hand on his right shoulder and pulled a little. He just jerked and said something that I didn't understand and went back to yelling. I grabbed his shoulder again and said in English, "Hey you asshole, look at me!"

He turned around and looked at me then! He was looking at my chest because he didn't expect to be looking at someone as tall as me. His eyes traveled upward until he looked straight into my eyes and I have never seen anyone's eyes get as big as his did! He was frozen for that moment. Then he had fear in his eyes and started to turn his head to look at the other men and shout something.

In that second I squeezed the trigger of the 45.

Silencers do not stop all the noise like in the movies, but they take away most of the sound. I could hear the slide of the 45 come back and eject the empty casing and pick up another round pushing it into the chamber. The round went right into his chest and his blood splashed all over me and in my face. The bad thing was that the round went right through his thin body and I didn't know where it stopped. But I didn't think it hit anyone else.

As he went down, the two other policemen turned their heads to see what was going on and saw the dead policemen. One started to bend over and the other one instantly saw me. In the next second, Trang's men quickly pulled out their knives and killed them both.

The two men who were standing in the doorway of the station couldn't see what was going on but could see something was very wrong and started to run out into the street. As soon as they came out the door, Trang's men quickly killed them, too.

This was so strange. This was too easy so far, but that was because the police were not in war mode. They were in police mode, just like our policemen back in the States. They rely on their badges and authority to control people. Our policemen would not have had a chance, either, if the same thing had happened to them.

Three of our men rushed into the station and Trang and I ran inside, too. They had the cell door open and were helping Bull out. One of them held a weapon on a guard who was still sitting in a chair.

I walked over to Bull to see if he was okay. His face was badly beaten and his left eye was swollen shut. He assured me he was all right though, and that he would be okay to travel. We all started to head for the door when we heard shooting going on outside and three of our men came running in starting to return fire out the door and windows.

They said an army patrol had come by and was out there now. There were about four or five men and I was sure they would call for help. Just as I walked by the guard who was sitting in the chair he jumped at me with a knife!

I turned just in time to grab his right hand holding the knife, and we both went down to the floor, with me on top. I had his right wrist in my left hand and I grabbed his hair pulling his head up. I smashed it back down hard on the floor. He was able to turn the knife enough to cut my arm but I smashed his head on the floor again and again until there was a big pool of blood and he stopped moving.

Shit, cut again! Well this is better than the last time I got stabbed through the wrist. That time it left a scar on my right wrist and this was going to leave a scar on my left arm.

Wow that makes the old scar about 17 years old. It was back in '67 and it started right near my birthday, 28 February, but it seems like it happened yesterday.

CHAPTER TWENTY-EIGHT

Operation Junction City

We were in War Zone C about 90 miles northwest of Saigon, just a few miles from the Cambodian border in Tây Ninh Province. The name of the operation was Junction City. We'd found a huge stash of rice in a field and we discovered a large tunnel complex. Our tunnel rats went in and found a multi-layer tunnel system which must have run for miles. Our men found some large rooms. There was also a small hospital room and a conference room. It looked like they could have hidden a battalion of Soldiers in there. There were all kinds of exits that came up everywhere, some even in villages under fire pits. Some came up in the jungle and some on the riverbank. After the operation was over our Soldiers spent weeks mapping the tunnels. They found tunnels that had as many as 17 levels.

We had been out in the jungle on reconnaissance for the main force. Ed, Joe, Song, Tuk, and I had been in the jungle for over 20 days. We were hot, tired, and hungry. The best food we had eaten in the last 20 days was that snake we killed. We had been out among the VC so we hadn't been getting much sleep.

It was about 1900 hours when we came out of the jungle, and there in a field was an artillery unit. An artillery unit stays about two or three miles back from the main unit to supply fire support for the forward units. Since they are positioned back about two or three miles from the fighting, they normally don't take fire as often as other units. So we thought we could stay there for the night and get some rest. It should have been a more secure area than out in the jungle. The unit was a battery of 105 Howitzers with about 50 men. It was Fire Support Base Gold, located 17 miles northwest of Tây Ninh.

We entered the perimeter, ate some great hot food, and slept well. I was up at 0600 and it was about 0645 hours, when suddenly we heard a lot of noise and gunfire!

"Holy shit!" There must have been 1,000 or 1,500 VC and they were coming from all sides! There were lots of mortars coming in and VC and regulars in uniforms with AKs. It turned out to be the 272ⁿᵈ VC Regiment. Before we could even get to a bunker, they were inside the perimeter and all over us.

I ran about 100 feet to my right; there were 2 VC coming inside the perimeter for about 50 feet along the line. I knelt down on my right knee and started to fire. I was so scared it felt like my heart was pounding out of my chest. There were a lot of them coming straight at me! I knew I couldn't kill them all and I didn't want to waste ammo. We had been in this battle for about 20 minutes and had already used up most of our ammo. I had no doubt we were going to die.

I think there were more VC inside our perimeter at this time than there were of us. I could hear someone firing at them on my right and left, but I didn't know who and didn't have time to look to find out. I had to kill as many as I could with the ammo I had. I only had ten 20-round magazines. I was down to one full magazine plus the one in my 16, and I didn't know how many rounds were left in it. I had to find a target, aim center of mass, squeeze the trigger, and then move to the next one. It sounds easy, but with so many of them coming at you it's really hard; you want to put it on full auto and try to kill them all. Unfortunately, that doesn't work. You only waste ammo.

We did kill most of the VC in just about a minute. I shot one of them 10 feet from me, turned a little to my left just in time to get a round off at second one, and hit a third one in the right hip. He was so close, the blood hit me in the face and he fell flat about a foot from me; his AK fell to the ground about three feet from him. He was yelling and grabbing his right leg and hip. I lowered my 16 and put a round in the top of his head. That was the last round in that magazine, and the bolt locked back.

I took my right index finger and pushed the magazine release and the magazine fell to the ground. At the same time I was reaching for my last full magazine with my left hand. I pushed the magazine into the 16 and was about to hit the bolt release with my left palm, but before I could do it,

I heard and felt someone to my right. When I turned to see who was there, I had my 16 in my right hand. Just as I turned, three VC jumped me! They were on me before I could react.

I fell back on the ground and my hands were over my head with my 16 in my right hand. At this point, everything seemed to happen in slow motion. All three VC had AKs and could have shot me – but they didn't. I found out later that they wanted to capture one of us as a POW. Thank God, they were trying to take me alive; if they had wanted to, they could have killed me as I turned!

One of them had a large knife. It was about 18 inches long, but only about one inch wide and had what looked like a water buffalo hoof for a handle. This guy was on my right with his leg pinning down my right arm, and he ran the knife though my right wrist. It went between the bones and came out the other side pinning my right hand to the ground, like when you crucify someone.

The VC to my left had his AK in his right hand and was trying to control my left hand and arm with his left hand. The third one was sitting on me. He had his right hand on the trigger of his AK and his left hand on the weapon's forearm. I started to lift up my head and chest. The VC sitting on top of me put the barrel of his AK over his left shoulder with the butt in front of him and smashed it forward, hitting me in the forehead above my left eye! It gave me a concussion and knocked my head back to the ground.

I looked to my right and could see the knife in my right wrist. I knew I couldn't try to pull my right hand up or it would just slide up the knife blade and do more damage. I really didn't think about what to do at the time, I just reacted from my training. I was hoping now was the time for all that hand-to-hand combat instruction to pay off. I remembered what the Army said was true: "What you practice is what you will do in combat. Train hard, because your lowest form of training will be your highest performance in combat."

The VC who was on my left trying to control my left hand was very young and had a small hand and wrist. I rolled my left wrist in and down and came around so that I had my fingers over his thumb and fingers. I rolled his hand and wrist over and back quickly and heard his wrist break. At this point he dropped his AK from his right hand and grabbed his broken left wrist instead. Finally, my left hand was free.

The VC to my right had his AK in his left hand and his right hand on the handle of the knife that was still in my right wrist. His right knee was still pinning down my right arm. I put my left hand on top of the VC's hand on the knife. I grabbed both the knife and his hand with my left hand and gave a hard pull. The knife came out of my wrist. I then rolled my hand to the outside and pushed forward at the same time. This snapped his wrist and turned the knife upwards. I was trying to break his wrist but was not trying to do anything special with the knife – just to get it out of my wrist.

I guess God was with me after all, because not only did I break his wrist, but the knife ended up about two inches away from the neck of the third VC who was on top of me. Now that my right hand was free, I hit the handle of the knife with the heel of my right hand and the knife slid into his neck! It entered on the left side of his neck near his Adams apple at an upward angle of about 30 degrees, and came out just below his right ear.

He let go of his AK and with both hands reached for the knife in his neck. I grabbed the AK that had fallen on my chest and with both hands hit the VC sitting on my chest hard in his face. This knocked him backward off of me. I pulled my legs up to my chest and rolled to my left and back up on my knees. The VC to my left was still lying on the ground holding his left wrist. The VC to the front with the knife in his neck was lying on his back not moving or making a sound. The guy to my right was on his knees trying to pick up his AK.

My 16 was still on the ground; I remembered that the bolt was open and there were no rounds in the chamber. I had the AK in my hand that the VC sitting on my chest had dropped on me when I shoved the knife through his neck. I moved it around so it was pointing at the guy to my left. The bolt was closed, so I didn't know if there was a round in the chamber or if there were any rounds in the magazine. With an AK, you have to take your right hand off the trigger to take the safety off. That takes time and I didn't have any time. The guy to my left looked at me and was about to get up so I pulled the trigger and hoped that they had ammo in their AKs and it was ready to go.

Again, God must have been there with me, because the AK went off. I hit him in the chest just above the heart and he fell back to the ground. I would have shot him again, but I didn't know how many rounds were in the AK. I still had to attend to the guy to my right. I turned and pointed the AK at him. He was trying to get his AK in a position to fire at me. Thank God he must have been right-handed and that was the wrist I had broken, so he was having a hard time trying to fire with his left hand!

The safety on an AK is on the right side and he had the AK in his left hand with his left hand on the trigger trying to get it pointed at me. I knew that my AK was not on safe because I had just shot the other guy, but I didn't *know if I had any rounds left and didn't have time to check. I didn't have time to aim; I just pointed it at his chest. I was only a few feet away and I was sure I would hit him if I could get my shot off before he could shoot me. I could see he was not going to be able to get his AK up to fire before I could fire. Just before I pulled the trigger I looked up from his chest and looked him straight in the eyes. When our eyes met, he knew he was about to die. I could see the fear in his eyes. At that moment I thought he might throw the AK down but he didn't. He was young, maybe only 17 or 18, but he looked down at his AK and started to raise it.*

I pulled the trigger and hit him just below the neck a little to the left of center, knocking him backward to the ground! I quickly turned to my left to see if the first guy I shot was dead. He wasn't dead but wasn't moving. I shot him two more times and then turned to the one that I had just shot, shooting him two more times. The third man who had the knife in his neck was dead from the knife wound. I pulled the knife out of his neck and I still have it. About this time, Song and Ed came over and took care of me for the rest of the battle.

To this day I have trouble with fine motor skills in my right hand because of nerve damage and I have a split in my skull over my left eye. This was my third Purple Heart, or as I like to call it, my VC sharpshooter badge.

We found out later that this tunnel complex went from Tây Ninh all the way to Saigon, and they were later used to transport personnel and weapons to the Saigon area for the Tet Offensive in '68. We also found out that on one occasion, Bob Hope was putting on a show for the troops while all through the show underneath the stage, there were VC in the tunnels making plans to attack us right below him. Amazing.

This battle lasted about four hours. After the battle, we found over 600 dead VC inside the perimeter. This was the biggest death toll for any single engagement for the VC to this date. We had 31 men wounded and nine killed.

CHAPTER TWENTY-NINE

Going to get Bull/The "Last Stand" Room

Back to the present and this battle. This time there were more of us than there were of them and we still had men outside. Now we were in a firefight!

This was no place to get trapped. It wasn't heavily fortified, although better than a mud and straw hooch. We had to get the hell out of there, not make a stand. Shit, here I was, trapped in a building again.

Two rounds just flew past me. We were going to have to fight our way out of this one; there was no safe room in this jail. But then there were not as many bad guys as the last time I was trapped in our hooch in the war. This was kind of like old times, only I was pretty sure we would get out of this one – back then I didn't think I was going to survive.

It was up north in the village of An Lộc in 1967.

We had been in this village for about six months. With the help of the people of the village, we had been able to hurt the VC's efforts in the area around our village, but for the last month or so the VC had been trying to stop us. They'd made five or six assaults on our village; we were able to repel them each time. There were four of us and about 15 locals who we had trained. The village had a 10-foot double fence all around it. All the attacks that had occurred before this one were with small forces of 20 VCs or so.

Because of the previous attacks, the villagers had dug small shelters around and underneath their homes to hide in, in case of a ground or mortar

*attack. Ed and four of the PFs were up the hill at the army camp. There was
a company of infantry from the 196ᵗʰ on a hill above our village about half a
mile away. Joe, Ron, Song, Tuk, and I were right around our hooch. The rest
of the PFs were scattered around the village when the attack came.*

*Our hooch was made of mud just like the rest of the homes in the village;
the walls were about eight inches thick, with a thatch roof. The whole building
was 15-by-30 foot, and there was a door on the front that faced the main
street with one door going out the back. There were three windows: one to the
front, one to the back, and two on the south side. We put screens over them
so the VC could not throw anything into the hooch, but there were no doors
on the door openings.*

*There were no homes within 50 feet of our hooch. It was about 20 feet
from the street with 50 feet of clear area at the back and 30 feet on each side.
We had barbed wire topped off with concertina wire. On the back side of the
hooch, we had a four-foot-high wall, 30 feet long, about five feet from the
hooch, as a fighting wall to the back. We had eight Claymore mines placed
all around the hooch. On the inside we had two rooms; the main room was
15-by-20 feet. There were sandbags three feet high all around the room. We
could get behind them fire. I'd made a desk that sat facing the front door. The
desk had sandbags on three sides with two layers on the front side and a piece
of plywood for the top. There was an American flag hanging on the front of
the desk with a Claymore under the flag and the plunger under the desktop.
We had four Claymores, one in each upper corner pointing into the room.*

*On the north end of the hooch we'd built a wall to make a small room,
15 x 10 feet. In this room we had three feet of sandbags on all the walls and
used 4 x 4s and plywood, then six feet of sandbags for the roof. This cut the
area in the room down to about four feet wide, nine feet long, and only three
feet high. We made an opening that was about two feet by two, and a shelf
with sandbags on it, so when we jerked on a pole, the sandbags would fall
and cover the opening. Inside the room we had a piece of plywood with all
the plungers for the Claymores that were in the outer room and one of the
radios. This was our "last stand" room.*

*When the attack came, it was at about 1400 hours, with a force of about
200 VC and at that time of day the gates were open.*

*The VC came in the north gate and down the main street. Our hooch was
right on the main street at the south end of the village. Two of the PFs were
near the gate when the VC started the attack. They started shooting and one
of the PFs called on the radio to tell us what was happening. We called to the*

village chief and he started to get the villagers into their shelters. I alerted the army company up the hill and the artillery battery to stand by, but we could not call in artillery at this time since the VC were in the village with our villagers.

The six PFs were no match for the 200 VC coming into the village. I called and told them to take shelter with the villagers. Joe and Tuk went out back to the sandbag wall and got ready. Ron, Song, and I each took a position at one of the windows in the main room. The VC took up positions in and around the homes near our hooch. They didn't have uniforms on, so it didn't look like they were NVA. They were not good at concentrating their fire, and were not very organized, just a lot of individuals firing at us.

Four VC tried to rush the back and Joe set off one of the Claymores, killing them instantly. There was a lot of fire coming into the hooch. Most of the VC were using AK-47s. They put out a lot of firepower.

We turned back four more charges with Claymores, and were only about 10 minutes into the attack, when all of the Claymores that we had placed in the field had been used. We were still taking a lot of fire. We had hit 50 or so of the VC, but that still left about 150 more! It was hard to throw grenades from inside the hooch. The firefight was so intense that all we could do at times was hold our 16s over the sandbags and fire without aiming. There are only two combat firing positions, over the wall and around the tree.

The inside of the hooch was being torn up! Every time three or four of the VC would rush us, we would concentrate our fire and stop them. There were still over 100 of them, and now they were 50 to 100 feet away from us. From the north side, about 20 or 30 of them rushed us and came right up next to the hooch! I stuck my 16 out the door without looking and fired; some of them were only five feet away when they dropped.

I could see we couldn't keep them out of the hooch, and in a minute, we would have a room full of VC. I yelled, "Def con, Def con!" This was the command for everyone to crawl into the small "last stand" room. Ron and I each threw a grenade; Ron threw one out the back and I threw one out the front door. Joe, Ron, and Tuk crawled into the room by way of the 2 x 2 foot opening. While they crawled into the room Song and I backed towards the opening.

As I turned and looked at Song who was just getting down on the ground to crawl into the room, two VC were coming in the back door about three feet from him! One jumped on Song; I fired and hit the second one in the face. Song was in a hand-to-hand fight with the VC on the floor. I heard something

behind me and turned, just as three more VC were coming in the front door!
I fired and hit all three of them, but I was out of ammo and had only killed
one of them. The other two were hit and down but still able to fight.

I turned around and Song was inside the "last stand" room. The VC that
had been fighting with Song, lay dead on the floor. I dove for the opening
headfirst and someone inside the room grabbed my hands and pulled me in.
I could hear voices right behind me! As soon as I was in, I pulled on the stick,
and the sandbags fell over the opening.

I yelled, "Fire the Claymores!" It was so dark in the room I couldn't see
who it was, but someone pushed all the plungers on the Claymores that were
in the upper corners of the main room. It was a very loud blast. That meant
all four Claymores went off and all were pointed into a 15 x 20 foot room.

I don't know how many VC were in the room but I'm sure it killed them
all. We could still hear a lot of voices though, and there was no way for us to
fight back at this point – we were on our bellies in the small space. We could
also hear the sound of a lot of gunfire and bullets hitting the wall that was
between our "last stand" room and the main room. Thank God, the small
room wall was three-feet thick with sandbags and their bullets couldn't
penetrate. But the VC would get to us soon, so I said to call the artillery in.
Ron had the radio and I could hear him call,

"Fire Base Red, this is OP Black, def-con, def-con, def-con!"

Def-con was the command for the artillery to fire on our position! They
knew that if we called for def-con, we had been overrun and they needed to
fire on us or we were dead anyway. Our hope was that in the "last-stand"
room we had a chance to survive because it had three feet of sandbags on the
walls and six feet of sandbags on the roof. This was our only hope.

In just a minute the artillery rounds started coming in on our position.
The artillery fire lasted for about 10 minutes and then there was dead silence.

Our roof and walls had collapsed on us, but everyone was alive. We
couldn't move; we could only hear each other. I told everyone to try to stay
still and wait because the army unit on the hill should be here soon.

In about 10 or 15 minutes we could hear voices – American voices.
We started to yell and in about 20 minutes they had dug us out. Ron had
a broken leg, and we were all bleeding from cuts on our heads. Other than
that we were okay.

One of the PFs was killed and eight villagers had been wounded, mostly
by the incoming artillery, not by the VC. One hundred and fifty-eight VC

had been killed. The artillery had destroyed our hooch and six other homes nearby.

We treated all the villager's injuries and paid to have their homes rebuilt, then we rebuilt our own hooch. It took a whole month to rebuild everything. While we were rebuilding the army offered to let us sleep up the hill with them, but we didn't want the villagers to think we had abandoned them and left them at the mercy of the VC. So until our hooch was rebuilt, we slept with the villagers in different homes each night.

In a month we were back in business and putting the "hurt" to the VC in the area. I was worried that the villagers would be upset, knowing the VC wouldn't have attacked their village if we hadn't been staying there. They had people hurt but as it was, they really appreciated that we stayed and fought for them. We had done so much for them on the medical side, they wanted us to stay.

The Last Stand Hooch

Well it was not going to be like that now, taking Bull out of here. I was sure no one wanted us to stay this time, and I didn't want to, either.

Soon the men from the ambush site showed up outside to help, and with us inside, this was not going to be much of a firefight. We quickly overwhelmed them and got to the vehicles heading out of town. We drove east toward Củ Chi and Saigon and fired at the locals without trying to hit them. We just wanted them to remember us and remember which way we went.

About two miles east of Tây Ninh we took a back road to the north and then west to Cambodia hoping this would give us time to get back to Cambodia before the police started after us. We hoped they would be looking to the east just like they did when they mistakenly thought a kidnapping had occurred earlier.

The General's family was now safely in Cambodia, and we had Bull back. We were finally getting close to the end of this mission. We were about six or seven miles from Cambodia and heading into the Hobo Woods; this was a place that had seen a lot of action back in the late 60s with the 25th ID out of Củ Chi.

We hadn't seen anyone chasing after us. Hopefully they were still trying to figure out what had happened back at Tây Ninh. It had only been about 90 minutes and I doubted that they were doing anything yet, just trying to put it all together. They didn't have much of a communication system, but they did have ground phones and may have been able to put the word out to other patrols in the area.

We arrived back at the spot where we entered the jungle, about a mile from the river. I told Bull to come with me, and that I was taking him to the States and freedom. He told me, "Thanks, but no thanks." He said that this was his country and his people, and he needed to stay and keep fighting. It looked like it was time to leave Bull and all of his men.

I looked into Bull's eyes. How do you say, "Goodbye," and "Thanks," to a man like him? This was one of those times when you understood that there are no words in our language that would have been adequate. I gave him a hug and we held on for a minute. I shook his hand, and then one at a time I thanked and shook the hands of each of the men who had risked their lives for this mission and me. I was sad; I knew they loved this country but there was not much of a life here for them under this government. This had been a hard mission. I was going home but they had to stay. This was their home.

Just then, two trucks came down the road and we could see they were carrying Soldiers! Bull yelled for me to run into the jungle and head for the river. When I got to the edge of the jungle I stopped to look back. I was about 50 yards from Bull and the trucks. Bull and the men were in a firefight but it looked like he and his men had things well in hand.

I stood up and headed for the river. I'd only gone about 10 feet when I heard rounds fly past me into the jungle. Just then my hat blew off my head and I hit the ground! A few more bullets flew by and the firing stopped. I looked for my hat but it was just a little out of my reach. I stood up and took one step picking up my hat, and headed for the river.

I started to put my hat on when I saw the bullet hole in it. How lucky was that? One inch to the side and I would have been dead…and just one mile from safety! Wow! This reminded me of a time back in An Lộc.

I was living in the village of An Lộc about 20 miles south of Da Nang with Joe, Ron, Ed, and four Vietnamese bodyguards. There were about 1,200 people that lived in the village. It was located right on the Gulf of Tonkin. An army infantry unit was up the hill from us about half a mile away.

One of our Vietnam villagers told us he heard there was a small VC unit of about 10 men living in a village 10 klicks north of us, so I decided to go have a look. I went up the hill and talked to 1st Sergeant Extrom at the infantry company. This was the unit from the 196th that lived out there near our village. I told Extrom what the villager had told us and asked if he would send some of his men with us. He said that he was tired of being stuck in the camp and that he would go with us himself and bring along a six-man squad. I told him I was going to take Ron, Song, and Tuk with me so we could bring as many as eight more men with the D Model Huey. His seven men and our four could all go together. We were only going out for the day so we didn't need much food, just lots of ammo and firepower. Top, the 1st Sergeant, had one of the guys bring an M-60, (belt-fed machine gun) in .308 caliber that fires 800 rounds per minute, and another guy bring an M-203, an M-16 with a 40 mm grenade launcher attached to it. We were ready.

The chopper came in and we took off. The trip only took about 10 minutes, and we landed on the beach about a mile away from the village. All along this part of the coast there was 100 feet or so of beach right on the Gulf of Tonkin; it had beautiful blue water and white sand. It was a gorgeous day, in the 90s and sunny. A large sand dune ran along the coast 50 feet high and 100 feet across at the top. We landed on the beach so the sand dune was between the village and us.

When the chopper was gone, we climbed to the top of the sand dune so we wouldn't get trapped on the beach with no place to take cover if we were hit from on top of the dune. It was hard climbing the sand dune, and while I climbed I thought how hard it would be for the enemy to climb up to get to us if we stayed on top. So when we got to the top we walked to the village, staying on top of the dune. We were back far enough that we wouldn't present a silhouette to any VC down in the village.

We could see smoke coming from fires as we approached. We kept low and worked along the dune until we overlooked the village. People were moving around; we had good binoculars and kept looking for people with weapons. The village was about half a mile long, so we kept working our way down the dune.

After about 30 minutes, we hadn't seen anything out of the ordinary, so I decided to take Song, Tuk, and Ron and go down to look over the village and talk to the villagers. Chuck said he wanted to go into the village with us, so we left the six men from his unit up on the dune to cover us. We looked around one more time but everything looked good. Ron, Song, Tuk, Chuck, and I stood up at the top edge of the dune about ready to start down the side when we started taking fire from the village!

It sounded and looked like maybe five or six AKs were firing at us. We all hit the sand and returned fire. The guy with the M-60 moved up next to me and was laying down a lot of fire. When the VC opened up on us, I could see the bullets hitting all around me in the sand. Chuck was lying to my left returning fire.

We exchanged fire for about five minutes and then there was a lull in the action. I looked at Chuck and that's when I felt something warm running down my right leg. "Shit!" I was hit again. I felt no pain but I knew sometimes you didn't feel the pain right away.

I yelled at Chuck that I was hit in the leg but that I was okay! We took more incoming and we laid down a heavy amount of fire until the incoming fire stopped. We were in a good spot; it would be hard for anyone to charge up the 50-foot tall sand dune and there would be no place to hide while they climbed up. We had the high ground. With me hit, we wouldn't go down into the village; they would come back with a larger force maybe a platoon of 50 men or so tomorrow, and really work the village over. They would search every hooch and interview everyone.

We set up a perimeter; Chuck called for a dust off and a slick to get the men out of there. Chuck asked me how I was and I reached down and felt my leg. It was all wet but still didn't hurt. I told him I was okay. Chuck put down the radio and came over to me and said to roll over so he could have a look at my leg. I laid back and asked him how it looked. He pulled at my pants and cut it open. Then he said it was a clean wound and that the bullet had gone in and out and didn't hit any bone. He had a big smile on his face and he said, "Do you want to see?"

"Of course," I said. "Sure."

That's when he held up the plastic canteen that I kept in my lower leg pocket. Sure enough it had a bullet hole going in and out of it. I had been shot in the canteen! He threw it at me and started to laugh. He called and cancelled the dust off, and of course he had to tell everyone who could hear on the radio that Coconut had been shot in the canteen. Everyone knew who Coconut was, so I thanked Chuck for announcing this to everyone on the radio!

Later the chopper landed right on top of the sand dune and Song and I waited until everyone was in the chopper before we got in. As I walked up to the chopper, I looked at the pilot and he looked at me. He held up his thumb and laughed. It had been less than an hour and even the chopper pilot had heard about me getting shot in the canteen. I knew I was never going to live this one down.

The chopper landed back at the camp and everyone was giving me the old "thumbs up," and laughing when I got off. I quickly went down the hill to our village where I thought I would be safe from all the fun that was going on at my expense since the village was full of Vietnamese. But oh no, I was down there about an hour when the villagers, especially the kids, kept coming by the hooch pointing and laughing thanks to Song, my body guard who I thought was my friend. He had apparently told everyone in the village!

Two days went by and the laughter had stopped. I thought it was over. Then I got a call on the radio from Chuck up on the hill asking me to come up and give an after-action report to the commander of the unit. I said I would be there at 1300 hours.

I got up there at 1300 and I thought it was strange because Ron, Ed, Joe, Song, and Tuk wanted to go with me. They said they wanted to get a good meal up at the unit since we normally ate like the villagers. The unit had a mess hall with hot food. I thought it was odd for them to want to go with me anyway, but I knew it could be true about the hot food. Right! When I got to the camp the whole unit was standing there with the Commander and Chuck out in front.

The Commander said, "Front and center!"

So I walked up there, all the time knowing everyone was going to have fun but me.

The Commander said, "1ˢᵗ Sergeant, read the award please." Chuck read something about me being wounded in combat and on and on that they were presenting my canteen with a Purple Heart. They handed me my canteen with a Purple Heart pinned to it. Then we ate cake so at least that was great! I was surprised later, although relieved to see that the story was not published in the Stars and Stripes Newspaper.

It was different this time. No one would know about this hole in my hat.

I stopped and called for the boat and told them I would be there in 30 minutes. I got to the river and onto the boat heading down river to the coast. I called Robe and said we were on our way and should be there in the morning. I told him to call the Navy and make the arrangements for us to be picked up.

CHAPTER THIRTY

Out of Vietnam

The trip down the river went without any problems, and here we were at Khum Angkol on the southern coast. Robe was there waiting to take me to the safe house. General Fong, with a sad smile on his face, came over and gave me a hug. Finally everyone was out of Vietnam, and there was only one more thing to do – get out of here and back to the States. Robe said the Navy was off shore about 20 miles, waiting for us. We had to leave in 30 minutes.

I realized that for the first time, I could let my emotions down and lower my level of alertness. It was like a heavy load was lifted off me.

We all got into the old boat. After it took us to the Navy ship, it would come back and take Ton and his men back to Bangkok with Ron. The rest of Bull's men would head back into Vietnam to meet up with Bull to continue the fight with the Communists.

At the start of the mission, I had to build up my emotions and my alertness as we traveled into Vietnam, but now it was time to let them down in stages. On the boat and in the open sea it was time to loosen up a little more. There was very little chance anyone could get to us now, but we still kept our weapons loaded and ready to go.

We got off the little boat and into a small Navy boat; I watched as the little boat turned and headed back to get Ton and the men. I could "step down" a little more now. It was time to unload my weapon.

Finally we were on the Navy Cruiser, at least that's what they told me it was. It could have been a battleship, for all I knew. It was big and steel and for the first time since this mission started I felt safe. I gave my weapon to a Marine for safekeeping; that was always a big moment when you could put your weapon away. We were served a home cooked meal and afterwards they shown me to my room.

Secured in my own room, I stretched out on the bed. It was so good to know that I would be sleeping for the first time in peace and safety since the beginning of this mission. As I started to relax, the events of the last few days began to move slowly through my mind. I began mentally sifting through everything that had happened, every phase of the operation, and what I might have done differently. It was always that way after a mission ended.

I realized I had planned well for this mission except for one thing. I had a plan and a backup plan that was good for almost everything, the weapons and communications were good. I had good backup plans for getting the General and his wife and daughters. But I could see that I didn't create a backup plan for extraction. I forgot about how Robe, and the General and his family would get out if I had been killed, or if something went wrong and the boat couldn't get there to pick them up. I guess I was just taking it for granted that I would be there to do it all.

If I had to, I would have just joined up with Bull and his men and figured out a way to get back to Thailand later, but I never thought about Robe, General Fong, or his family. Robe had no experience like this, and he wouldn't have lasted long in the jungle alone. If the boat hadn't gotten there, what would have happened to the General and his family?

I should have had a backup plan for that and should have briefed everyone on what it was. I should have relied more on Bull and his men to be the backup plan to get everyone out if something went wrong. Thank God, he was on our side and we hadn't needed another plan. I realized now that this is what happens when you're out of the business too long.

Back when I was doing this all the time, I would have never made a mistake like that. Everyone was counting on me to run this mission, and it would have been entirely my fault if it had failed. Hopefully, this is the last time for me to lead anything. I just wanted to go home.

CHAPTER THIRTY-ONE

❧❦❧

End of a Mission or Beginning of a New One

We ended up at Clark Air Force Base in the Philippines. This was like being on U.S. soil. The next day there was a plane waiting for us. When we took off, it felt like back when I had flown out of Vietnam at the end of the war. The only thing that could stop us now was if the plane crashed.

Robe was talking to some men from The Company and I knew there would be a long time of writing and debriefing coming, but not now. I just needed to sleep. I was so tired and now I did feel safe and could sleep.

About an hour later, Robe came over and said I had a phone call, so I went up front to pick up the phone. It was Raines. He said, "Kurt, congratulations on a mission well done!" I could hear the satisfaction in his voice.

I told him, "Thanks," but I was glad this was over.

There was a pause and then Raines said, "Well . . . come by and see me at my office when you get back Kurt. Okay?"

I laughed at that and jokingly said, "Why, do you have another mission for me?"

There was a long pause . . . too long . . . and then he said, "Maybe. Just come and see me –okay?"

I'm sorry I can't my friend. It was a successful mission and I saved lives and rescue some people from Vietnam, but the cost was too high; I sold my soul. I can never enjoy the peace and comfort I had as an

Eagle Scout, although there will always be a part of that Eagle Scout in me. There will always be the memories of the things I had to do to save people's lives. I can see that I will struggle for the rest of my life with a moral conflict between my actions in the war and the actions expected of me as an Eagle Scout. It is so strange that the goals in the war were the same as my goals as an Eagle Scout: to love, protect, and serve people. I guess I just never imagined the things I would have to do in war to accomplish that.

AFTER WORD

***

Life After Vietnam

Now that you've heard my story, I hope you can understand the emotional and moral conflict Soldiers face in war. What is "right" and "wrong?" I guess, that depends on where you are and what you are doing.

When we enter the military, it's a totally different world; it is not about being kind, it's about being aggressive. We learn hand-to-hand combat, how to kill with the bayonet, and how to use a rifle to kill people. We are told that it is our duty to fight and kill. We go off to war and find that we are rewarded for doing all the things we were taught not to do, growing up. The more aggressive I was and the more I killed, the more I was rewarded, promoted in rank, and given medals for doing so.

Counting the Cost

If you're a combat veteran, there is no need to explain all the repetitive and specific details listed in this book. For those of you who have never been in the military or endured traumatic situations, let me explain. The war was 50 years ago, yet I can still recall every step, every smell, and every drip of sweat rolling off my face. I can still hear the sound of my heartbeat, and fearing that the enemy would hear it, too. I remember every scratch on my weapon, every face of the villagers, and every crack of artillery as if it was happening right at this moment. I can still see the palm trees and hooches, and smell the food; I recall in slow motion, the limbs and lifeless bodies of my fellow soldiers flying out of a bunker wired with explosives. I smell their blood that saturated my uniform while I carried their body parts back to the Huey. These details may seem redundant to you, but I live them every second, of every minute, of every day.

As you might guess, I was looking forward to getting away from all of that and coming home. I longed to be in a place where I was safe, and could get more than two hours of sleep at a time, without having to sleep with my finger on the trigger of my gun. I hoped that I could leave that part of my life behind, and pick up where I left off back home. I just wanted to find a job, a girl, have fun hanging around with my friends, and pursue a college degree under the G.I. Bill.

It would be great to be able to sleep in bed and clean clothes, instead of on a hard cot in my uniform and combat boots.

When I returned home, I arrived at O'Hare International Airport in Chicago. I departed the plane and started walking through the airport. For the most part, there were just a lot of people walking around. There were two or three small groups of individuals around 20 or so, and they were holding up signs saying, "Baby killers," and "We hope you die!" I couldn't believe it. They were also yelling profanities and spitting on us as we walked by.

A wide array of conflicting emotions swept over me. On the plane, I was glad to be coming home, but angry that our politicians didn't keep their promise to rescue those who had helped us in Vietnam. I was looking forward to getting back to safety and to the country I loved so much, only to find that I was more hated by my own people on my own soil, than I was in a foreign country. I couldn't go back to Vietnam, but I wasn't welcome here, either. What happened to my country and how did I end up in the void

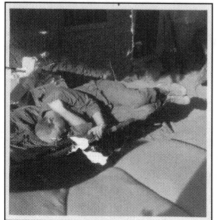

that lies between? My dreams of finally being able to live in peace and safety when I came home, quickly diminished when we were faced with such hatred and opposition.

That was my first introduction to the phenomena of the anti-war group. Instead of taking out their aggression on the individual soldiers, they should have been protesting the politicians who sent us there. Most of us weren't even old enough to vote.

The culture shock and trauma of the war was difficult enough, but coming home to be treated like this was extremely traumatic for me. It set the stage for a lifelong battle with PTSD and Moral Injury. My emotional struggle came from the conflict between the decisions I had to make to carry out my military duty, and the values I was raised with. Public opinion caused me to question myself. They deemed me as some kind of monster. The things they said and the way we were treated, triggered a constant fear in me that I would end up in hell for what I had done.

I quickly discovered that the medals I had earned were negative symbols to some of my friends and people back home. I believe the things I did were honorable. I was saving lives and defending my country. Yet I was looked upon as a heartless, cold-blooded killer by some and still am, today. To the villagers in Vietnam, I was a hero who saved their lives.

So which is it? Am I a hero or a cold-blooded killer? Am I a little of both? Am I that Eagle Scout that would help anyone in need, or a heartless killer? I guess only God knows.

Every day, Veterans struggle with the answers to these question and will continue to do so, for the rest of their lives.

Awards for Being Good or Bad?

I found that by far, the majority of the people in my area had very little interest in the war, pro or con. There was a small minority who were anti-war (and as it turned out anti-soldier), who had a great negative impact on my life. My friends had jobs, wives, and a normal life; I saw the world completely different than they did. They were easy-going and carefree, but

 I could not let go of the images I had seen and the things I had done.

It wasn't long before I realized it was hard to laugh and enjoy the pleasures of life. I never felt safe. I always had to have a gun with me, even though I knew that I wasn't in any danger. I just didn't feel safe anywhere, and still don't to this day.

Every Fourth of July, I would lock myself in the house, and close the windows. Once the house was secure, I would turn up the radio to try to drown out the sound of the fireworks. To me, it was like an artillery attack.

I love nature and being outdoors. I felt more at home in the woods by myself than I did among people. I went squirrel hunting once, and out of the corner of my eye I saw movement. Without thinking, I had rolled onto the ground and acquired a man in my sights, who was also squirrel hunting. I was about to squeeze the trigger when I realized he was just another guy out there hunting squirrels like me.

Going to war right out of high school, I didn't have the opportunity to learn social skills like my friends back home did. For them, when somebody looked at their girl, they would give them a dirty look or say something. They may walk up and push each other, but it would rarely go past that. Even if it did, it was no more than a minor altercation.

One night, I was taking my girl to the movies when three local college students came up and made lewd remarks about her and her miniskirt. I said something, and one of them came up and tried to push me. Before he could reach me I punched him, and his two friends came to his aid. I reacted quickly, and in a matter of seconds had broken one of their noses, and the right arm of another. All three were on the ground and in need of medical attention.

They filed a complaint and I went to court. Fortunately, the Judge said since they started it, and there were three of them and only one of me, that it was self-defense. Then he reminded me that I needed to act like an adult and said I couldn't solve my problems with physical violence. That's when I got in trouble with the Judge.

I said, "You mean the way President Kennedy and President Johnson could not solve their problems with Ho Chi Minh and the North Vietnamese, so they sent us there to kill them? Is that what you mean by acting like an adult?"

I had been solving my problems for the last few years with deadly force, and it saved lives, including my own, but that's not how things are handled here. It was obvious to me that I just didn't fit in and never would. I made it a point not bother anybody and to leave people alone. I needed to get on with my life. That's all I wanted, but it just didn't seem to happen.

I tried to get a job and was called for an interview. When I arrived, the man acted sincere. He opened his book and skimmed over the jobs available at his factory. Then he looked up and said, "I just don't see any jobs available for a machine gunner and a killer."

He seemed genuine at first, which is why his response caught me so off guard. I felt hurt, angry, demoralized, and betrayed. It was because of people like me, that he got to sit in his plush office and go to sleep without a care in the world, yet somehow I disgusted him. Between the "less than warm" welcome we received upon returning home from Vietnam and people like this, I quickly learned that I couldn't even trust my own people.

I hoped that going to college and getting my degree would help me find a good job, so I signed up under the G.I. Bill. I didn't want anyone in the school (especially the professors), to know I was using the GI Bill, much less anything else about me. Word spread, and several of the teachers made it a point to make negative comments to me about being a soldier in Vietnam. One day I came out and someone had spray-painted "Killer," on my car in the school parking lot. When I went to the administration to complain, they said, if I didn't like it, I should quit. I didn't, and eventually graduated two college degrees.

The War Within

It wasn't long before I started having anxiety attacks, nightmares, and other emotional problems. I really didn't understand why. It would've been easy to turn to drugs or alcohol to deaden the pain, but I found a wonderful woman and married her. We found a church to attend, and the comfort I received grounded me and helped clarify the line between right and wrong.

Up to that point I had found little or no help for PTSD and Moral Injury. I'm not sure they even knew what it was back then. When I would have an anxiety attack, I never knew when it was coming or how long it would last. My heart and mind would race, my palms would sweat, and I had an urgent need to get out of there. The only thing that seemed to help was to get in my car, turn the music up really loud, and just drive around. If I couldn't do that, I would put on my Walkman, turn the music up loud, and walk around for hours.

Because of the anxiety attacks, I was unable to find work that fit my college degree, and had a hard time holding down a job. I never knew when one was coming, but when it did, I had to get out; I couldn't just sit there. That cost me a job or two. It was unfair to me as well as the employer. I understood why they couldn't keep me on the job, but I still had a family to support.

At some point I realized that my only option was to be self-employed.

If I had an anxiety attack, I could leave the job, not be fired, and make up for lost work by working late or on the weekend. I've been self-employed ever since, but have never been able to make as much money or have the retirement benefits that I could have had, if I had been able to utilize my college education.

I don't know how my wife and family put up with me. I was never angry or violent with them; I love them deeply, but because of the way I had to work and the anxiety attacks, I was not there for them all the time. I was not the best husband or father. I was not even good for me. I found the only people I could talk to were fellow veterans. I also realized that the only time I didn't have anxiety attacks was when I was in the military, so I re-enlisted and ended up staying a little over 24 years.

Addiction to Combat

This is a strange phenomenon that I suffer from. Trauma, stress, or being in a state of "high alert" for long periods of time, causes the brain to release dopamine, cortisol, and adrenaline. The adrenaline gets us focused and our hearts racing, and cortisol prepares our body for a state of shock. Dopamine plays a major role in reward-motivated behavior, and is part of what causes the "high" when someone uses heroin or cocaine. Likewise, being in a "hyper-alert" state for that long of time period actually becomes an addiction.

When I wasn't in combat, I was like an addict going through withdrawal. I was edgy, nervous…off. It was only when I was engaging in high risk activities that I felt like I was "in my element." I took jobs working as an undercover agent for the police department buying drugs and doing things that carried high personal risk to them. I was in my 50s when I worked security for a private contractor during Hurricane Katrina and went to Iraq in my 60s as a security contractor. I did any work I could that had the potential to satisfy my craving for action and risk.

Now I'm in my 70s and too old or incapable of doing those types of things, but I would if I could. Being gone all the time and putting my life in constant danger wasn't fair to my wife and kids. Unfortunately, that was the only time I didn't have panic attacks, flashbacks, or nightmares. PTSD feels like a demon I've been carrying since the war. I hate it. How could I have controlled an entire village of people or a group of men under constant fire, but can't control my own emotions? I don't understand it, and deep down I long to be able to live like others around me who enjoy their friends, family and jobs. I just want to be able to sleep peacefully and feel safe.

Changing Times

I was called back to active duty for Desert Storm almost 20 years after I had returned from Vietnam. I had to fly out of Chicago with my group, dressed and ready for battle. The thought of returning to O'Hare in uniform struck more fear in me than returning to war. I didn't want to go through being treated badly by the people of my own country again. It took every ounce of courage I had to return to that airport in uniform.

Fortunately, it was a different time in the world. Public opinion had changed toward soldiers and the people were supportive of military personnel, even if they were not supportive of the military action. To my great surprise and pleasure, I found people coming up to us shaking our hands, and bringing coffee to us as we waited to board the plane. Up to this point, this was without a doubt the best therapy I had received in the last 20 years. It was the start of the healing process for me and the struggles that I'm still dealing with 50 years later.

Long Term Effects

Around 2005, I went to the VA because I incurred several physical injuries when I was in the military. While I was there, I enrolled in the mental health section that dealt with PTSD. My therapist, Dan Bishton, truly saved my life, along with my wonderful wife, of course. I have medications to help with my nightmares and my anxiety attacks, but they don't completely eradicate them. They take the edge off and settle me down enough to be able to wait them out, knowing they will pass.

When I eat in a restaurant or go to a movie, I still sit with my back to the wall, and I always have my gun. I know that's irrational because I'm not paranoid or think somebody is after me, but without it, I just don't feel safe. When I walk in a mall, I walk to one side so people can get around. I don't feel comfortable in crowds.

I sleep better now, but in the summer I have to have all of the windows closed and locked. Thank heaven for air conditioning! I always check the doors and the windows before I go to bed. For about a year, when I first came back, I slept on the floor with my back to the front door, and my gun in my hand the entire night. That was the only way I could get any sleep.

I never understood when I came back why the people were angry with us soldiers. In those days it was not a volunteer army. They just drafted us, took us away from our home, family, job, and school, and paid us $78 a month to kill or be killed. We weren't even old enough to vote or buy a house or car until we were 21. I often wonder how the politicians rationalized that we were responsible enough to go kill people, but not responsible enough to vote for the people who sent us there.

I honestly thought the people back home who were opposed the war, would at least feel bad for what we went through, but they didn't. Many of them took out their frustrations over the war on us soldiers, and I just can't seem to get over that.

I cannot forgive the people who treated us badly when we came home. They left us there to fight and die, instead of picking up a weapon and coming to help us. It's easy to take the moral high ground, when you're not the one being shot at, having to decide who lives or dies, watching children get butchered, or carrying your best friend's body parts back to the chopper.

In today's world, everyone has a voice. Protestors and their opposition stand on the street shouting each other down. People express their opinions and argue their point through social media. Back then, we didn't have a voice, and we had no one coming to our aid or standing up for us. We had to hide in our own country, from our own people. Those who didn't hate us, were not willing to stand up or speak up for us. The media gave the protestors a platform and continuous news coverage in an effort to push their narrative, only fueling the public's hatred for us. I get that people opposed the war, but why protest the soldier who had no choice in the matter?

There were Soldiers who protested the war when they got home, but they didn't protest their fellow Veterans. I don't have a problem with that. What I have a problem with is the people who, in an effort to further their public career, took advantage of the spotlight and attacked their fellow soldiers repeatedly on national television. In my book, that is the epitome of a traitor. Doing that is offering for slaughter the very men who had their backs during the war, for their own personal gain. There is no excuse or forgiveness for that.

I have often said, I would be happy to sit down with a North Vietnamese

Soldier and talk about the war. They were our enemies at one time, but they were just soldiers doing their job like we were, and I respect that. Who I will never accept, respect, or forgive, are my own countrymen who treated us like garbage when we came home. They are my perpetual enemies. The way they treated us caused as much harm as the trauma of war, itself. We expected to get shot at over there, but we never dreamed we would be treated so badly by our own people in our own homeland. Our only place of refuge, and the people we needed support from the most, turned on us like rabid dogs.

Time to Talk

For over 30 years, I never talked about the war or what I had done, to anyone except other veterans. Even then, I only spoke superficially about some of the things. I've never talked to anyone, including my wife, kids, family, or friends, in detail about my emotions or how I felt about my time in Vietnam. It was about 10 years ago, around 2008, when one of the local teachers asked me to talk about my experiences in his history class. That scared me emotionally, but I thought it may do me some good, and I was right.

As I began addressing the classroom, I realized that the students weren't even born yet, when I was in Vietnam. After telling them some of my story, they started asking those same questions. They said, "Why would people take it out on you? You didn't make the war, you only had to fight in it."

Telling my story to this class helped me start talking with other people about it, at least on some level. It was my therapist who thought it would be good to write down some of my thoughts, and that's when I decided to write this book. Hopefully it will allow Veterans, combat or not, to understand: there is help for what you're feeling, you're not alone, and to seek help. Even military personnel who were not in the middle of combat, were still torn from their homes and witnessed the atrocities of war all around them.

Educating the Public

Many people suffer from PTSD. It can stem from domestic violence, rape, or many other social issues they've experienced. It can be debilitating if left untreated. Realizing how PTSD develops from war, and how it goes hand in hand with Moral Injury, I hope the struggles we face will be easier for you to comprehend. The war may be over, but we will fight our internal battles until our last breath. There is no rest for us. Throughout the day we are plagued with flashbacks and memories of the horrors we've endured, and at night while you sleep peacefully, we are tormented by nightmares.

Being able to justify our actions in war, doesn't mean that we aren't still struggling with the emotional conflict and need support and treatment. Just because we don't feel guilty, doesn't mean we don't feel at all. It is a trauma that you can't possibly understand unless you've been forced to take the life of another human being.

Many of my friends died in the war and they missed out on so many wonderful things. They never had the chance at love, life, and all the things I have had the opportunity to enjoy, yet at the same time, there are days when I think they are the ones who are better off. Sometimes, I would rather have died for my country than to have killed for it. At least I wouldn't have had to live all these years with the memories, nightmares, and emotional trauma. The suffering stopped for those who died in the war, but mine continues, 50 years later.

Fortunately, with the help of my wife, my therapist, and my church, I am able to function in society. There are many who don't. The medication helps make that possible, too. It is my sincere hope that this book will help both Veterans and non-military have a better understanding of the emotional consequences of war.

To Veterans

1. PTSD and Moral Injury are nothing to be ashamed of. It shows you were able to survive hell and still maintain your humanity.
2. You are not alone. Many people suffer from PTSD and Moral Injury, but not everyone talks about it. Don't assume what you're experiencing is unique to you.
3. Talk about it to people you can trust. It helps to get it off your chest, and it helps them better understand what you're going through.
4. There is help available through the VA, seek it out. I can't promise that it will completely cure you, but it definitely helps.

To Civilians

To those who have never served in the military, I hope you see how your actions can make or break a Soldier, especially those who are already struggling with PTSD and Moral Injury from war. When you are tempted to protest, please consider the big picture and how many lives you may be taking with your actions. Carrying signs and marching in the street doesn't stop or start wars. When you publicly protest, it only fuels the enemy's morale and gets our soldiers killed. During the Vietnam War, the protests back home cost us American lives on the battlefield, because the politicians were more worried about public opinion polls than our military personnel. If you want to be effective, contact your politicians and voice your opinion to them, and don't protest the Soldiers.

It's okay to have an opinion, but unless you have walked a mile in our shoes, you have no right to stand in judgement of the choices we made or the things we were forced to do in war. I would ask that you put yourself in our position before rushing to judgement, and consider how your words and your actions will affect our Soldiers. A kind word and a little compassion, and some appreciation go a long way. We are losing 22 Veterans a day to suicide. How you respond to them may be what keeps them from it, or pushes them to it.

There is a song protesters love to play. It says, "War. What is it good for? Absolutely nothing." I hate that song, because it's not true. Someone once said, "The only thing required for evil to prevail is for good men to sit back and do nothing." There are times when war is necessary. Keep in mind that it is the U.S. Soldier who fought in wars that have provided you your freedom to protest today. If it wasn't for our Soldiers going to war in WWII, we would all be speaking German right now.

To oppose good men and women who were trying to stop Ho Chi Minh from slaughtering his own people, is the same as helping him do it. The men and woman who served, bled, and died fighting to save the Vietnamese people, were right to do so. Our country owes our Soldiers respect for what they do, and for the sacrifices they make, as well as an apology for how we were treated when we returned home from Vietnam.

"You sleep safely in your beds at night, only because soldiers stand ready to do violence on your behalf." ~ Author Unknown

"War is an ugly thing, but not the ugliest of things. The decayed and degraded state of moral and patriotic feeling which thinks that nothing is worth war is much worse. The person who has nothing for which he is willing to fight, nothing which is more important that his own personal safety, is a miserable creature and has no change of being free unless made so and kept so by the exertions of better men than himself." ~ John Stuart Mill (1806-1873)

VIETNAM FACTS VS. FICTION

For over 30 years, I, like many Vietnam Veterans, seldom spoke of Vietnam, except with other Veterans, when training Soldiers, or in public speeches. It's time the American people learn that the United States military did not lose the Vietnam War, and that a surprisingly high number of people who claim to have served there, in fact, DID NOT.

<u>Below are some assembled facts most readers will find interesting</u>:

- 9,087,000 military personnel served on active duty during the official Vietnam era from August 5, 1964 to May 7, 1975.
- 2,709,918 Americans served in uniform in Vietnam
- Vietnam Veterans represented 9.7% of their generation.
- 240 men were awarded the Medal of Honor during the Vietnam War
- The first man to die in Vietnam was James Davis, in 1958. He was with the 509th Radio Research Station. Davis Station in Saigon was named for him.
- 58,148 were killed in Vietnam.
- 75,000 were severely disabled.
- 23,214 were 100% disabled.
- 5,283 lost limbs.
- 1,081 sustained multiple amputations.
- Of those killed, 61% were younger than 21.
- 11,465 of those killed were younger than 20 years old.

- Of those killed, 17,539 were married.
- Average age of men killed: 23.1 years.
- Five men killed in Vietnam were only 16 years old.
- The oldest man killed was 62 years old.
- As of January 15, 2004, there are 1,875 Americans still unaccounted for from the Vietnam War.
- 97% of Vietnam Veterans were honorably discharged.
- 91% of Vietnam Veterans say they are glad they served.
- 74% say they would serve again, even knowing the outcome.
- Vietnam Veterans have a lower unemployment rate than the same non-vet age groups.
- Vietnam Veterans' personal income exceeds that of our non-Veteran age group by more than 18 percent.
- 87% of Americans hold Vietnam Veterans in high esteem.
- There is no difference in drug usage between Vietnam Veterans and non-Vietnam Veterans of the same age group (Source: Veterans Administration Study)
- Vietnam Veterans are less likely to be in prison – only one-half of one percent of Vietnam Veterans have been jailed for crimes.
- 85% of Vietnam Veterans made successful transitions to civilian life.

Interesting Census Stats and "Been There" Wanabees:

As of the current census taken during August, 2000, the surviving U.S. Vietnam Veteran population estimate is 1,002,511. This is hard to believe, losing nearly 711,000 between '95 and '00. That's 390 per day. During this Census count, the number of Americans falsely claiming to have served in country is: 13,853,027. By this census, FOUR OUT OF FIVE WHO CLAIM TO BE Vietnam vets, are not.

The United States sought to minimize and prevent attacks on civilians while North Vietnam made attacks on civilians a centerpiece of its strategy. The National Liberation Front assassinated 36,725 Vietnamese and abducted another 58,499. The death squads focused on leaders at the village level and on anyone who improved the lives of the peasants such as medical personnel, social workers, and school teachers.

Vietnam Veterans were no more likely to die from suicide than non-Vietnam Veterans. A myth is the common belief that a disproportionate number of blacks were killed in the Vietnam War. The fact is that 86% of the men who died in Vietnam were Caucasians, 12.5% were black, and 1.2% were other races.

It is a myth that the domino theory was proved false. The fact is, that the domino theory was accurate. Philippines, Indonesia, Malaysia, Singapore, and Thailand stayed free of communism because of the U.S. commitment to Vietnam.

It was a myth that Kim Phuc, the little nine year old Vietnamese girl running naked from the napalm strike near Trang Bang on 8 June 1972 ... shown a million times on American television ... was burned by Americans bombing Trang Bang. The fact is that no American had involvement in this incident near Trang Bang that burned Phan Thi Kim Phuc. The planes doing the bombing near the village were VNAF (Vietnam Air Force) and were being flown by Vietnamese pilots in support of South Vietnamese troops on the ground. The Vietnamese pilot who dropped the napalm in error is currently living in the United States. Even the AP photographer, Nick Ut, who took the picture, was Vietnamese.

The incident in the photo took place on the second day of a three-day battle between the North Vietnamese Army (NVA) who occupied the village of Trang Bang and the ARVN (Army of the Republic of Vietnam) who were trying to force the NVA out of the village. Recent reports in the news media that an American commander ordered the air strike that burned Kim Phuc are incorrect. There were no Americans involved in any capacity. "We (Americans) had nothing to do with controlling VNAF," according to Lieutenant General (Ret) James F. Hollingsworth, the Commanding General of TRAC, at that time. Also, it has been incorrectly reported that two of Kim Phuc's brothers were killed in this incident. They were Kim's cousins, not her brothers.

It is a myth that he United States lost the war in Vietnam. The fact is that the American military was not defeated in Vietnam. The American military did not lose a battle of any consequence.

The United States did not lose the War in Vietnam, the South Vietnamese did.

The fall of Saigon happened 30 April 1975, two years AFTER the American military left Vietnam. The last American troops departed in their entirety 29 March 1973.

As with much of the Vietnam War, the news media misreported and misinterpreted the 1968 Tet Offensive. It was reported as an overwhelming success for the Communist forces and a decided defeat for the U.S. forces. Nothing could be further from the truth. Despite initial victories by the Communists forces, the Tet Offensive resulted in a major defeat of those forces. General Võ Nguyên Giáp was the designer of the Tet Offensive. Still, militarily, the Tet Offensive was a total defeat of the Communist forces on all fronts. It resulted in the death of some 45,000 NVA troops and the complete, if not total destruction of the Viet Cong elements in South Vietnam. The organization of the Viet Cong units in the South never recovered. The Tet Offensive succeeded on only one front and that was the news front and the political arena. This was another example in the Vietnam War of an inaccuracy becoming the perceived truth. Regardless of how inaccurately it was reported, the news media made the Tet Offensive famous.

GLOSSARY

Item	Description
196th	196th Light Infantry Division
25th	25th Infantry Division - camp at Củ Chi about 40 miles northwest of Saigon in War Zone C or The Iron Triangle
AK-47	Russian assault rifle, full-auto, produced by most Soviet block states, 7.56 x 39 ammo
C-Rations	Food in cans; some dated from WWII – tasted good but hard to carry
C.I.A.	Central Intelligent Agency
C-4	Plastic explosive. Soft and hand malleable, usable over a wider temperature Range than pure explosive.
Charlie	Name given to the Viet Cong, VC, Victor Charlie
Chinook	Large, two-bladed cargo helicopter
Chopper	Some type of helicopter
Christians in Action	name for the CIA
Claymore mine	8.5 in long, 3.25 in high, and weighs 3.5 pounds, 700 steel spheres & 1.5 pounds of C-4 explosive, electric blasting cap

Klick	1,000 meters
CO	Commanding Officer
CP	Command Post
Dustoff	Medical Evacuation Helicopter (HUEY)
Eagle Flight	Lightning fast operations carried out by several troop laid in HUEYS on a VC village or suspected area
Flank Man	Man on right and left of unit for security - right flank & left flank
G2	Army Military Intelligent
Grenade Concussion	No shrapnel; loud noise, breaks ear drums
Grenade M2	Smooth - high explosive - filled with wire that breaks into many pieces
Grenade pineapple	Looks like a pineapple-filled with flaked TNT-not as powerful as M2-used in WW2 and Korea & marines in Vietnam
Grenade Smoke	Uses different colors to mark something. No delay on fuse
Grenade WP	Filled with white phosphorus-used to start things on fire
Grunts	Nickname given to the Infantrymen (GIs)
Gunship	Armed helicopter
H & I	Harassing-and-Interdictory fire
H E	High explosives
Hooch	Hut
HQ	Headquarters
HU-1D	The workhorse helicopter of the Viet Nam War (the HUEY)
Huey	Bell-model C or D Helicopter - used to haul troops and supplies-holds 12 - 30 mile range - 130 MPH
K-Rations	Dehydrated food-easy to carry but did not taste good
KIA	Killed in action
LAW	Light Antitank Weapon

Line Unit	Army infantry unit that does most of the grunt work in Vietnam
LP	Listening Post
LRRP	Long-Range Reconnaissance Patrol
LZ	Landing Zone
M-14	Standard rifle (7.62mm) of the Infantry in Viet Nam, replacing the older M-1
M-16 or 16	Full auto rifle. 5.56 or .223 ammo
M-60	Standard (7.62mm) light machine gun
M-79	Grenade launcher (40mm)
MEDEVAC	Medical Evacuation helicopter
Mikes	Minutes or meters depending on the context
Military Time	A 24-hour time period beginning and ending with midnight.
Nasty Boat	A specially built shallow draft high speed craft
Núi Bà Đen	Black Virgin Mountain just north of Tây Ninh
Nung	Mercenary troops of Chinese dissent paid by the U.S. Government
NVA	North Vietnamese Army or Regulars
O2	A small single engines Cessna used for recon and to spot and mark targets
PF	Local Vietnamese Pacification Force
Dong	South Vietnamese Currency equating to approximately 85 cents to the
Piaster	U.S. Dollar
Point Man	Man out in front of a unit for security
PRC 10	Hand held radio
PRC-25	Lightweight Infantry Field Radio / about 18 in H - 12 IN W - 4 in D / carried on the back

Reaction Force	Standby, reserves or reinforcements
Recon	Stands for reconnaissance - to go and look
RTO	Radio Telephone Operation
S & D	Search-and-destroy
S-2	Staff Intelligence Officer
Saigon	Capital City of South Vietnam
Slick	Another name for a Huey - used to haul troops and supplies
Tay Nin	A town about 80 miles northwest of Saigon-home of the 196th light infantry division
The Company	Name for the CIA
VC	Vietnamese Communist
WIA	Wounded in action
WSO	Weapons System Officer

ABOUT THE AUTHOR

I grew up in the 50s in a small rural town of about 200 people. I had loving parents and went to church every Sunday. Basically, the whole town was a big family that took care of each other. I was in the Boy Scouts, along with most of my male friends, and I earned my Eagle Scout in 1960. I took it seriously and tried to do more than just earn it. I tried to live as an Eagle Scout with honor, and live up to the oath and mottos of the Scouts.

I graduated from high school in May and by September, I was at Fort Knox, Kentucky, learning to be a Soldier. This was scary and stressful, because up to this time, I had never been more than 100 miles from home. I quickly adapted to being a Soldier and enjoyed the camaraderie and the opportunity to be a part of something that was contributing to my country. It only paid $78 a month at that time. I re-enlisted, was sent for more training, and soon found myself in Vietnam, 12,000 miles from my home. It was both scary and exciting at the same time. I had a real gun with real bullets, and of course, I thought I was invincible. I believed it was only the other guys who would end up dying for their country, not us, we were the good guys.

At first, it wasn't a geo-political question of why I was there or what I was doing. It was about the "here and now," living one more day, and surviving the next battle. The things you don't see or hear on TV or radio, are the things that soon put me in emotional conflict between being an Eagle Scout and being a good Soldier. It didn't take long for me to realize that the world was not as simple as I thought it was.

Like many of the Soldiers, I began to wonder why I was there and why I was doing these things. I could see early on what I was fighting for, and it was not for all my friends and family back in the States. It all became clear when I witnessed the atrocities perpetrated by the Communists on the South Vietnamese people. They were people who just wanted to live in peace, yet, they were being killed and slaughtered by the Communists. It didn't take long before I started seeing every shot I took as "saving a life," rather than "killing the enemy."

I couldn't stop the war. I wasn't old enough to vote at that age, but I was responsible enough to kill. When I saw a mother murdered and a child left to die, is when my emotions came in conflict with what I was taught in church, by my mother, and my oath as an Eagle Scout. The sorrow, hatred, and rage I felt seeing these acts, went against everything I knew to be right. I was there to help them, but "helping" in war is not like back home, where you just had to talk in order to help people. Here, I had to kill to save them.

I have never committed atrocities. I have never killed, just to kill. I killed to save lives. I've had doctors and people ask me if I feel guilty about what I did, and I do not, but that does not make everything okay. I feel sorrow and sadness, as if somehow I had let God, my mother and father, and many others down with the things I have done. Yet at the same time, I had helped people like they had taught me to do.

The conflict within me never goes away, not for a day, or an hour. I don't feel guilty, and therein lies the conflict. I feel alone when I am in the church. I saved lives and yet I feel unworthy to be there. It is hard to find someone to talk to. If you haven't been there and done what we have done, then you can never understand.

Returning home, I was not the same young man I was when I left, and certainly not like my friends that stayed home. I didn't, and still don't fit in anywhere. Some people treated me badly, and it was hard to hold down a job. I never felt safe without a gun, and still don't.

I was lucky to have a supportive family, and to have found a wonderful woman to marry, as well as a good church to support me. As a result, I didn't turn to drugs or alcohol to survive, unlike many Vietnam Veterans. In those days there was no mental health support in the military. It wasn't until 2007 that I was able to find help through the VA system with Dan Bishton, who saved my life many times. There are times when I feel guilty that I survived. It seems it would have been better to die for my country than to have killed for it, but I am sure the people I saved do not believe that.

Printed in the United States
By Bookmasters